The Ascent of Man

The Ascent of Man

of

Man

A Philosophy of Human Nature

James F. Harris

Transaction Publishers
New Brunswick (U.S.A.) and London (U.K.)

#494691812

Library of Congress Catalog Number: 2010020386
ISBN: 978-1-4128-1421-8
Printed in the United States of America

Library of Congress Cataloging-in-Publication Data

Harris, James F. (James Franklin), 1941-
    The ascent of man : a philosophy of human nature / James F. Harris.
        p. cm.
    Includes bibliographical references (p.   ) and index.
    ISBN 978-1-4128-1421-8
        1. Philosophical anthropology. 2. Human behavior. I. Title.

    BD450.H288 2010
    128--dc22
                                                                2010020386

For Andrea

Ought we not to consider first whether that which we wish to learn and to teach is a simple or multiform thing, and if it is simple, then to inquire what power it has of acting or being acted upon in relation to other things, and if multiform, then to number the forms; and see first in the case of one of them, and then in the case of all of them, what is that power of acting or being acted upon which makes each and all of them to be what they are?

—Plato, *Phaedrus*, 270d

The most useful and least advanced of all human knowledge seems to me to be that of man.

—Rousseau, *Discourse on the Origins and Foundations of Inequalities among Men* (the Second Discourse)

Contents

Preface

Why write a book attempting the development of a rigorous, systematic theory of human nature when such an endeavor has been apparently so studiously avoided by the giants of intellectual history? It is not that major thinkers have avoided making claims about human nature; it is rather that those claims have not been seated in and justified by a broad, metaphysically modest, theoretical framework. Consequently, disputes amongst differing claims about what it means to be human have frequently come down to the trading of unfounded aphorisms or brief clichés. Generally, this has meant that more heat has been generated than light has been shed.

Whenever philosophers, social scientists, or natural scientists have written about the nature of human beings, there has usually been unqualified agreement about the fact that human beings are unique creatures that are different from other things in the known universe—both living and non-living. At the same time, it is equally true that there has usually been little or no agreement about how that uniqueness and difference are to be explained or upon what grounds such an explanation is even possible. In other words, there has been significant agreement about the fact that human beings are unique, but there has been little agreement about what it *means* to claim that human beings are unique. It is the meaning of "human" in "human beings" about which there has been so little agreement, i.e, about what is the *nature* of human beings.

Natural scientists are geared towards accounting for the uniqueness in biological terms—morphological or genetic differences or differences in DNA-while social scientists usually appeal to social and cultural phenomena. Philosophers and theologians usually appeal to a range of properties or attributes of varying degrees of abstractness ranging from "being rational," or "being a political animal," to "possessing an immortal soul." The net result is a variety of different accounts of human nature, some of which are "thin," i.e., claiming a small or minimal difference between human beings and other known living things, and some of which are "thick," i.e., claiming a large or significant (usually metaphysical) difference between human beings and other known living things.

Another characteristic of the way in which human nature has been treated by philosophers, theologians, and scientists is the way in which human nature has been cannon fodder for various intellectual battles that are being waged. One kind of such intellectual battle involves what might be called "turf wars," e.g. evolutionary biology v. theology and psychology v. neuroscience. Political and/or economic theories, e.g., democracy v. fascism and socialism v. capitalism, have frequently argued their differences across the battle ground of human nature. Ideologies that have defined epochs, e.g., the divine right of kings, manifest destiny, and liberalism and the Enlightenment have based their claims upon characterizations of human nature. Appealing to some vague notion of human nature has been used at various times to justify preferential treatment or discriminatory treatment for different racial or ethnic minorities, "the lower classes," women, and children. The Greeks famously regarded all non-Greek speaking peoples as *barbarians* (or "lower classes" who spoke Greek poorly). Even philosophers (who presumably should know better) have generally shaped their positions regarding human nature in the shadow of taller trees so that human nature has simply been used as a stalking horse for other political (e.g., Locke) or theological (e.g., Augustine) interests. Frequently then, in the course of philosophical or, more recently, scientific examinations of human nature, there have usually been different and larger fish to be fried. Repeatedly, vague, intuitive, or stipulated short, aphoristic claims about human nature have been the grease for frying those larger fish.

Intellectual interest in what it is that makes human beings human dates from the earliest periods of recorded history. For example, Herodotus reports the account of what may be the first documented, controlled experiment regarding human beings in human history. According to Herodotus, Psammetichus I, Pharaoh of Egypt, (also known as Psamtik I), sent two children to live in a secluded location with a shepherd in the seventh century BC to try and determine if there is a basic, "natural" language that is the root of all human languages. A similar such experiment was reportedly conducted by James IV of Scotland when he sent two children to live on a remote island with a mute woman. Given that the use of human language is one of the most obvious ways in which human beings differ from other animals, it is easy to understand the motivations behind these crude experiments as inquisitiveness into whether there is something basic, fundamental and "natural" about such human linguistic ability. Such inquisitiveness and speculation (and controversy) continue to the present day as illustrated in the work of Noam Chomsky and other generative linguists.

The important thing about these observations concerning the interest in human nature over the ages is that although there has regularly been interest in and appeals to human nature, i.e., what it *means* to be human, there has rarely been attempts to develop a systematic theoretical account of human nature. *Claims* about human nature have been plentiful, e.g., humans beings are basically good, human begins are basically evil, human beings are fundamentally selfish, human beings are fundamentally generous, human beings are rational animals, human beings are emotional animals, human beings are political animals, human beings are social animals, etc., but attempts at providing a theoretical framework within which such claims can be justified are rare. Even more rare are attempts at providing such a theoretical framework that do not appeal to abstract metaphysical claims that are at least as much in need of justification as the original claims about human nature.

In an attempt to provide exactly such a theoretical framework within which differing claims about human nature can be addressed in a systematic fashion, I develop in this book a comprehensive theory of human nature called the "cluster theory." According to the cluster theory, human nature is a complex emergent property that supervenes upon the causal nexus that is created by the interactions amongst a cluster of properties. In this regard, this book is likely to be a disappointment to those who wish a simple, single "catch" word or phrase or some simple aphorism to answer the questions, "So, what *is* human nature? What *does* it mean to be human?" One of the fundamental lessons from the cluster theory is that there are no simple, short answers to these questions. Hopefully, it will not be possible for anyone to capture how the cluster theory provides answers to these questions with a cliché.

In an attempt to avoid much of the existing conceptual confusion about the bases for differing claims about human nature, I distinguish between being an individual with human nature, being biologically human, and being a person. The focus in this book is upon the concept of human nature. I leave exploring the concept of being biologically human, i.e., the biological species, *Homo sapiens*, to biologists and the concept of personhood to the moral and political philosophers. While there may well be some overlap and other conceptual and empirical relationships amongst individuals described in these different ways, I explore very few of those relationships in this book.

I take as my point of departure Plato's comment in the *Phaedrus* that in learning what a thing is we should look to the ways in which it acts upon or is acted upon by other things. The focus then is upon describing how human nature has developed in the natural world in which human beings have developed and how that natural world has affected, how it continues to affect, and how it might affect in the future what it means to be human. In developing this theory, I commit explicitly to methodological naturalism, and I draw shamelessly upon what I consider to be the most recent and highly regarded experimental data and theories from both the natural and social sciences.

I do not pretend (or even dare to hope) that the cluster theory of human nature will resolve all of the disputes that have been waged through the ages about what it means to be human. I do not attempt to address all of the questions raised or claims made by others about human nature. Neither do I regard the cluster theory as constituting *the* philosophy of human nature as others have regarded their claims about what it means to be human. The subtitle of this book, "*A* Philosophy of Human Nature," is conscientiously chosen to indicate that the cluster theory is offered as *a* theoretical account. It is to be put alongside whatever other theoretical accounts there may be so that the advantages and disadvantages of each can be examined. I *do* expect the cluster theory to provide a new, unique theoretical and conceptual framework within which the old disputes may be addressed anew, the result of which being that the old battles may be waged along new battle lines.

I wish to express my gratitude to the College of William and Mary and to the family of Francis Haserot for support and the opportunity to devote time to writing this book. I also wish to express my gratitude to colleagues, friends, and family—especially my wife, Andrea—for graciously tolerating my sometimes compulsive fixation upon the various aspects of what it means to be human.

James F. Harris
August, 2009

1

Introduction: Theories of Human Nature

The title of this book, *The Ascent of Man: A Philosophy of Human Nature*, was chosen deliberately and unapologetically to indicate clearly its philosophical relationship to Charles Darwin's *The Descent of Man*. While some might object to the generic use of "man" to refer to human beings, the subtitle should make clear that the purpose of this book is to develop a general theory of *human* nature. As will become clear momentarily, the title has also been chosen to capture an essential feature of the kind of theory of human nature that is developed in this book and to highlight a crucial difference between this theory and others. There are several ways of characterizing the different approaches that philosophers have taken to theorizing about human nature. The different kinds of theories regarding human nature overlap and crisscross in a number of different ways generating a significant variety of different possible approaches to the investigation of human nature. Except for a few very preliminary remarks here for the purposes of explaining the approach that is taken in this book and contrasting that approach with other ones, I will not discuss these different views or engage in lengthy or detailed criticisms of them.

One illuminating way of distinguishing different views of human nature is by juxtaposing *descending* views of human nature with *ascending* views. This distinction focuses attention on the division between those philosophers who generally favor what I call *top-down* views of human nature and those who favor *bottom-up* views. Perhaps ironically, given the title of Darwin's work explaining the application of his theory of evolution based on natural selection to human beings, his use of "descent," which trades upon the notion of biological *descendant*, does not represent the top-down view as much as it does the bottom-up view.

Compare, for example, the claim that human beings descended from angels or from some other divine being(s). Such a top-down view of human beings descending—whether metaphorically or literally—from some other metaphysical realm or spiritual dimension does not trade at all upon the biological notion of descendent but rather, upon a much more metaphysically-laden notion of "originating from or in." Top-down views of human beings thus generally originate within a dualistic metaphysical framework within which some spiritual or mental component of human beings is identified as being the human-making quality that is somehow implanted in the physical realm, i.e., this material world. Such views are ontologically generous to the point of being ontologically careless.

In the history of philosophy, Plato is a major figure who is representative of such a top-down view of human beings. His account of the nature of human beings is based upon the claim that each person has an immaterial soul, which existed prior to that person's birth and which continues to exist eternally after that person's death. Plato envisioned the soul as a metaphysical substance that is "imprisoned" in the physical body of a human being. The soul is the seat of reason and knowledge and is in constant conflict with the physical body. In his well-known, tripartite division of the soul, Reason controls and regulates the competing interests of Passion and Spirit. The important aspect of Plato's theory of persons to emphasize at this point is that the human soul—the human-making aspect of human nature—metaphorically *descends* (or, perhaps for Plato, even *literally* descends) from the realm of the Forms. Human souls are imported from a different metaphysical world, the world of the Forms, and injected into physical bodies in this world to form human beings. Human nature is thus best regarded as a fragile and temporary amalgamation of the spiritual and the physical.

Neo-Platonism is responsible for importing a great deal of Plato's theory of the nature of human beings into Christian theology. Although it is somewhat misleading to describe Christian theology as having a single, definite view of human nature given the wide spectrum along which a large number of widely diverse beliefs are spread, it is safe to attribute a certain, general view of human nature to mainstream Christianity. Although Christian theologians might disagree about whether human nature is basically good or inherently evil, basic Christian theology holds that man is made "in the image of God." Plotinus' reformulation of Plato is responsible for converting Plato's notion of the Form of the Good into the notion of the One, an absolutely transcendent God from which all human souls (as well as two World Souls, all Goodness, and the rest of the physical universe, including Earth and the natural world) emanate. These neo-Platonist views—in particular, the emphasis on a metaphysical dualism and the *ex nihilo* origin of the universe—made their way easily into Christian theology. While there may be other more disputed ways in which human beings are said to be made in the image of God according to Christian theology (such as having free will, for example), the most fundamentally important way (and the least disputed way) is that a human being is said to possess something of the "spark of the divine" by having an immortal soul, which, in some fashion or other, survives death. The Christian view is another obvious top-down view of human nature, according to which one's immortal soul, the essential aspect of human nature, is designed and created by God and then placed in this world. Human nature descends from God's creation (or, to use Plotinus' notion, human beings "emanate" from the One) in such a manner that what it is that makes human beings the unique creatures that we are originates in a metaphysically different world and then is imposed upon this natural world.

Descartes' view of human beings based upon his famed "Cogito" and the characterization of himself as "a thinking thing," and his thorough-going dualism with its complete, metaphysical separation of the immaterial mind from the physical body is perhaps one of the best-known and arguably one of the most influential top-down views in the history of philosophy. Famously, not only does Descartes claim that he exists as a mental substance, but he claims that this is the most epistemologically-certain claim possible, a claim that cannot possibly be false or even reasonably doubted. If in fact, Descartes can be absolutely certain that he exists while still doubting that he has a physical body, then his physical body, which is a part of the mechanistic, material world, must be incidental to his existence and hence his nature. A substance is identical with its essential attribute, and the only essential attribute of a mental substance is thinking, i.e., *consciously experiencing*, for Descartes. Hence, to be a human being is essentially to think. Furthermore, a Cartesian immaterial mind not only originates in a different metaphysical realm and is then implanted in a physical body in this world, but it remains metaphysically distinct and separate from the rest of the material world while it "occupies" a human body. This perpetual metaphysical separation is what Descartes calls "the Real Distinction between Mind and Body...." Explaining just what the connection is between the two and how the mind and body are able to interact, if indeed they do, has generated as much controversy and as much literature as perhaps the debate concerning human nature itself. Attempted possible explanations have run the gamut from occasionalism to pre-established harmony to epiphenomenalism; however, arguably, there is no satisfactory explanation to the problem of explaining the nature of the interaction of an immaterial mind and a physical body that has won wide philosophical acceptance that preserves the original Cartesian dualism.

In contrast to top-down views, what I call *bottom-up views of human nature* account for human nature through some kind of process(es) in this world whereby human beings develop or come to be the kind of creatures that we are. According to bottom-up views, human beings came into being at some point in our natural history as a result of such certain processes. There is significant disagreement about exactly what the process(es) might be through which human beings came to be human and exactly how the proposed development might actually have taken place. Generally, although not necessarily, bottom-up views are meta-physically naturalistic, and generally, although again not necessarily, such bottom-up views are non-theistic. There are theists, for example, that attempt to combine theism with evolutionary theory by proposing that some divine providence intervenes at certain points in the evolutionary process to produce desired results and that human beings are thus the result of both natural and divine processes. While such claims might be interesting from a theological point of view, the method here will be to attempt to provide an account of the nature of human nature without any such appeal to speculative, theological claims and thus to contrast bottom-up, naturalistic views with top-down, theistic views. The fundamental methodological commitment of this book is thus to naturalism.

Some philosophers who have favored the bottom-up approach on completely naturalistic grounds have emphasized biological processes while others have emphasized social ones.

One obvious example of a major figure in the history of philosophy that represents a bottom-up view and who accounts for human nature in terms of social processes is Karl Marx. Human nature, according to Marx, is to be accounted for simply in terms of "the totality of social relations" into which human beings enter. For Marx, it is thus society that determines and produces fundamental human nature, and this understanding of how human nature came to be what it is explains Marx's political philosophy: change society and human beings (and presumably, human nature) will be changed.

The use of evolutionary psychology to explain human nature is also a bottom-up view. Evolutionary psychology, as a discipline, owes its inception to sociobiology and the work of E. O. Wilson. Sociobiology was based upon what proved to be the controversial (and now generally discredited) claim that certain social behaviors and patterns of social activities of human ancestors (originating mainly in the Pleistocene era) were based upon traits that would have favored survival and reproduction and were therefore selected for by natural selection. Taking general Darwinian evolution by natural selection as a given, evolutionary psychology developed from sociobiology by shifting the focus of attention from different traits and behavior to various "psychological modules" that collectively make up the human psyche. These different psychological modules, according to evolutionary psychology, have evolved because they provide psychological mechanisms that have allowed human organisms to adapt to various environmental problems and challenges by directing human behavior. The only important point to be made at the moment is that both sociobiology and evolutionary psychology are bottom-up theories that attempt to account for human nature as the result of certain natural processes. The claim is that human nature evolves or emerges as a result of these processes.

Top-down views have the distinct advantage over bottom-up views in providing a much clearer and more definitive claim about exactly what it is about human nature that accounts for the *uniqueness* of human beings. The uniqueness of human beings, according to top-down views, is usually accounted for in metaphysical terms by an infusion of some metaphysically distinct soul or spirit into the natural world from a different metaphysical realm. The advantage gained by top-down views thus will not be regarded as an advantage by naturalists favoring bottom-up theories of human nature since it comes with a high metaphysical price tag. Accounting for the uniqueness of human beings within a completely naturalistic metaphysics is more difficult since the characteristics that account for human nature—whatever they may be—must be characteristics within the same metaphysical domain shared with other living things. Thus, for example, distinguishing between human beings and other animals is simple, in one respect, according to Christian theology or Cartesian dualism: human beings have immortal souls (or immaterial minds), and other animals do not. Of course, the main difficulty with top-down views of human nature, including Plato's view and Christian theology, is that such views are irrevocably tied to highly-speculative and widely-rejected metaphysical views. The history of the long disputes regarding such claims about metaphysically-distinct souls is evidence of the problems attached to top-down views.

Bottom-up views of human nature tend to be empirical. Indeed, the great advantage of bottom-up views of human nature is that they draw their support from observations, evidence, and data provided by the natural and social sciences so that such theories can be examined, analyzed, and evaluated in light of those scientific claims. This is, in fact, a description of the exact process whereby sociobiology both initially came to be proposed and then came to be regarded as a wrong-headed theory. It just does not square with the empirical data. However, if human beings are to be accounted for within a completely naturalistic metaphysical framework that puts human beings on the same metaphysical level as other animals, then one of the major tasks will be to provide an account that contains some compelling explanation of the unique position that human beings occupy in the natural world. This is one of the major objectives of this book.

A second way of categorizing different attempts to provide theoretical accounts of human nature is by distinguishing *essentialist* from *non-essentialist* accounts. Essentialist views of human nature account for human nature in terms of either a single quality or characteristic or some set of qualities, characteristics, or features that is/are both necessary and sufficient to account for the nature of a human being. Again, Descartes is an obvious example of a major figure from the history of philosophy who holds an essentialist view of human nature. "I am," Descartes famously said, "a thinking substance—a thing that thinks." According to his metaphysical dualism, which divides the universe into physical and mental substances, human beings are the single, unique place where the two different kinds of substances are conjoined. However, other aspects of human nature and other qualities or features that a person might possess having to do with one's physical body or other aspects of the physical universe are accidental and non-essential. The essential and defining part of human nature—the necessary and sufficient condition that sets human beings off not only from other animals but from every other thing in the mechanical universe—is, for Descartes, the existence of an immaterial, mental substance in which essentially private mental events occur. It was this view of a metaphysically-distinct mind occupying a physical body in a mechanistic universe that Gilbert Ryle derisively referred to as the "Ghost in the Machine" in *The Concept of Mind.*

There are many other examples from the history of philosophy of essentialist views of human nature. Some such views are teleological, claiming that the essence of human beings consists in having a certain purpose or aim, e.g., seeking happiness or seeking a beatific union with

God. Other essentialist views account for the essence of human nature in terms of reason, moral agency, or free will. Most essentialist theories of human nature are top-down views in that the essence of human nature is usually attributed to a metaphysically distinct, non-natural ingredient–either spiritual, mental, or teleological. Top-down, essentialist theories, which identify some non-natural aspect of human nature as essential, also usually regard that non-natural essence as unalterable. Human beings are what we are because of a certain essence, like it or not; so we simply are who we are, and that is the end of the matter. However, some essentialist views take a bottom-up approach. Jean-Paul Sartre, for example, is noted for claiming that "existence precedes essence." For Sartre, the human condition and the fact that human beings are forced into making free choices of great consequence determine the essence of human nature; so, uniquely human actions produce a uniquely human essence.

Non-essentialist theories of human nature do not identify any single feature or set of features that are essential to human beings being the unique creatures that we are. Different features might be emphasized to a greater or lesser extent as contributing to human nature, but, on non-essentialist views, human beings are not thought to have a single, unalterable essence. Non-essentialist views tend to be empirical, drawing from evidence and data supplied by the natural and social sciences. The results of the scientific study of the brain by neuroscience, as well as the study of human development and human culture by anthropology and sociology, are gradually and constantly becoming more complete and detailed, and our understanding of the different features—both biological and cultural—as well as the different ways in which those features contribute to human nature—are constantly changing. At one time, for example, the size of the entire brain was taken to be a significant contributing factor to human nature, but it is not now. Some now take the development of the cerebral cortex and cognitive intelligence as the essential feature of human nature (a scientific version of Aristotelianism), but there is significant disagreement as to how important the *size* of the cerebral cortex is to the complex functions that take place there. At one time, anthropologists attached great weight to the fact that human beings use tools. However, then it was discovered that other animals use tools as well. Then, social scientists claimed that human beings are unique in that we both make and use tools. But we now have learned that other animals both make and use tools also. For non-essentialists, the different qualities or features, whether biological or cultural, that collectively account for human nature tend to be moving targets. Careful attention must be paid to what the scientific evidence is from the latest and most highly-regarded scientific discoveries and experiments. An important characteristic of the approach taken here is an attempt to draw from the most salient information from the most recent and the most highly regarded scientific evidence regarding human beings to try and assemble a composite view of human nature.

On the far side of the spectrum on which essentialism and non-essentialism both lie is the postmodernist claim (made, for example by Richard Rorty) that there is no single, ahistorical or acultural human nature but that different human natures are culturally *constructed* by different societies in different places at different times. Such a view might be called *anti-essentialist*. Although non-essentialists deny that there is a single essence of human nature, they still maintain that there is such a thing as human nature that is, as least to some extent, ahistorical and acultural. Thus, according to non-essentialist views of human nature, although there may not be an identifiable essence of human nature, there are still some qualities or features in terms of which I may be said to have the same "nature" as Socrates or other individuals from different cultures and different times. Anti-essentialists such as Rorty maintain, in contrast, that there is no single quality or feature or specific set of qualities or features that characterizes anything that is identifiable as a nature of human beings that is transhistorical or transcultural, i.e., no human nature exists independently of a culture that constructs that nature in terms of certain qualities or features. Postmodernists thus maintain that human nature (as well as such epistemological notions as truth and human reason) is *constructed* by the cultures in which human beings live and does not exist independently of those cultures.

Although there can be reasoned debates between essentialists and non-essentialists, anti-essentialists take reasoned debate "off the table" since their extreme, relativistic position is usually more the result of politics than it is of rational arguments. There is no doubt that the social sciences have identified a wide variety of different traits and behaviors from different cultures that are all human traits and behaviors, and that these differences have led to different understandings of what it means to be human. However, the fact that such differences exist and such different understandings of the nature of human beings exist does not prove that everything human is socially constructed. On the contrary, there can be no doubt that nature imposes upon different cultures certain limitations within which each culture operates. The existence of such limitations does not mean that there is a biologically-determined essence, but it does mean that human nature is not completely or infinitely malleable. One of the crucial tasks of a theory of human nature is to sort out, to some satisfactory degree of preciseness, exactly to what extent human nature is fixed by our biology and to what extent it is not. Even given the differences that exist amongst different human beings in different cultures of the world, there is still a difference between those different human beings and other animals, and even given those same differences, there is still some sense in terms of which we want to say that those different individual human beings are the same kind of creatures as were earlier human beings. Identifying, explaining, and defending the exact qualities or features in terms of which such comparisons are made is the substance of the theory of nature developed in this book. While I do not discuss anti-essentialism explicitly later in this book, the view developed here, taken as a whole, is intended as a general rebuttal to anti-essentialism.

Focusing on the different contributions made to human nature by biology on the one hand and by culture on the other explains another way of characterizing the different kinds of theories regarding human nature. If it is granted that the malleability of human nature is limited to some degree by nature, i.e., biology, then determining exactly the kind and degree of that limitation provides the backdrop upon which the *nature versus nurture* dispute is waged. If biology is responsible for determining *some* of the features of human nature, then the crucial issues become identifying which features are determined biologically and how those features are essential for making human beings independent of environmental influences. In contrast, the biologically-determined features may simply be the fundamental, "raw materials" that are then shaped and molded by experience into the essential features of human nature. There is perhaps no older or longer-lived continuing dispute than the one concerning whether human nature is essentially fixed by biology or by environment.

The nature/nurture controversy can be argued in several different ways and on several different grounds. The positions taken, favoring either nature or nurture, tend to line up with other claims about human nature forming a picture that is something of a jigsaw puzzle with interlocking pieces. Significant philosophical issues in political philosophy, moral philosophy, and epistemology are related to this basic question of just how much nature or nurture is responsible for the kind of creatures that we human beings are. Examples of related philosophical problems are abundant, but, to illustrate the point, consider just one or two of the more influential philosophical theories about these problems. On the side of nature, perhaps Thomas Hobbes' view of man is most illustrative. For him, human beings are helplessly selfish, self-centered, and self-interested. According to Hobbes, selfishness is a natural quality of human nature. His view of human nature was a bottom-up, materialistic view. He vehemently attacked the top-down, spiritualistic view and the notion of a soul or an immaterial mind. He also insisted that the only justification for political authority is to deliver and protect human beings from the "state of nature," the pitiful condition of war in which every man is pitted against every other man in which each individual is primarily concerned with survival and procreation. Only the power of political authority can save us from the condition, which Hobbes famously described, where human life is "solitary, poor, nasty, brutish, and short." Ironically then, Hobbes' view thus implicitly incorporates hints of both evolutionary theory and original sin. The selfish drives described by Hobbes are indelibly stamped on human nature. They are never erased. They are simply controlled and moderated. The Leviathan provides a kind of secular deliverance and salvation from the hellish state of nature in a manner similar to the way in which divine grace does the same thing according to some theists. In terms of the nature/nurture debate, Hobbes clearly falls into the nature camp. The Leviathan nurtures man, in a manner of speaking, by providing for the conditions necessary for human civilization; however, the raw power of the Leviathan does not change human nature itself in any way, i.e., there is nothing that might be called the "rehabilitation" of human beings. There is only the possibility of controlling human conduct through the fear generated by a powerful political authority. For Hobbes, human nature remains brutish and nasty although the human condition might be improved if people are forced to accept the fact that tolerating or supporting certain political arrangements actually serves our own self-interest.

To counterbalance Hobbes's view of human nature and to illustrate the significance of nurture in forming human nature, it is perhaps most illustrative to juxtapose John Locke's famous claim that human nature is a *tabula rasa*, a blank slate where everything that is uniquely human is written by experience. Discussions of Locke's view are usually connected with treatments of either liberalism or Christian theology, and certainly, Locke deserves special mention in connection with both. As is the case in many instances, Locke's view of human nature was driven by other philosophical concerns, including, primarily, his rejection of the Cartesian notion of innate ideas and his political views having to do with human equality and human rights. His liberalism and his accompanying rejection of authority, both political and ecclesiastical, were theologically motivated, as was his justification of the importance of property and the ownership of property. Thus, on the one hand, Locke's view is a top-down view since he accepts the theological claim that human beings have immortal souls, and this claim underlies his views having to do with equality. However, on the other hand, for purposes of illustrating the role of the environment in the development of human nature, it is more important to emphasize Locke's empiricism as opposed to his theology. The *tabula rasa* metaphor is used by Locke to depict an initial condition where nothing is written or etched that is determinate of human nature. His view is a rejection of both original sin and innate ideas. For Locke, in terms of knowledge, human beings do not come into this world "ready-made" or even partially made. In what one might say is a theological sense, the possession of an immortal soul might make human beings unique, but in terms of an actual *nature*, human beings are the exact, unique creatures that we are because we are what this world makes us to be. Or, perhaps more correctly, one might say that human beings are what our *experience* of this world makes us to be. The blank slate is a receptor of ideas imprinted upon it by experience, and those ideas constitute the whole of what a person is. It is one's environment, or the experience of that environment through one's senses, that thus determines the kind of creature that one is. This view attributes an extreme plasticity to human nature since the blank slate itself is entirely passive in the process of acquiring ideas. Ideas are casually flung at the experiencing mind through the senses, and some ideas "stick" there while others do not. This lack of direction or control by the mind of the process of acquiring ideas has been a major criticism raised by many against Locke's view, including Leibniz and, more elaborately, Kant.

Locke's empiricist view of human nature has been adopted, perhaps most influentially, as a dominant theme of the social sciences. Undoubtedly motivated by the attempt to be "scientific," most social scientists, until relatively recently, have attempted to account for human nature completely as a function of culture. Such social scientists tend to ignore the top-down aspect of Locke's theory while developing some form of his empiricistic, blank slate theory. Many of the major figures (and, in some cases, the founding figures) of the social sciences, such as John B. Watson and B. F. Skinner in psychology, Émile Durkheim in sociology, and Margaret Meade in anthropology, have emphasized the extreme plasticity of human nature. For all of these influential social scientists, whatever part of human nature that is provided by nature serves simply as the raw material, similar to Locke's blank tablet, that is given some substance and some definite content by experience. According to the social sciences, an important part of such experience is provided by the culture into which one is born and in which one lives. This gives some clue as to why such disciplines are known as the *social* sciences. There can hardly be a science of the blank slate since there would be, according to Locke himself, nothing for such a science to study—or precious little, at best. The view that culture determines and constructs human nature can easily slide into the kind of post-modernist relativism according to which the existence of any single, universal form of human nature is rejected. Since human cultures differ significantly around the world, if culture constructs human nature, it would be reasonable to suppose that human nature is constructed in significantly different ways by different cultures around the world.

The nature/nurture controversy leads naturally into another way of understanding different theories about human nature. There are those who maintain that human nature is *perfectible*; while others maintain that it is *non-perfectible*. Those who favor the perfectibility of human nature tend to be optimists about the human condition and its future, while those who do not favor the perfectibility of human nature tend to be pessimists. The non-perfectibility of human nature and the pessimism that frequently accompanies such a view are clearly evident in Hobbes' description of human nature. Human beings are what we are, and the picture is not a very pretty one. Driven by selfish desires, self-interest, and the fear of death, the best that can be said of human beings is that we are able to reason sufficiently to see that it is our own self-interest to cooperate with a powerful political authority *in order to preserve our own safety and to pursue our own self-interests.* Things will get better only in the sense that the Leviathan is able to control the beast within human nature, but the beast remains, and it remains unchanged. Such a view of the innate corruption of human beings, which finds its theological expression in the doctrine of original sin, provided the general, philosophical framework for the notion of the divine right of kings, according to which only especially chosen or endowed individuals were recognized as having legitimate political authority. Those selected for genuine political leadership were thought to require some special, divinely-bestowed quality that set them apart from ordinary human beings who remained fundamentally polluted and in need of divine guidance and assistance.

Although their views are disparate in most other respects, Rousseau agrees with Hobbes that human beings are non-perfectible, but for very different reasons than those proffered by Hobbes. Rousseau begins with the view that human beings, in the "State of Nature," are in as near a state of perfection as it is possible to attain. "Savage man" lives in complete harmony with Nature, according to Rousseau, including complete, peaceful harmony with the beasts and freedom from diseases and other maladies. It is only in such a condition that man is completely free. Society, culture, and governments are responsible for all of the ills and misfortunes of man. *Perfectibility* thus has an ironic meaning for Rousseau since it is responsible for man's "progress" from a more perfect state to a less perfect one.

Others have championed what is considered to be the innate ability of human beings to learn, change, and improve. Such a view characterizes the Enlightenment view of human nature upon which modern liberal democratic theory is based. Locke, Rousseau, and other figures of the Enlightenment shared a view of human nature according to which human beings are capable of developing our own systems of government and our own social, political, and economic arrangements. It was this view of human nature that was adopted by Thomas Jefferson and incorporated into the *Declaration of Independence* and the *Constitution of the United States*. With such a view of human nature in place, Jefferson, following Locke, insisted that human freedom is an intrinsically good thing and that the best government is the one that restricts freedom the least—only in those circumstances in which it is necessary to provide security and protection of the citizenry of the democracy. Jefferson was so optimistic about human nature and what he took to be our inexhaustible capacity for knowledge and the inestimable power of education that he thought, like many Enlightenment figures, that human reason could overcome any obstacles and correct any ills. If Hobbes is on one end of the pessimistic-optimistic spectrum, Jefferson is on the other.

At least some of the differences amongst theories concerning the perfectibility or non-perfectibility of human beings and the accompanying optimism or pessimism about the human condition can be traced to differences concerning *descriptive* versus *normative* claims about human nature. In other words, bottom-up, non-perfectibility views tend to emphasize empirical or otherwise descriptive claims about what human beings actually are or historically were while top-down, perfectibility claims tend to emphasize what human being *could be* like or what human beings *ought to be* like. Such normative claims are usually not held completely independently of factual descriptions of human beings or human history (except in the cases of claims that are purely theological or speculatively metaphysical), but such claims tend to emphasize certain incidents or figures from human history that are taken to be illustrative of the particular normative feature that is claimed for human nature. Thus, one might identify particular examples of human actions that are claimed to represent some ideal of what all human beings ought to be like or some ideal towards which all human beings should strive. For example, one might suggest what are taken to be acts of altruism or what are taken to be acts of heroism. Alternatively, one might identify acts of self-denial that are supposedly prompted by parental love for one's children or acts of sacrifice for others. Theological versions of perfectibility views tend to select what is described as a spiritual quality or an aspect of human nature that is taken to be "divine-like" so that *perfecting* human nature really amounts to moving away from *human* nature towards a more *divine* nature.

Finally, theories of human nature differ in their thickness. Some theories are very *thin* theories, by which I mean that such theories draw faint, subtle, and vague distinctions between human beings and other animals or other parts of the natural universe. Other theories are *thick* theories, by which I mean that such theories draw clear and distinct differences between human beings and other animals and other parts of the natural universe. Thin theories tend to make the differences between humans and other animals a matter of degree while thick theories tend to account for the differences between humans and other animals in terms of qualitative, indeed sometimes metaphysically qualitative, differences. Thin theories tend to be non-essentialist theories while thick theories tend to be essentialist theories. Naturalistic theories tend to be thin theories, making human beings just another member of the animal kingdom. Theological, or other top-down theories, are usually thick theories, making human beings such metaphysically distinctive, unique creatures in the universe that we become "strangers in a strange land"—creatures that are significantly out of place in the rest of what becomes an alien, natural world. Descartes' view is a perfect example of a thick theory. His claims that human beings are unique combinations of soul and body and that other animals are inanimate automata create a deep and wide metaphysical chasm between human beings and the rest of the natural world.

Top-down, thick theories also tend to be *static* theories while bottom-up, thin theories tend to be *dynamic* theories. Essentialist theories are necessarily static and non-essentialist theories are nearly always dynamic. Non-perfectionist views are necessarily static while perfectionist views are nearly always dynamic. Static theories of human nature claim that there is never a change in whatever is taken to be the essential human-making quality or qualities that constitute human nature. Static theories are immune to new discoveries by the sciences or new theories developed by either natural or social scientists about the natural history of human beings or our social development. Dynamic theories of human nature claim that human nature changes, or has changed, within a certain range, as a result of certain natural processes identified by the latest and best views from the natural and social sciences. Thin, bottom-up, non-essentialist views of human nature are constantly fine-tuning their claims about exactly what it is that makes us human in light of what is taken to be the best science available at the time. For dynamic theories, if the science changes, then the theory of human nature changes. Dynamic, fluid theories force one to think in terms of what human nature was, what it is now, and what it might be in the future. The fundamental conceptual issue becomes one of focusing upon the question of just how *plastic* and *elastic* the notion of human nature is, i.e., just how far can the concept of human nature be stretched before it breaks? In other words, just how different might we imagine human beings to be—either in the past or in the future—and still be human beings, in the sense that we still possess whatever it is that accounts for a unique human nature? Answers to these conceptually puzzling questions will be developed as the theory of human nature is developed in the following chapters. The theory of human nature developed in this book is a thin, descriptive, dynamic, bottom-up, non-essentialist, naturalistic theory. A general and preliminary description of this theory is the subject of Chapter 2.

2

The Cluster Theory of Human Nature

Arguably, few topics have interested philosophers through the ages more than the question of what it is that makes human beings the unique creatures that we are. Most of the major figures in the history of philosophy have had something to say about human nature even if they have not attempted to develop a full-blown, systematic theory. Unfortunately, most of the more recent attention given by philosophers to the question of human nature has come from moral philosophers, political philosophers, or metaphysicians interested in some particular aspect of human nature. For example, moral philosophers have focused on moral psychology and the psychological make-up of human beings that allows us to make moral judgments and have moral sentiments. Metaphysicians have focused on the questions of whether human beings have free will and, if so, how that affects other philosophically important issues such as moral responsibility and punishment. Some moral philosophers have first determined *what* the moral law is and then argued that human beings must have a certain nature in order to follow that moral law. Others have claimed that human beings have experiences of the supernatural, the divine, or, perhaps more generally, that human beings have religious experiences or "the religious spirit" and have then proceeded to determine what sort of nature human beings must have in order to have such experiences. In other words, most of the more recent or contemporary philosophers interested in a theory of human nature have had other philosophical axes to grind or fish to fry. These other philosophical interests and, in some cases, prior philosophical commitments or assumptions, have determined the starting place of philosophical inquiry concerning human nature and significantly shaped the nature and direction of that inquiry. This explains why more philosophers have been interested in the notion of "person"

17

than in a theory of human nature since, in the current nomenclature, personhood maps more directly onto legal and moral questions about such issues as abortion or euthanasia, which, in many cases, provide the primary impetus for the inquiry in the first place.

Indeed, one of the most dominant features of the notion of "person" is the degree to which it reflects an individual's social and political status; however, the understanding of this status differs from culture to culture. Slaves and women and children have not been recognized in some cultures as full-fledged persons and thus have not been deemed deserving of the same legal privileges and protections as adult men. Often one must attempt to abstract, decipher, or infer what a contemporary philosopher's view of human nature is from what is needed to be consistent with other views developed concerning other philosophical matters. This approach explains why considerably more in-depth systematic treatments of the subjects of *human nature*, *man*, and *human beings* have been produced by anthropologists, biologists, and sociologists than have been produced by philosophers. Given that the concept "person" is so heavily ingrained with moral and legal features, the focus in this book is on the concept of human nature, and it is therefore left it to others to analyze how different treatments of the concept "person" map onto the treatment of human nature developed here.

Rarely does philosophical inquiry concerning human nature proceed explicitly and directly. Perhaps, as many have claimed, inquiry cannot proceed with no assumptions at all. However, in this present inquiry into human nature, I intend to proceed with as few prior commitments as possible to particular philosophical or theological positions, and I intend to make explicit and defend whatever kind of assumptions I do make during the inquiry. I begin then with no particular view of the nature of moral judgments or free will or the relationship, if any, between free will and moral responsibility. I begin with no view concerning human rights or human reason. I also begin with no assumptions about the origin of the universe or the eventual destiny of human beings—before or after death. I begin with no metaphysical assumptions beyond those that involve a commitment to the existence of the natural world. I do begin with a commitment to the natural and social sciences and to the best scientific theories and data that they can provide us with about human beings upon which a theory of human nature can be based. I thus begin with a commitment to methodological naturalism.

There are major ambiguities about the meanings of "human" and "human nature" that pervade much of the literature about human nature.

Thus, a major conundrum has developed concerning human nature and such surrounding and related concepts as "person," and "human being." I do not try and resolve this conundrum; however, I do begin with the assumption that there is a difference in meaning between being biologically human and having human nature—a distinction that I argue for at length throughout the book. Not only might an individual be biologically human (whether determined by human DNA or by certain anatomical or developmental features) without possessing human nature, but it is consistent with the theory of human nature developed here that there could be an entire species of creatures that are biologically human no single individual of which possesses human nature. It is also consistent with the theory developed here that there might be individuals that are non-human biologically (e.g., aliens from some distant galaxy) but who possess human nature. While some of these possibilities might seem extremely controversial, in reality most are not very problematic. The ambiguity between being biologically human and having human nature and the distinction between the two is revealed regularly in common speech when we say about someone—whether it is a psychopathic killer or someone in a permanent vegetative state—that he or she is not "really human." The non-controversial nature of the claim that being biologically human and having human nature are different will become more obvious as a systematic theory of human nature is developed.

The theory that is developed here can best be described as the *cluster theory of human nature*. The cluster view is informed by the current, most highly-regarded theories from biology and neuroscience as well as the latest views from the social sciences, and, as such, it is thus a naturalistic, thin, bottom-up, dynamic, non-essentialist view. The careful consideration of the best-informed theories from the natural and social sciences makes it possible to identify a cluster of different characteristics, features, traits, qualities, abilities and/or behaviors that collectively provide a causal nexus—a causal environment upon which human nature depends and from which it arises. Some of these distinguishing features of human nature are biological traits that have been selected for. Others are the result of cultural or societal influence. Other features are more difficult to characterize as either biological or cultural and are "up for grabs" in the competition between the natural and social sciences and in the nature/nurture debate. Still other features are more likely be to regarded as "spiritual" or, at least, mental, and the challenge will be to account for such features using a completely naturalistic methodology. For the cluster theory to account for all of the features of human nature and the causal relationships amongst those features completely naturalistically does not logically require a stance on metaphysical naturalism, i.e., it does not require the formal denial of any other kind of metaphysical existence beyond the natural world. It does mean that the cluster theory is committed to methodological naturalism, according to which, to repeat the claim made above, all of the various characteristics, features, traits, qualities, abilities and/or behaviors that collectively provide the causal nexus—a causal environment upon which human nature depends and from which it rises—can be found and accounted for in the natural world.

Given the wide range of different features that collectively make up human nature and the different *kinds* of features that belong to the cluster, the use of different terms, e.g., "trait" or "behavior" is often taken as prejudicing a theory in one way or another towards biologically-determined or socially-conditioned views. Thus, I will use what I take to be the philosophically-neutral term *"property"* to refer generically to the different features that belong to the cluster of features that comprise what we call human nature. I intend the term "property" to be understood as the most generic, inclusive, and unbiased term for referring to the set of traits, behaviors, features, abilities, qualities, or characteristics that might be considered as belonging to human nature.

Exactly how the *properties* of human nature are to be understood, however, requires some explanation because even the use of the term "property" may be misleading, suggesting a set of essential characteristics for a complete definition of "human nature." However, since the cluster theory is a non-essentialist view of human nature, the claim is not that there is a set of different essential characteristics, traits, behaviors, etc., that *define* human nature. The notion of a *cluster* of properties is intended to convey a very different picture. In the first place, and most importantly, the *properties* of the cluster theory are, individually, *non-essential* features, characteristics, traits, or behaviors, a *core cluster* of which make up human nature. According to the cluster theory, it is not a single feature or trait or behavior that accounts for what we call human nature. Furthermore, it is also not a specific, identifiable definite *set* of features, traits, or behaviors that makes up the core cluster. While some particular property or some particular set of properties in the cluster might be deemed more important than others and might occur more frequently than others or even occur nearly all of the time, none is essential.

What exactly is it then, one might ask, that makes up the core cluster of *properties* of human nature if it is not a specific, identifiable definite set of *properties*? The answer to this question constitutes the very heart of the cluster theory and occupies the remainder of this book. The core cluster of *properties* is composed of a set of features, traits, and behaviors, of which no single one is essential for constituting human nature and of which no unique set is essential for constituting human nature but of which *some* set or sets, i.e., *some* combinations of properties, are responsible for producing what we regard as human nature. One might say that human nature can best be thought of as the result of a combination of different, non-essential *properties* that are related to one another in a way such that *certain combinations* of those properties—but no single, particular combination of those properties—produce a causal nexus sufficient for human nature to exist. In other words, there is a large set of properties that are sometimes (or regularly) instantiated in human beings, and there is a large range of different possible combinations of the instantiations of those properties, possible subsets of those properties. It is essential that *some* one subset (i.e., one cluster of properties) be instantiated in order for the causal nexus upon which human nature is dependent to be produced, but no one *particular* subset of properties (i.e., no one cluster of properties) is essential. *Some* cluster of properties is essential for human nature, but no *particular* cluster is essential. This leaves a rather wide range of possibilities of different combinations of properties that might theoretically subvene human nature.

At least part of what must be meant by the resemblance of the *properties* in the core cluster of human nature must be causal and historical, which also greatly multiplies the possible numbers of clusters that might be used to explain human nature. The properties themselves are the functions of a complex set of interrelationships that exist between members of the human species and our environment. Such interrelationships include the relationships to other members of our own species, the relationships to other living and non-living things, the ways in which we both act upon and are acted upon by our environment, and the ways in which we experience different parts of our environment.

Furthermore, the cluster of properties that comprise what we call human nature form a *causal nexus* within which the properties are related to one another in such a way so as to form an irreducible complexity, i.e., the individual properties are causally related to one another in such a way that properties in the cluster cannot be removed or altered *significantly* without affecting others significantly. The cluster of properties that comprise human nature is not present as a set of discrete, individual properties like marbles in a jar or peas in a pod where one can easily be removed while the others are left undisturbed. What we call human nature *emerges* from the causal nexus created by the casual interactions amongst the properties in the cluster.

Human nature thus *supervenes* upon the *causal nexus* of the cluster in a Gestalt manner. More precisely, the complexity formed by the causal nexus of properties that constitute human nature should be called an *imperfect* irreducible complexity since the removal or significant alteration of one of the properties of the nexus might not completely abolish or eliminate human nature. However, the removal or alteration, whether minor or significant, of one of the properties contained in the nexus might very well eventually threaten to destroy human nature and, as I shall argue, can easily set into motion a causal "chain reaction" that could eventually destroy human nature. Historically and descriptively, human nature is thus the emergent result from the causal nexus resulting from the instantiation of a cluster of properties in a biological species over a fairly stable period of time. It is the result of a felicitous convergence of properties, perhaps some major and some minor, just as a bay might be the result of the convergence of large rivers and small streams. By saying that the convergence is a felicitous one, nothing is implied about purpose or design. The convergence is felicitous in the sense that it is a fortunate thing for the existence of human nature itself.

It is difficult to settle upon just the appropriate metaphor to capture the way in which human nature supervenes upon the causal nexus of the cluster of properties identified in the cluster theory. One might think of a recipe for baking a cake (an often used metaphor used to explain emergent properties); however, cakes, once baked, are what they are, and they *emerge* in a manner that is irreversible and irreducible to their original components. Unlike cakes, human nature has evolved and changed and might very well evolve and continue to change in the future. Also, human nature is a property that may be instantiated to different degrees in different individuals. In order to capture that reality, any systematic theory of human nature must be dynamic. Thus, the cluster theory is dynamic in the sense that it recognizes and embraces fluctuations that occur in individuals in the degree to which certain properties in the cluster of properties upon which human nature supervenes are instantiated as well as similar fluctuations amongst numbers of individuals in a general population.

Perhaps it is helpful to think of a very complex, multidimensional puzzle with numerous pieces. The puzzle in question must be a very special kind of puzzle in which not only do the different pieces interlock and fit together but the nature of one piece of the puzzle is a significant factor in determining the natures of other pieces of the puzzle and *where each and every piece of the puzzle is a linchpin that keeps the puzzle from eventually falling apart.* There are reflexive causal connections amongst all of the pieces of the puzzle such that keeping the whole thing together supervenes upon not only the different pieces of the puzzle but the unique relationships amongst those pieces. Borrowing from the original, literal meaning of "linchpin," each piece of the puzzle can be understood as a linchpin because any significant change in any one piece threatens to allow, in the colloquial expression, "the wheels to come off" and the whole that is human nature to come apart.

However illustrative the metaphor of a puzzle with linchpin pieces might be, in the end it is misleading and unsatisfactory because it too strongly suggests a relationship between the properties of the cluster theory and the physical pieces of the puzzle. It is the causal nexus of the cluster of properties upon which human nature supervenes. The notion of a linchpin is ultimately too weak to capture the notion of the causal nexus. Consider, however, a Rubik's Cube. With a Rubik's cube, the solution to the puzzle is a particular configuration of the colored squares on the sides of the cube, and the desired configuration is not produced by a physical arrangement of the squares but by a *process* of moves—of twists and turns—performed in a certain order (or in one of a very limited number of possible orders). The "solution" of the puzzle—the particular desired configuration of colored squares—*emerges* at a certain point in the process of moves and as a result of the preceding moves. The properties of the cluster theory of human nature might be thought of as akin to *configurations* of colored squares of the Rubik's Cube. If human nature is understood as the final configuration of colored squares on the observable surfaces of the cube, then the cluster of properties upon which it supervenes can be understood as the additional configurations of colored squares in the interior of the cube upon which the final configuration supervenes. Changing one of the interior configurations slightly threatens to destroy the final solution (or, perhaps in the actual case of the Rubik's Cube any change of the other configurations *does* destroy the final solution).

Perhaps because human beings are such unique creatures with such a unique nature, there is no metaphor for explaining that nature that is completely appropriate. In using the Rubik's Cube, for example, I do not mean to suggest that there is any linear progression of "moves" or changes that take place in human development to produce human nature, nor do I mean to suggest that whatever the processes are that, in the end, allow human nature to emerge are mechanical, nor do I mean to suggest that there is some "intelligent designer" or game player manipulating the process, nor do I mean to suggest that there is an identifiable, definitive set of "moves" that can be made to produce human nature.

Like other dynamic, biological processes, the exact combination or processes that produce the cluster of properties upon which human nature supervenes are likely never to be sorted out, and thus, the "solution" to the puzzle that is human nature is likely never to be found. So, in the end, the concept of human nature is a vague one; however, just because the concept of human nature is vague does not mean that we cannot gain some understanding and clarity about it. For example, and in particular, the understanding of human nature that emerges with the cluster theory does not identify any particular order of processes or set of properties that is *essential* to producing human nature. This is perhaps the most important respect in which the cluster theory of human nature differs from the metaphor. Still, with these significant differences, the notion of an emergence of a combination, pattern, or configuration of properties, interrelated in a manner that produces a causal nexus, upon which human nature supervenes is most illustrative for understanding the cluster theory of human nature.

In this context, considering another metaphor that is illustrative of the cluster theory of human nature might help to correct some of the misleading aspects of the example of the Rubik's Cube. The attempt here is simply to help get some conceptual purchase on the cluster theory. Imagine yourself listening to a live performance of Tchaikovsky's *Sixth Symphony*, the *Pathetique*. In the First Movement, as the familiar theme begins to swell, the full orchestra is playing at full volume. Let us ask exactly how it is that the theme emerges from the actions of the various musicians playing different instruments in different sections of the orchestra. The interest here is not in questions about the aesthetic object or what actually constitutes the *thing* that is Tchaikovsky's *Sixth Symphony*, i.e., questions concerning whether the aesthetic object is the written score or the performed music. The focus instead is on the causal relationship between the audible music and the instruments, musicians, and actions of the musicians in the orchestra. The theme that is *the* theme of the First Movement of Tchaikovsky's *Sixth Symphony* emerges only as a result of certain successive actions of the musicians using certain physical instruments. Now the original score calls for a certain number of specific instruments and a specific succession of notes that is supposed to emerge from those instruments, creating what I regard as a causal nexus from which the theme then emerges. Just as the theme of the First Movement of Tchaikovsky's *Pathetique* emerges from the interrelated processes that take place in different sections of the orchestra (in this case, the fingering, bowing, plucking, blowing, and striking in various precise manners by members of the orchestra), so human nature emerges from the different properties that are the result of different natural processes in the great orchestra of nature. Explaining how this takes place is the general purpose of the cluster theory of human nature.

There may be differences that are distracting (as there are with any metaphor) between these metaphors and human nature. However, considering the final configurations that are the baked cake, or the solution to a puzzle, or the musical theme and how these configurations are produced as the results of complex causal processes gives some idea of how I intend the supervenience of human nature upon the causal nexus of the properties of the cluster to be understood. Although these metaphors will not be discussed again in any detail, explaining and elaborating upon their meanings and how they illustrate the emergence of human nature according to the cluster theory will occupy much of the attention of the remaining chapters of this book.

The understanding of human nature that lies behind these metaphors is that it is a complex, emergent property that is produced by certain combinations of instantiations of properties, i.e, *clusters* of properties. The *instantiation* of those properties must occur within a natural world, thus, as I argue in the next chapter, a significant causal factor involves the nature of that natural world. In a very important and fundamental sense, human nature is a relational property that is a function of how human beings experience, interact with and respond to that natural world. To understand this aspect of human nature, consider the property of *buoyancy*. Buoyancy is a property of objects that is properly not simply a property of the object itself but a function of the relationship between the object and a liquid. An object *floats* when the pressure of the liquid pushing upwards on the object cancels the weight of the object. The property of being buoyant thus involves not simply characteristics of the object itself but, just as importantly, factors that obtain in the natural world, including the existence of liquids and the chemical compositions of those liquids, the force of gravity, etc. Should those conditions be significantly different than they are in this actual world, the property of buoyancy would also be significantly different or, perhaps, non-existent. In this actual world, a flat steel bar has no buoyancy, but a flat piece of

Styrofoam does. However, when configured to form the hull of a ship, steel can float. Whether a thing floats is thus, like human nature, the function of a complex emergent property of a certain causal nexus that is the product of the multifaceted interaction between an individual thing and its environment. Again, in this actual world, if an object floats it is orientated to its environment in a completely different way from an object that does not float. Instead of simply sinking, like the Proverbial stone, an object that floats can be propelled by wind or current or other means to travel great distances and interact with other objects in numerous ways. The force of the quote from Plato's *Phaedrus* (at the beginning of this book) is clear: to understand what makes *buoyancy* or *human nature* to be what they are is to understand their power of acting or being acted upon in this world.

The comparison with buoyancy can be used to illustrate another important feature of human nature. Human nature is a property that is multiply realizable. In this context, to say that human nature enjoys multiple realizability is simply to emphasize the difference between an individual being biologically human and having human nature. Buoyancy is a property that may be instantiated in varying degrees and in a multiplicity of different ways by a number of different kinds of objects. Just as buoyancy may be multiply realized in different objects, composed of different materials and characterized by different designs so human nature may be multiply realized in different individuals—some biologically human and some perhaps not. This is not to say that either buoyancy or human nature can be instantiated in just any old way. Given the natural laws and the physical and chemical properties of the known universe, buoyancy can be realized only within a somewhat narrow range of possible ways, and the same is true of human nature. Hydrostatics is given to sorting out the details and principles of how buoyancy comes to be instantiated within a certain range of possibilities, and the cluster theory is given to sorting how human nature comes to be instantiated within a certain range of possibilities.

As an effect that supervenes upon the causal nexus of the core cluster of properties, human nature is an organic notion. It has come into being gradually, over a significant period of time, as the result of natural processes and the rather complicated ways in which biological creatures of a certain species have interacted with their environment, which itself has been characterized by certain vital features. Since Darwin's evolution by natural selection has undermined the immutability of the species, in order to grasp fully what human nature is, it is necessary to think in terms of human nature of the past, the present, and the future. What circumstances in the past, and over what period of time, were exactly as they needed to be in order for the biological species that we now call human beings to develop the core cluster of properties that comprise human nature? Within what range of present circumstances might human nature be preserved? And within what range of changes in those circumstances in the future might human nature be preserved? Within what latitudes are the proper "moves" made to produce the configurations of biological and social properties that are comparable to the configurations of colored squares of Rubik's Cube? Just how different might an orchestra be constituted or Tchaikovsky's *Pathetique* be scored and performed and still be said to produce the same symphony or the same musical theme? What if the entire string section of the orchestra were to be missing in a performance of the *Pathetique*? What if there were no cannons or timpanis used in a performance of Tchaikovsky's *1812 Overture*? The audience would still be hearing *something* for sure, but would one want to say that the audience is hearing *the Pathetique* or *the 1812 Overture*? The most likely answer is, "Probably not."

Pursuing answers to these questions, and others similar to these, serves to focus attention on the important, underlying philosophical questions concerning the properties of the core cluster themselves and how (and to what degree) they might vary. If human nature is taken to be the property h that supervenes upon the core cluster of non-essential properties a, b, c, d, e, f, g, then the crucial issue becomes the one of determining just which particular combinations of those properties are sufficient for producing the nexus upon which human nature depends and just what variation is possible in the presence of those properties, in the exact nature of those properties, and in the causal interaction amongst those properties. To pursue answers to these questions, it is necessary to engage in some conceptual "stretching" to see just how far the concept of human being might be stretched and under what modalities it might be stretched to what lengths.

Consider Wittgenstein's often quoted remark to the effect that if a lion were able to speak, we would not be able to understand it. There are varying interpretations of this comment under which it might be taken to represent some important philosophical insight. Since speaking a language is a part of *a form of life* for Wittgenstein, the most common understanding attributed to his point is that it is not possible for individuals within a particular form of life to understand and communicate with those within a significantly different one. More recently, interest in such issues has led to consideration of the question of the incommensurability of different conceptual schemes. However, if we keep the focus more narrowly on Wittgenstein's comment, there are at least two scenarios under which one might explore why this claim would be true. It might be, for example, that the lion is speaking the Lion language and we human beings are not tutored in Lion. By this I mean that the lion is not just producing grunts and roars but distinctive and recognizable phonemes whose *meanings* are unknown to human beings. Under this scenario, assuming that speaking lions do so at regular times and familiar circumstances, some may claim that it would be a relatively short time before teams of enterprising young biologists, anthropologists, and linguists, working with government grants, would study lions and Lion and produce translations and dictionaries of Lion. We have gone through similar processes of trying to decipher and understand various animal "languages" without generating baffling philosophical puzzles with no apparent, adequate solutions. As provocative and challenging as this situation might be, this surely does not capture the philosophical significance of Wittgenstein's point.

Perhaps the puzzling philosophical problem might be better revealed if we imagine a different scenario in which the lion *simply* speaks common English. The conceptually provocative nature of this suggestion might be hard to grasp initially because of the overexposure of Disneyesque cartoon characters behaving and speaking in a human manner. However, imagine a *real* situation in which one is walking through an unexplored jungle and happens upon an ordinary-looking lion that offers a friendly, even exuberant, greeting: "Top of the morning to you, Governor. Dr. Livingston, I presume?" On the one hand, one might wonder just what is so difficult about *understanding* the lion's greeting. One might just think that the lion has just gotten the wrong impression that *I* am Dr. Livingston. But exactly what could it mean to attribute to the lion such a misapprehension and to take the spoken words as evidence of this misapprehension and as convening some *intended* greeting or other meaning? Wittgenstein's point is that it is impossible to bridge the staggering conceptual chasm between recognizing meaningful uses of language—including attributing understanding and intentionality to the speakers of human language in the case of human beings and doing the same thing in the case of lions. Imagining the lion speaking in ordinary English drives home the point that engaging in meaningful uses of language with others involves an assumed attribution of a whole set of shared attributes to those other speakers.

It is easy to agree with Wittgenstein that, no matter the circumstances, because of the conceptual difficulties, one could never bring oneself to attribute the ability to discourse meaningfully to a lion and to believe that one is actually engaged in a meaningful conversation with an actual *lion*. Why would this be conceptually impossible? For Wittgenstein, the answer would be something like the following: speaking a human language is part of a *form of life*. The uttering of a meaningful sentence in modern English (or any other human language) or issuing a greeting is not something that occurs *by itself* in isolation from other features or characteristics that we take to be salient features (or perhaps even essential features) of a particular *form* of life. Conceptually, we do attribute the requisite intentions and understanding for meaningful discourse only to other creatures that we recognize as human beings, and that means we recognize those creatures as possessing or demonstrating the shared characteristics with other creatures that we take to be human beings. We do not, Wittgenstein might say (if he were less cryptic and more direct about the point) recognize lions as possessing or sharing those salient characteristics that are necessary for attributing the requisite intentions for meaningful discourse; so, although the phonemes are those occurring in common English, we would not recognize them or understand them as conveying any meaning. Thus, we could not be said to *understand* the lion.

All of which suggests a different but equally interesting question. Could it ever come to be the case, *at some point in the future*, that a lion might speak in a manner that we human beings could understand and regard as meaningful? In other words, can we *imagine* ourselves carrying on a humanesque conversation with a lion under very different circumstances than those that exist presently? Perhaps, Wittgenstein intended that we cannot imagine such a situation in the *weak* sense of imagine, i.e., that is, in the sense where we try to imagine a lion speaking while everything else in this world remains unchanged. But, consider whether we can imagine the possibility of understanding a speaking lion in a *strong* sense, i.e., can we imagine a world in which everything or at least many things might be different than they are in this world, including our notions of human beings and human nature? With a dynamic, fluid theory of human nature, one ought to expect that the concept of human being and the core cluster of properties and the causal relationships amongst those properties upon which our understanding of human nature supervenes might change over a period of time. Just how much those properties and their causal relationships can change and just how elastic and malleable

the notion of human nature is are questions that will occupy much of the
attention for the remaining chapters of this book.

Considering the possibilities and the extent of the plasticity and elas-
ticity of the notion of human nature just might give one a very different
slant on Wittgenstein's puzzle. Without giving a specific answer at the
moment to the question of whether it might ever come to be the case that
a lion might speak in a manner that *we* would recognize as meaningful, it
is important to realize that to answer the important, underlying question
about human nature, it is necessary to consider not just the modalities that
might result in the lion taking on different properties or characteristics
than it currently possesses. One must also consider how, over a period of
time, what we now consider to be human beings might change—perhaps
by taking on properties that we human beings do not now possess but
that lions do. The point is that one must consider not just what might
change so that the lion might become more like human beings but what
might change so that human beings become more like lions (but still,
of course, remain human beings). Considering such modalities is a way
of pursuing the issue of how conceptually elastic the notion of human
nature is and how far it can be stretched before breaking.

Some years ago, I was a participant in a workshop on creative thinking
when my group was asked to come up with an answer to the following
question: If human beings were to be redesigned with a third eye, where
would you put it? This problem certainly provoked interesting and creative debate amongst the members of my group. One person suggested
putting the eye on the end of a forefinger or another finger. Initially, the
increased practical benefits and the expanded visual possibilities of this
location (e.g., seeing around corners or under heavy objects without
having to move them or kneel down) seemed promising. However,
then the liabilities of having an optic nerve running all of the way from
a person's finger up the arm to the brain weighed heavily against this
suggestion. Some people wondered if the result of putting an eye on the
end of a finger would result in people being "right-eyed" or "left-eyed"
(depending upon which hand was chosen) comparable to the way in
which people are now right-handed or left-handed. Since I am actually
missing the tip of my right forefinger as the result of an earlier accident,
I pointed out the increased vulnerability of such an exposed location.
The second suggestion, and the one that was, in the end, preferred by
the members of the group, was to put the third eye in the back of the
head. In this location it appeared that one would gain the advantage of a
significantly-increased visual field while the location provided the kind

of protection that would be lacking elsewhere on the human body. The members of the group discussed but never resolved the details of how a third visual stimulus could be incorporated into the existing binocular vision that human beings have, how the cerebral cortex might need to be altered, and how hats might have to be redesigned.

Prompting such creative thinking was exactly the purpose of the exercise, and it served its purpose. However, since I was the only philosopher in the group, I had to ask the following question: "Would human beings still be human beings if we had third eyes?" This question prompted a new exercise, which might best be described as one of creative "conceptual stretching." The problem might be put this way: In terms of anatomy or in terms of perceptual apparatuses or in terms of perceptual experience, how different might the creatures be that we now regard as human and still be human? Answering this question is not a simple, straightforward process. A carefully-considered answer requires one first to identify all of those predicates that belong to the core cluster of predicates that comprise human nature and then to consider where and to what degree the particular anatomical and perceptual properties fall in this group. It will also be necessary to consider, given the causal nexus within which the different properties in the core cluster occur, what the effects on the other properties in the cluster might be of a significant change in one those properties. That is, the assumption in asking the question about adding the additional eye appears to be that the addition could take place *ceteris paribus* and that thus, we are asking if we can imagine, in the weak sense, that humans could have a third eye. However, it is not obvious at all and it may not even be true at all, that if human nature is taken as supervening upon an imperfect, irreducible complex of a cluster of properties, that even a relatively insignificant change could take place in one of the properties of the complex without eventually, over a long period of time, affecting or perhaps undermining the process of supervenience. With a dynamic theory of human nature, adding a third eye to the human anatomy is certainly more than a minor, insignificant change, and making that change (or any other such changes—whether they are regarded as minor or significant at the time) might very well eventually necessitate a change in our concept of human nature depending upon the "ripple effect" that we judge that one change to have upon other properties in the cluster and the causal nexus of those properties. "Well," we might come to think, at some point in the future, "human beings used to be the kind of creatures that only had two eyes, but we have gradually evolved into creatures with three eyes." Or, alternatively, some human-like creatures might come to think, at some point in the future, that human beings with two eyes were early prototypes or progenitors of their species.

Consider also, what if adding a third eye resulted in a *significantly altered* (and one would assume *significantly improved*) sense of vision—one of those qualitative "quantum leaps" of perceptual ability? And what if some individuals acquired the third eye through some quirky mutation while others did not? Then there would be a significant difference between "the two eyes" and "the three eyes"—perhaps on the level of the present difference between blind and sighted individuals. How such large scale changes in the way in which human beings experience the physical world might affect the notion of human nature and just how closely human nature is tied to human sense experience is the subject of Chapter 5.

Our understanding of human nature, according to the cluster theory, is thus something of a moving target. With apologies to biologists and anthropologists, even getting a clear aim at the target requires thinking counterfactually about the past and hypothetically about the future. Of course to think counterfactually, we must begin with what we take to be the most accurate factual account that biologists and anthropologists can provide of the past. Starting with that account, we then ask, "Just how differently might things have developed in the past and just how different might the consequences of those different developments have been for producing whatever it is that we now regard as making human beings human?" And just how might events transpire in the future and what might the possible effects of those events be upon the core cluster of properties and their causal nexus upon which human nature supervenes? On the one hand, such questions might initially seem to be the kind of subject matter only of science fiction and comic books. On the other hand, and upon more reflection, such questions are the subject matter of serious science and serious philosophical inquiry. For example, in a different context, when Philo is speculating in Part XI of David Hume's *Dialogues Concerning Natural Religion* about the ways in which this world might have been created differently by an omnipotent God to minimize the existence of evil, he suggests that God might have tweaked human nature in a particular way to produce significantly different results. Philo points out that most living creatures appear to have the bare minimum of features necessary for survival, and that this appears to be true of human beings as well. When he considers how human beings and their nature might have been different, he does not insist that human beings be gifted with the eye of the eagle, the strength of the ox, or the swiftness of the deer. He suggests that God might have simply made man more industrious and given more naturally to labor rather than naturally given to sloth and laziness. Just this one small tweak, Philo suggests, would have been responsible for significant differences in human nature (and for the better).

Now the problem of evil is not the present concern; however, in Hume's suggestion we have the suggestion of a possible world approach to thinking about human nature that might prove to be helpful in dealing with the problem of sorting out the modalities that might affect human nature. Perhaps Hume is suggesting that the human genotype might have been different, i.e., perhaps he means that different character traits might have been genetically encoded in the human genome. However, exploring possible ways in which human nature might be different need not commit one to the position that all of human nature is genotypic; thus, questions about God, creation, or the human genome need not even enter the picture if the question about how human nature might be different is considered within a completely naturalistic methodology.

Human nature is neither completely biologically determined nor completely the result of what the environment has imprinted upon a "blank slate." Consequently, following Hume's suggestion, we must think in terms of how differently human nature might have evolved if certain events in the past had transpired differently. Pursuing this line of inquiry leads to several related, very poignant questions that must be addressed by any adequate theory of human nature: if certain events in and features of the universe had been different in the past, and the resulting consequences had been responsible for certain differences in human nature, just how significant could those changes be before human nature would be destroyed? What range of differences might our current understanding of human nature tolerate in the human genotype? Similarly, what range of differences might our current understanding of human nature tolerate in the properties of the cluster that are phenotypic and what would the effect of those changes be upon the causal nexus of those properties? In a different possible world with certain differences in its natural history, would the creatures that evolved in that world, which might be very much *like* the creatures that we now regard as human beings, actually *be* human beings and possess what we regard in this actual world as human nature? Or, perhaps, most poignantly, could human beings, possessing what we now regard as human nature, *only* exist in this actual world?

To explore an explanation of human nature in terms of methodological naturalism, it is necessary to understand a great deal about natural history. If what is commonly known about natural history is taken seriously along with the part of that natural history that affects human history, then the part of natural history about which we might think counterfactually is more narrowly circumscribed. In other words, given what science has demonstrated about natural history, certain modalities concerning how humans might have developed differently are ruled out, and others come more sharply into focus. Also, if what science tells us about the *process* through which human beings developed is taken seriously, then certain modalities, e.g., divine acts or other metaphysically-distinct explanations, for how human nature came to be what it is are ruled out, and again others, e.g., those affecting human evolution, come more sharply into focus. Thus, we can adapt the general, possible world approach apparently presupposed by Hume's suggestion to a more narrow and realistic context whose limits are drawn by modern science. To consider the effects of different modalities upon the development of human nature, we can imagine the consequences of certain situations in which most of what we know about man's natural history is held constant but in which particular conditions and events of that natural history, within a very narrow range, are imagined to have gone differently. In such a process, it is axiomatic that small, subtle differences in the beginning of a long, slow, developmental process can result in large, significant differences at the end of that process.

Thinking counterfactually about natural history specifically within a context circumscribed by those natural conditions and events that might have been different and thus might have affected the specific way in which human nature has developed suggests an approach that makes use of a particular form of the *anthropic principle*. There is no single version of the anthropic principle that is commonly accepted by scientists, and some versions of this principle are quite controversial.[1] There is, however, a common element of the different versions of the anthropic principle that commands some degree of agreement amongst scientists. That fundamental notion captured by different versions of the anthropic principle is this: given what scientists now know about the initial conditions from which the universe eventually evolved, even very minuscule variations in any number of those initial conditions, which are apparently causally unrelated, would have precluded the development of carbon-based life. Thus, given what science tells us about the conditions and circumstances regarding the very beginning of the universe, according to the anthropic principle, the antecedent probability that intelligent, human life would evolve in the universe was infinitesimally small. All of this means that the various physical conditions and properties of the universe had to be *almost exactly* as they in fact were in order for carbon-based life, and thus human life as we know it, to evolve.

Suppose we assume that the fundamental claim of the anthropic principle is true and that the initial conditions of the universe had to be *extremely* exacting, with minuscule tolerance for variation, for carbon-based life ever to exist. We can then ask, given that carbon-based life *did* evolve, what range of conditions was necessary for it to evolve *exactly* the way that it has in order for human beings finally to emerge with the particular cluster of properties that constitute what we now take to be human nature. This kind of question suggests an evolutionary version of the anthropic principle that we might call the *evolutionary anthropic principle* according to which the conditions under which any given species has evolved must have been *extremely* exacting for that organism to have evolved in *exactly* the way in which it has with *exactly* the set of traits that the members of that species possess which have been selected for. In other words, the *evolutionary anthropic principle* suggests that human beings and human nature would have been different if we had evolved in a slightly different environment. And, in a significantly different environment, the *evolutionary anthropic principle* suggests that nothing closely resembling human beings would have evolved.

The following questions then naturally arise: Just how different might the environment have been in which human beings did evolve and still have the same (or *nearly* the same?) characteristics as the species that did actually evolve? And just how different might those conditions under which human beings did evolve have been and just how different might the product of those conditions be before we would say that they produced a *different species*, perhaps one very similar to human beings, but a different kind of creature with a different kind of nature, nonetheless?

Darwin maintained that human *reason* allowed human beings to adjust to a wider range of variations in the environment and thus survive across a wider geographical and climatic range than other species might be capable of doing. For example, human beings were able to use reason to design and construct clothes, which allowed human habitation in areas with greater variation of temperature. But Darwin was thinking *factually* about the actual, natural development of human history. If we think counterfactually about the past to try and define the limits of the modalities within which human beings could survive (and still be human beings), it is obvious that, at the extremes, human beings with a particular nature could not exist. Human beings and human nature could never have existed on the surface of the sun or on the surface of

Pluto. But within these extremes exactly what are the limitations within which human beings with a particular nature might have developed and survived? If one considers the degree to which a certain range of perceptual experiences belongs to the cluster of properties that subvenes human nature, then it is immediately obvious that however that range of perceptual experiences is defined, it is a function of the evolutionary development of certain perceptual organs and a certain physical environment. In a physical environment in which there is no light, for example, no eyes would evolve, and no visual perceptual experiences would ever take place. Even if some range of perceptual experiences is taken as one of the cluster of properties upon which human nature supervenes, we ought not expect that the range be *exactly* the actual range that is now attributed to human beings. But if the range of perceptual experiences currently enjoyed by human beings might be different, then just how different might the physical environment, the developing perceptual organs, and the range of perceptual experiences be for human beings (and still have those creatures be considered human)? Pursuing some sort of insight and partial answer to this kind of question is the focus of the following chapters.

Considering the range of modalities within which human perceptual experience might have developed and the range of variations in human perceptual experience is a way of understanding one part of the gradual, evolutionary ascent of humans from our progenitors. The ascent of man was a slow, gradual climb out of the primordial muck and slime, a climb up from the bubbling primordial soup that once covered the face of the Earth. A fortuitous confluence of conditions and circumstances produced a unique cluster of certain natural properties that causally interact with one another to create a causal nexus that has resulted in human beings having a unique nature and gaining the current position of preeminence that we occupy in the natural world. The next steps are to identify those properties belonging to that cluster of properties and to sort out the causal connections that create the causal nexus upon which human nature supervenes.

Note

1. For a discussion of the different versions of the anthropic principle, see James F. Harris, *Analytic Philosophy of Religion* (Dordrecht, The Netherlands: Kluwer Academic Publishers, 2002), 133. For the most thorough treatment of the anthropic principle, see John D. Barrow and Frank J. Tipler, *The Anthropic Principle and the Cosmological Argument* (Oxford: Oxford University Press, 1986), 16ff. Much of the philosophical discussion of the anthropic principle has taken place in the context of the cosmological argument for the existence of God.

3

The Natural World and Human Nature

Perhaps it will seem too obvious and simplistic to some to point out the importance of the fact that human beings are biological organisms that live in and interact with a natural environment; however, most philosophical inquiries into human nature (or, more commonly, philosophical inquiry about the concept of "person") have ignored this fundamental and crucially important factor. What has been described earlier as the felicitous convergence of properties that produces the causal nexus upon which human nature supervenes has occurred, for better or worse, in the natural world in which we live. An important, unresolved question is to what extent this natural world is causally responsible for those properties. Thus, an examination in some detail of exactly what it is about the natural world that has enabled human beings to be able to develop, live, interact, and thrive in the particular natural environment in which we have evolved (and in which we now find ourselves) should be revealing of important information about what kind of creatures we are and about how the convergence of properties in the cluster upon which human nature supervenes came about. Such an examination should also be revealing of, or at least demonstrative of, important information concerning the kind of natural environment in which we have managed to become the kind of creatures that we now are and the ways in which we are able to interact with that environment. An investigation into such matters should also provide evidence concerning whatever limitations there may be upon the natural world in which human beings might exist and possess anything like the nature that we currently possess as well as evidence about whatever limitations there may be upon the ways in which human beings can interact with whatever natural environment in which we find ourselves. These are all crucial matters that have been largely ignored by those interested in theories of human nature.

Evolutionary biologists are aware, of course, that natural selection only works in a particular environment. Traits that facilitate adaptation only develop and are selected for vis-à-vis adaptation to that environment. In a phrase first coined by John Bowlby, the environment with which the interaction of the organism results in the adaptation of particular traits is called "the environment of evolutionary adaptation" (EEA).[1] The importance of the EEA in developing those properties that are regarded as uniquely human, however, has generally been ignored or simply assumed and left in the background in the treatment of the evolution of human beings. In this chapter, I will focus direct attention upon the role of the EEA in producing those properties in the cluster of properties upon which human nature supervenes.

Upon the basis of the best available scientific evidence at the moment, it is as certain as any empirical fact can be that it would be impossible for human beings or any other known living organism on Earth to survive on the surface of the Sun or in a black hole. In the one case, any living organism would be instantly vaporized, and in the other, instantly crushed into oblivion. Obviously, there are certain physical constraints upon the kind of natural environment in which anything similar to the kind of creatures that we now call human beings can or could exist. On the basis of the best scientific information available at the moment, it is safe to say that for human nature to exist the cluster of properties upon which it supervenes must be instantiated in some living, biological organism. Whether this will remain to be true is yet to be determined. Exactly what that biological organism must be and how closely that biological organism must resemble modern, biological human beings are topics addressed in Chapter 4. For present considerations, we can simply say that the cluster theory of human nature requires that some properties be instantiated in a living, biological organism. Any contingently existing object or organism exists only given certain conditions that are necessary for its existence; however, the point here is a more specific one. A *particular* object or organism exists as the unique thing that it is only given certain *particular* conditions that are necessary for that object or organism being what it is. The metaphysical point is at least as old as Aristotle: there are general metaphysical conditions (or now "*cosmological* conditions" is preferred) for things existing, and there is a unique subset of conditions under which a particular thing exists as it is, i.e., as the unique thing that it is or the unique *kind* of thing that it is. The issue then becomes one of determining the unique set of conditions under which human beings can exist as the kind of creatures that we are, i.e., as possessing human nature.

In recent years, some scientists and some philosophers, particularly philosophers of religion, have given a great deal of attention to what is now known as the Anthropic Principle. First formulated by Brandon Carter, the Anthropic Principle (AP) emphasizes the extremely low antecedent probability that intelligent, carbon-based life could ever exist in the universe given what cosmologists now know to be the initial, and presumably unrelated, properties of the universe.[2] While there is much disagreement and controversy over different formulations of AP and whether it is a scientific or philosophical principle (or, indeed, whether it is a principle at all), there is an important insight buried in AP that is revealing about the ways in which human beings are able to exist in and interact with our natural environment. This insight is usually lost in the grand, sweeping cosmological emphasis given AP by some philosophers and the ensuing theological debates. The original basis for AP was recognized by Alfred Russel Wallace, co-developer with Darwin of evolutionary theory, in a much more narrowly-focused context. Wallace was interested in the largely ignored feature of biological evolution that requires the natural world to exist in rather precise ways in order for organic life as we now know it to have evolved. Wallace thus was interested in what I have called an evolutionary form of AP in the previous chapter. Via extrapolation from Wallace's concern, it is illustrative to investigate what ways the natural world had to exist for creatures with what we now regard as human nature to evolve.

According to AP, the world had to be finely tuned in terms of its initial conditions in order to become a place that supports carbon-based life, and it is reasonable to assume then, that the Earth had to be even more finely tuned to become a place that supports *intelligent*, carbon-based life. The phrase, "finely tuned," is not intended here to suggest anything in the way of intelligent design or a designer. This has simply become a commonly-used phrase to capture the extremely complex arrangement of different properties of the early universe that eventually allowed life as we know it on Earth to develop. Theological debates about intelligent design and other debates about different versions of AP have largely ignored some rather obvious and important consequences of AP. For example, it is quite compatible with AP that there are other possible natural worlds, different from this actual natural world, that would support carbon-based, but *non-human,* life and that there are even other possible natural worlds, different from this actual natural world, that would support *intelligent but non-human* life. The additional claim that is made here is that there could be other possible natural worlds, different from this actual natural world, that would support intelligent *human* life, *but with a different human nature!* As one moves conceptually from a natural world conditioned to support carbon-based life to a natural world conditioned to support intelligent, carbon-based life, to a natural world conditioned to support intelligent, *human* carbon-based life, to a natural world conditioned to support intelligent, human carbon-based life *with what we now regard as human nature,* the conditions become more and more exacting, and the range of possible worlds that could produce and support such life becomes more and more narrow.

Taking a clue from Wallace, so far as a theory of human nature is concerned, it is important to ask just how it was that what we regard as biologically *human beings* came to exist and thrive and just how it is that we are able to continue to exist and thrive in the natural world. Let us call the principle that captures these conditions the *Human Anthropic Principle* (HAP). It is clear that there must be a subset of conditions identified in AP captured by HAP. In other words, there might well be possible worlds with conditions that are precisely formulated, i.e., "finely tuned," with non-human intelligent life; thus, there must be a subset of conditions found in AP that explains how it is that human beings came to be. These are the conditions captured by HAP. HAP thus incorporates Wallace's evolutionary AP.

Furthermore, given whatever conditions are identified in HAP, there must be another even more "finely tuned," i.e., precisely formulated, set of conditions that explains how it is that human beings came to exist and are able to continue to exist *with the particular human nature that we do possess*, i.e., under what exact conditions of the natural world was it possible for human beings to come to be and to continue to be with what we regard as human nature? Let us call the principle that captures these conditions the *Human Nature Anthropic Principle* (HNAP). It is important to note that the conditions identified in HNAP are not necessarily (need not be) a discrete subset of conditions found in HAP since the claim here is that there may be possible worlds in which human beings as a biological species exist but without the particular human nature that human beings possess in this actual world. While there has been significant disagreement concerning exactly what a species is, there has been little or no attention focused upon the relationship between being biologically human and having human nature. Traits that are selected for biologically are preserved because those traits are more adaptive *given a particular environment*. The same is true of the properties that are to be found in the cluster of properties that creates the causal nexus upon which human nature supervenes. Given a substantially different natural environment, few would disagree that different traits would be selected for biologically; similarly, given a substantially different natural environment, different properties would be found in the cluster of properties responsible for human nature.

Obviously, some of the conditions in HNAP would be of the grand, sweeping cosmological variety emphasized in AP or of the biological variety emphasized in HAP; so, there would be some overlap of membership of the conditions in HAP and HNAP. However, of interest here, more particularly, are the *additional, unique* conditions in the natural world that are responsible not just for the existence of carbon-based life, or intelligent life, or even human life, but for the existence of human beings that possess the core cluster of properties, upon which, according to the cluster theory, human nature supervenes. The focus of attention upon the natural world in which human beings have evolved thus serves to provide some explanation for how it is that the cluster of properties and the causal nexus created by those properties upon which human nature supervenes are the result of a unique set of conditions found in the natural world. It is impossible to isolate completely the role played by the natural world in producing human nature from the roles played by human biology and human experience. The importance of some of those roles to the cluster theory is explored in the next chapter, and the ways in which human beings experience and interact with the natural world are the focus of Chapter 5. I claim that the unique features of human biology and the unique ways in which human beings experience our sensible environment are crucially important factors in our having the nature that we possess. The present concern is with identifying the increasingly narrow range of modalities of conditions and features of the natural world that could conceivably result in the existence of creatures with what we now regard as human nature. The recognition of the delimiting force of that range of modalities is the result of the fundamental insight captured by HNAP.

Usually ignored in the theological debates over AP is the fact that it is easy to imagine possible worlds in which AP holds and in which neither HAP nor HNAP holds. This claim, of course, assumes that it is logically possible to imagine a world in which the person doing the imagining does not exist and in which human beings generally do not exist. This assumption appears to be a safe one. Science fiction books and movies are replete with stories about intelligent, extraterrestrial life that exists in the far reaches of the universe in which human beings do not exist. However, one need not even appeal to science fiction to validate such a possibility. If one is not completely anthropomorphic in defining the concept of intelligence, this actual world, although devoid of human existence, would still contain intelligent life. One might think that such a world would not contain such products of intelligence as books and skyscrapers. However, as I demonstrate later in this chapter, such products are not simply the result of intelligence or even *human* intelligence but human intelligence combined with a unique *nature* that is the result of the cluster of properties, which, in turn, are the result of a pattern of different ways in which human beings experience and interact with our natural environment. For the moment, I will leave the matter of speculating about different forms of intelligent, extraterrestrial life to the science fiction writers (and, increasingly to astrophysicists and cosmologists) and focus here on examining the conditions of the natural world responsible for allowing the development of *human* intelligence in beings that also possess a unique *human nature*.

Perhaps the best approach for focusing upon the crucial conditions of the natural world that have allowed the development of the properties upon which human nature supervenes is to consider the range of possibilities for human existence but a kind of human existence in which human beings lack the particular nature that we now attribute to ourselves. To consider the range of modalities within which human nature might exist, one need only consider the kind of creatures human beings are now and then think counterfactually about the past of the natural world. If certain facts or processes or conditions had been different in the natural world, but not so different that human beings could not exist at all, just how different might human beings be now, i.e., just how might our nature be different from what it actually is in this existing world? Proceeding in this manner amounts to engaging in a variation on David Hume's question, mentioned in the previous chapter, about just how different human nature might have been from what it is now. Considering the different possibilities under which it might turn out that creatures that are biologically human exist but with a different human nature is revealing about the plausibility of different theories of human nature. Since, according to the cluster theory of human nature, the cluster of properties upon which human nature supervenes includes many of the biological features that identify human beings as mammals, the range of possible worlds in which human beings can exist with the nature we now possess is very narrow, and arguably, might include only this actual world. However, other theories of human nature maintain that human beings (with whatever it is that is regarded by these theories as comprising human nature) might exist (or might have existed) in very different worlds.

Consider the story of the origin of human beings that is described in Genesis, which is proffered by some on the basis of theology and held in conjunction with a top-down, essentialist view of human nature, according to which human nature is accounted for in terms of the possession of an immortal soul. According to this account, Adam and Eve, the original human beings, existed in a Garden of Paradise in which there were no diseases, no labor, and no pain. After the Fall, on this account, when Adam and Eve were made to leave the Garden, they were forced to live lives that were characterized by "pain," "toil," and "sweat"—conditions that are then taken to characterize the existence of all human beings.

In an effort to avoid the usual theological disputes surrounding this account and the disputes between this "creation" account of human nature and an evolutionary account, the focus here is simply on the importance of this account for theories of human nature.[3] Notice that on this theological account, human beings existed in a Paradise that was very different from the natural world in which we now find ourselves. According to this story, the natural environment in which human beings exist changed but human beings did not, i.e., human beings are taken to be *essentially* the same kind of creatures before and after the exit from the Garden of Eden. But such a claim stretches credulity to the breaking point. Suppose we grant, for the sake of argument, that creatures with human DNA that were biologically identical to what we now regard as human beings might have existed in such a natural setting as that described in the Genesis story. When one focuses upon the implications of such a claim, it is impossible to imagine that such creatures would be the same *kind* of creatures as those we now regard as human beings, i.e., such creatures could not have anything like a *human* nature. While it might be plausible to claim that human beings were biologically the same before and after the Fall, it is not plausible to claim that human nature was the same. In other words, although HAP might be compatible with the story of the Garden of Eden, the HNAP is not.

Once what existence would be like in a complete paradise is examined closely, it becomes clear that human beings with what we now regard as human nature could not exist there—even if creatures that are regarded as human beings biologically did. Adam and Eve would be missing too many of the properties that provide the causal nexus from which human nature emerges, and such creatures begin to sound more like humanoids from some science fiction story than like "real" human beings. Thus, while the HAP *might* allow for human existence in such a paradise, the HNAP does not does not allow for the existence of human nature. Such an idyllic natural world would not be *natural* at all and could not permit the existence of the *kind* of creatures that human beings are.

Some proponents of an essentialist, top-down, spiritual view of human nature insist that such creatures would still have the same nature because of the possession of an immortal soul. This view has dominated one strand of Christian theology, which ties human nature essentially to the possession of an immortal soul. If the possession of a soul is taken as *the* essential property of human nature, then it seems the proper response is to show the implausibility of such a claim by *reductio ad absurdum*. The usual interpretation of this view is that one's soul is "imprisoned" in one's body and that the body is simply a temporary and incidental locale of the soul. If the possession of an immortal soul and the related spiritual nature of human beings is what is essential about human beings being the *kind* of creatures that we are and if the human body is simply a convenient and temporary place of lodging for the soul, then all of the physical properties of the universe, the biological features of the human body, and the interactions of human beings with the natural environment are all inconsequential to human beings being the kind of creatures that we are. Such properties and features would thus be inconsequential to human nature. The implication of such a view is that human souls might theoretically be housed temporarily in *any* physical location *without changing the essential ingredient of human nature.* Indeed, the usual view is that human souls might be completely *disembodied* without disturbing the essential ingredient of human nature, but if a soul can be disembodied without loss of identity, then why can it not be *re-embodied* or *other-embodied*? In other words, the consequence of this form of a top-down, theological view appears to be that the human soul might be implanted in a cockroach or a fly or even a rock or a pile of dung without affecting the soul or changing its human-making influence. Such implications clearly constitute a *reductio*. It was perhaps of such obvious difficulties of this form of Christian theology that Thomas Aquinas emphatically declared, "I am not my soul." This chapter and the next one are devoted to demonstrating the importance of both the physical environment and human biology to human beings being the kind of creatures that possess the unique nature that is human nature.

It is not necessary, however, to consider such a fanciful past in order to gain insight into the importance of the limitations of our natural environment and the ways in which we might interact with that environment for understanding human nature. While the importance of the ways in which we human beings are able to experience our surrounding environment is examined in detail in Chapter 5, the focus here is upon the features, conditions, factors, etc., of the natural world that act causally to produce the core properties in the cluster of properties upon which human nature rests. While it is impossible here to explore all of the differences between life such as that attributed to existence in the Garden of Eden and life as we know it in the present natural world in which we now live and in which, according to evolutionary theory we evolved, it is possible to point out a few major differences. The most important difference as far as human nature is concerned can best be explained by beginning with what Charles Sanders Peirce calls the metaphysical category of *Secondness*.[4] For Peirce, whereas the category of *Firstness* is simply the pure qualitative aspect of things and simply the "possibility of appearance," *Secondness* represents the *haecceity*, the resistance or *thisness*, of things. It is this *Secondness* of things, again, their *haecceity*, that provides human beings with a sense of *externality*, i.e., the existence of things that are external and independent of ourselves. The notion of *Secondness* is used by Peirce to account for how it is that one comes up against a thing in the world and through the resistance of that thing, one is able to come to experience the *thisness* of the thing, i.e., the externalness of the thing.

Peirce's use of his categories occurs on the metaphysical level; however, there is also a human-nature counterpart to his metaphysical category of *Secondness*, and there is a human-nature corollary to his notion of *haecceity*. In other words, Peirce's notions of *Secondness* and *haecceity* have important implications for the nature of the subject as well as the nature of the object of an experience. It is *Secondness* that provides the resistance to our actions on the part of the natural world in which we actually live and that consequently provides us with an important element of human nature. It is the *haecceity* of the environment that is the most fundamental aspect of the EEA within which human nature has evolved. The *haecceity* of the external world accounts for the *come-up-againstness* that provides the backdrop of resistance that allows us to become agents by forming desires and then intentions to act against, or perhaps in accordance with, that *haecceity*. On the most fundamental level, this is what allows human beings to become practitioners of practical reason. It is the actualization of agency against the thisness of *haecceity* that provides some kernel of underlying truth to Karl Marx's claim that labor is species-defining for man. Of course, for Marx, his notion of labor is loaded with political and economic baggage. There is, however, a more politically neutral and palatable understanding of his claim that the *productive life* is "life-engendering" and "the life of the species." Productivity is, indeed, fundamentally constitutive of human existence if this claim is taken as meaning that what is produced is not some good or commodity for economic exchange but a state of affairs that is brought about by the actions of a rational agent.

As John Dewey has correctly noted in a different context, "it was not enjoyment of the apple but the enforced penalty of labor that made man as the gods, *knowing* good and evil instead of just having and enjoying them." Thus, "necessity is the mother of invention, discovery and consecutive reflection."[5] In other words, what some religious believers and defenders of a top-down, essentialist view of human nature believe to have been the *Fall* of man (according to the creation story in Genesis) was really the first step of the *Ascent* of man. Why? Well, it is because the natural environment in which human beings live on Earth is as it is, i.e., it is because the natural environment presents problems and challenges, threats and dangers and the potential for gain or loss through appropriate or inappropriate actions (*come-up-againstness*) that human beings are stimulated into noticing or understanding anything at all about the natural world. For Dewey, it is dangerous and threatening primary experience that provokes the process that results in unique human knowledge, resulting from reflective imagination, which then allows human beings to interact satisfactorily with a dangerous and threatening natural environment.

Dewey has captured an important element of human nature, which has been largely neglected. On the most elementary epistemological level, even our most fundamental categories for categorizing our experiences such as space and time, cause and effect, and means and ends are tied up with the human organism's interaction with the natural world in ways that require actions to produce certain, desired results. This is true whether or not one is a Kantian or a Lockean about the nature of such concepts. Even if there are such things as *a priori* categories of the understanding, such categories are empty and useless without experience, as Kant himself emphasized. While it is difficult to imagine exactly what such an existence would be like, in a complete paradise, where there are no dangers and no labor, presumably no *effort* would be required to produce whatever might be the objects of one's desires; thus, it is difficult to see how one would ever come to understand the notion of cause and effect. It is also difficult to imagine how there could be intelligent, *intentional* human actions since such actions involve the awareness of a current situation, the contemplation of a future desired state of affairs and a consideration of alternative courses of action that might bring about that future desired state of affairs. Dewey is correct, indeed, in saying that it is only *acting* and seeing the good and bad consequences of one's actions that one is able to come to an understanding of good and evil and thus become a moral agent. The main point here, however, does not concern the question of moral agency or the problem of evil. More importantly, and more fundamentally, in a complete paradise where there would be no unfilled desires, and thus, no futile courses of action for bringing about desired states, there would be no intentional actions at all since such a world would provide no *come-up-againstness* to resist any of one's actions. It is impossible, under such conditions, to understand how such an existence would provide the basis for human beings ever coming to understand ourselves as *agents* acting with purpose or employing practical reason. If some actions are not better suited to producing some desired consequent than others, i.e., if one is never thwarted in one's desires, if there is no resistance from the natural world to bringing about those desired results, there is no agency. Indeed, it is difficult to see how such an existence would be *rational* since anything one might do in a particular situation would be just as likely as anything else one might do to satisfy a desire. Indeed, it is questionable whether it is meaningful to ascribe desires or purposes at all to such creatures that might exist in such circumstances.

Furthermore, contrary to some popular, post-modernist claims, the concepts and categories that human beings employ to act as agents in interaction with the natural world cannot be simply conventional or cultural posits. Unless the *haecceity* of the natural world comes fixed with regularities and patterns ingrained in it, the notion of a tool or the connection between forming intentions and actions that are suited to bringing about those intentions would not make sense or be successful in practice. The design and use of a tool are functions of both the way the world is and the specific way in which one wishes to alter or otherwise influence the way the world is. It is the recognized *repeated* patterns of circumstances in an otherwise changing natural environment that are predictable and allow anticipation on the part of an agent and that then allow that agent to act in rationally selected ways and to suit actions to circumstances in order to bring about some desired result and to achieve some held desire. It is this interaction of an individual with a natural environment whose regularities and patterns are, for a large extent, easily detectable to human beings who are equipped biologically to experience the world in certain ways (see Chapter 5) that is responsible for human agency, rational choice, and what is usually called inductive reasoning.

Contrary to the line of argument suggested by Dewey's emphasis on secondary experience and the contribution that human beings make to shaping nature through the impositions of interpretations of primary experience, the amount of flexibility allowable in that regard is very limited. Human beings acting as rational agents are, for the most part, *products* of a changing natural environment whose *come-up-againstness* "regulates" and delimits the ways in which individuals can interact with that environment successfully. In terms of priority, the role of man in the interaction between man and environment must be understood as a reciprocal one. Human beings have become rational agents because of a successful adaptation to what has earlier been called "environments of evolutionary adaptation" (EEA). Given that those environments have changed regularly and dramatically over a long period of time, it is per-haps best to understand human rational agency as the result of effective adaptation through interaction with a unique pattern of changes in such environments. Consider again the property of buoyancy. Just as an object that floats has a unique pattern of ways in which it acts and is acted upon, given the physical laws and features of this universe, an individual with human nature has a unique pattern of ways in which it acts and is acted upon, given those same laws and features. What all of this describes is a human nature corollary to the EEA of evolutionary biology. Human nature has evolved and developed only in interaction with a particular environment, and if that environment changes radically, one ought to expect that human nature will change radically also.

Without *haecceity* and *come-up-againstness* presented to us by our natural world, human experience would simply be a succession of unre-lated events. *With* the *haecceity* and *come-up-againstness* presented to us by our natural world, human beings are provided with a context within which we can fit our actions to the circumstances in an effort to bring about a desired result. To do this requires some understanding of the relatedness amongst the events in the natural world, some understanding of how an array of potential actions might be causally efficacious with those events, and then the understanding of how some of those actions lead to an ordered, consummatory experience. For Dewey, this process is an aesthetic experience—the phenomenological feeling of complete-ness, the culmination or fruition of the chaotic flux of experience, the coming together of means and consequences, the "felt whole," and the basis of his naturalistic theory of aesthetics. His description of how we come to understand our place in the natural world and the consequences of our *actions* in that world is definitive:

> That appetite as such is blind, is notorious; it may push us into a comfortable result instead of into disaster; but we are pushed just the same. When appetite is perceived in its meanings, in the consequences it induces, and these consequences are experimented with in reflective imagination, some being seen to be consistent with one another, and hence capable of co-existence and of serially ordered achievement, others being incompatible, forbidding conjunction at one time, and getting in one another's way serially—when this estate is attained, we live on the human plane, responding to things in their meanings. A relationship of cause-effect has been transformed into one of means-consequent.[6]

Since the cluster theory of human nature is a "bottom-up" view, it holds that human nature gradually comes into being through several different processes. Dewey can be understood as describing one of the most important of those processes, the one by which we come to be rational *agents*. Making and using tools is one manifestation of rational agency wherein we act in concerted ways to impact our natural environment to bring about desired consequences and to turn circumstances that are "indifferent" or even "hostile to life" into ones that are friendly and beneficial to human flourishing. For Dewey, this process takes place in reflective imagination. In a world that resists one's actions, i.e., in a world with *come-up-againstness*, certain actions, which are better suited for bringing about the desired result, are met with success while others are not. It is by coming to identify those successful actions, i.e., the felicitous ways and means of achieving desired results, and by linking them to the production of the desired result that one becomes a rational agent and a practitioner of practical reason. "Ah," one thinks, "*this* is how it is done. *This* is what I must do (how I must act) using *this* to manipulate *that* to bring about what I desire, to produce what I want. I thus will to do it *this* way using *this*." It is through such a process, using the human nature counterpart of Peirce's notion of *haecceity* that one becomes a rational agent acting in one's natural environment. Rational agency thus comes about by actions that are based upon and the result of the identification of *thisness* to resolve the challenges presented to us by the *come-up-againstness* of the natural world. A careful reading of Dewey's description of this process reveals that there is a fundamental reciprocity between the natural world and human agency. The process whereby one comes to the "deeper understanding" of the natural world by transforming cause-effect into means-consequent is one of trial and error in which the human agent learns to adjust and fit behavior to the circumstances to order successfully the consequences of one's interaction with one's natural environment.

But, since the cluster theory is also a non-essentialist view, this means that, in the case of agency, perhaps unlike Dewey's claim, there is no magical demarcation point at which it is possible to say that human beings cease being "mere animals" and move to "the human plane," on which we then operate with a distinctive rational agency. For this reason, it is better to say that, in the process described above, we move from being "mere animals" to the plane of agency. Some human beings act on a "higher plane" than others, and some either act on such a lowered plane or are unable to act at all so that we either deny rational agency to such people or seriously question it—as in the respective cases of the psychopath or the person in a permanent vegetative state. Again, individuals can be biologically human without having human nature.[7] The cluster theory also has no difficulty in recognizing that other animals employ practical reason and act as agents. Questions about agency notwithstanding, an existence that requires no work and no effort would furthermore provide no sense of accomplishment, the satisfaction of a job well-done, or perhaps even the understanding that one had completed a task or achieved a desired result.[8]

On the other end of the spectrum, the *come-up-againstness* of nature can be so extreme, severe, or demanding that it overwhelms any attempt at agency and hence any existence of human nature. In some cases, the severity is so extreme and overwhelming that it threatens or actually extinguishes human life, and in other cases, the severity is so extreme that it threatens or overwhelms human nature. The differences may be explained by the variations in individuals' relationships to and responses to the circumstances in question; however, some circumstances are so severe that no human being might be expected to retain his or her human nature even if that person manages to survive biologically. The properties in the cluster of properties that subvene human nature that are the result of human culture are especially and most easily vulnerable to extreme fluctuations of environmental circumstances. Consider natural disasters. As both historical and recent world events reveal, natural events such as floods, hurricanes, earthquakes, etc., and the resulting effects on the human population such as plagues, famine, etc., threaten not only the biological existence of human beings but the existence of human nature. Frequently, when an individual or a group of individuals teeters on the brink between survival and death, few of the properties in the cluster of properties upon which human nature supervenes are able to survive. Arguably, in the most extreme cases, the properties are eroded to the point that human nature is lost. While those eroded properties and human nature might be restored at some later date, bare biological survival does not guarantee the survival of human nature.

Perhaps, extreme torture is most illustrative. Contrary to romanticized representations, while prolonged subjection to excruciating pain might not result in the death of a person, it will undoubtedly result eventually in a complete erosion of the properties that account for human nature. Assuming that physical harm could easily destroy the biologically-based properties discussed in Chapters 4 and 5, such as bipedalism and sensory experience, the only remaining issue concerns what the effect of continual exposure to extreme torture would be on such properties as agency and the cultural properties. The realistic and obvious answer is that all such properties are vulnerable and fragile and are contingent upon the absence of prolonged, intense pain. Thus, for biologically human creatures to possess human nature, not only must the HAP operate to circumscribe a range of conditions within which human beings can survive, but the HNAP principle must also operate to circumscribe a rather narrow range of conditions within which human beings can be "fully human," i.e., not only survive but thrive to a certain extent. Usually, discussions of the interaction of the human species with its natural environment are focused solely upon the survival of human beings as a biological species, i.e., the role of HAP; usually ignored is the question of the survival of human nature and the role of HNAP. So far as the development and survival of human nature is concerned, HNAP limits the *come-up-againstness* of the natural world on both ends of the spectrum and circumscribes a rather narrow range of resistance form the natural world that allows for the development and flourishing of human nature.

The focus here has been upon the way in which HNAP facilitates the development of human agency; however, this description of the gradual development of rational agency is much too general and metaphysical to explain adequately the uniqueness of human agency. What has been described thus far is simply the big or general picture. What about the specifics, i.e., what is it specifically about this natural world that has contributed to the development of human, rational agency? If rational agency is taken to be one of the properties in the cluster of properties upon which human nature supervenes, the question might be put in terms of how it is that the natural world is construed in such a manner so as to provide not only the conditions for HAP but for HNAP as well. Accounting for the uniqueness of human nature is a notoriously difficult issue that is fraught with pitfalls. The lightning rod of controversy is how human beings are or are not different from other animals. The cluster theory embraces the fact that many non-human animals act on a higher plane of agency than is recognized by or admitted by most philosophers. Also, some non-human animals act on a higher plane of agency than do some humans. Non-human animals are now commonly known to make and use tools, and arguably, many animals regularly act more convincingly on a higher level of agency than do human infants, idiots, or those in a permanent vegetative state. So, what is it that accounts for the special nature of human agency? The answer will be disappointing to those searching for some essential aspect of rational agency that, in turn, can be used to grind some theological ax or to provide, in an Aristotelian sense, the essential nature of human beings. Whatever is distinctive about human, rational agency is accounted for simply in terms of the degree to which, the level to which, and the complexity to which human beings have managed to confront and resolve the conundrums presented by the *come-up-against-ness* of the natural world. There is no difference *in kind* between human rational agency and non-human animal rational agency. There is only a difference of degree and the position human beings occupy (compared to non-human animals) along the continuing "plane of agency." Those relative positions are determined by the relative success in responding to and resolving the specific challenges of our natural environment. If men were to be placed in a significantly different environment, the results would be quite different. Consider Lewis Carroll's Alice when she falls down the rabbit hole and into Wonderland. In such a strange place, rational agency takes on a completely different meaning.

There are important and, as yet unaddressed, issues about exactly how it is that human beings have been able to identify, address, and resolve such a wider range of infinitely more complex problems presented by the *come-up-againstness* of the natural world than any other species. To this point, the claims about the importance of the role of the *haecceity* of man's natural environment has been long on generalities and short on particulars. Part of the explanation for the lack of specificity to this point is that more of what the cluster theory of human nature has to say about the importance of the particulars is to come later—particularly in Chapters 4 and 5. In addition, there are at least two challenging obstacles to being more specific about the various particular characteristics of the *come-up-againstness* of the natural world that have been responsible for providing environments of evolutionary adaptation for man. First, this area is the purview of scientists and social scientists, and while the cluster theory makes use of the latest and best science, it must be acknowledged that scientists themselves are in significant disagreement over many of the specifics about exactly how the interaction of man with certain conditions and features of the natural world has resulted in certain adaptations. Secondly, perhaps the most important thing that might be said about the specifics of the *haecceity* and *come-up-againstness* of the natural world delimited by HNAP is that what is in question is not a simple set of specific conditions in the natural world but a unique path through different sets of specific conditions that human beings have traveled, i.e., a unique human history. Specifically, the particular aspects of the world's *come-up-againstness* against which human agency is measured and by which it is determined have changed significantly over long periods of time. The particular forms of *come-up-againstness* will also continue to change in the future. Thus, what accounts for the uniqueness of human agency is not simply the interaction of human beings with a particular natural environment of evolutionary adaptation but to a particular history of interaction with a set of changing environments.

In terms of interaction with the natural world, what distinguishes human beings from other animals is simply the fact that humans beings have been able to adapt more successfully to the changing natural environments than have other animals. More than anything else human beings have proven to be extremely flexible and adaptable to a variety of different natural environments. It is futile to attempt to account for this success in terms of a single or single set of features or attributes possessed by human beings since those features or attributes have changed also. The success is to be accounted for in terms of differences in degree and complexity and not differences in kind between human beings and other animals. There is no doubt that other animals exhibit what can only reasonably be described as intelligence in their dealings with the natural world. In order to preserve the unique place of human beings in the natural world, such intelligence is usually attributed to instinct or qualified as "animal" intelligence. But intelligence is intelligence. About some matters, especially those having to do with *immediate* interaction with the natural world, some animals exhibit a greater degree of agency and intelligence than do human beings; however, the agency and intelligence of human beings exceed those of other animals in respect to a broad spectrum of matters—especially those having to do with more spacially and temporally remote ones, i.e., more theoretical matters. These differences are accounted for in terms of several factors, most of which have to do with differences in biology and the correspondingly different ways in which different animals experience their natural surroundings.

Different species in the animal world are spread across a wide spectrum upon which different behavior resulting from differences in sensory stimuli can be measured. The cluster theory has no reticence about saying that intelligence and agency are also spread across a similar spectrum. Attempts to preserve these designations exclusively for human beings are the result of a residue of Christian theology and anthropomorphism. The behaviors of some animals are very impressive. The migration of some birds and butterflies can only be accounted for in terms of their awareness of and interaction with their natural environments in ways that biologists are still trying to understand. What is called "flock behavior," i.e., large numbers of birds flying together in formation with individual birds in very close proximity to one another, moving together, and changing directions as a single flock, is evidence of their ability to perceive and react to subtle changes in their immediate environment that even the most agile human athletes or dancers cannot approximate. Some animals sense impending natural disasters in ways that still mystify animal behavior experts, but those animals do not worry about global warming or its effects upon their offspring. It is true that some animals make and use tools, but no other animal makes or uses anything approaching the sophistication or complexity of an automobile, computer, airplane, or space craft—all devices to alter or enhance the ways in which human beings interact with the natural world. Elephants go to the elephant graveyard to die, but they do not buy life insurance or engage in estate planning.

Because of various differences in sense perceptions, various animals might recognize members of their own species or members of different species much more readily than do human beings—usually to identify prey or predator. However, it is extremely doubtful that any other animal theorizes about or speculates about what *makes* its own species unique as humans do. Many species of animals—especially birds—migrate hundreds or even thousands of miles in feats of navigation that still mystify ornithologists, but only human beings have figured out a way to take the giant leap to leave Mother Earth. It is exactly this significant difference in the degree of abstraction of interests and concerns that has permitted human beings to construct governments, create religions, and organize other permanent social institutions.

The cluster theory of human nature is a theory that describes human nature as it actually exists, i.e., a nature that supervenes upon a cluster of natural properties that actually exist and can be observed and explained in empirical terms. To repeat, there is no single set of necessary and sufficient properties in that cluster that then magically and necessarily produces human nature. There are many possibilities to consider. There may well be possible worlds or even other remote parts of this actual world in which human nature can be found supervening upon the same, or *most* of the same, or *some* of the same, or (contrary to intuition), even *very few* of the same properties. In such a possible world, or even in some distant corner of this actual world or some temporally remote state of this little corner of this actual world, conditions may be so dramatically different that some or even many of the properties upon which human nature actually supervenes at this point in human history on Earth may not exist.

Whether human nature might still exist under such dramatically different conditions is not clear. While it is not possible to specify exactly where the line might be drawn, it does not seem possible that human nature might exist in creatures that possess *none* of the same properties. It is even possible to imagine this actual world changing, i.e., evolving to the point that human nature could be found supervening upon different sets of properties instantiated in creatures that are very different biologically. One must resist saying "in very different human beings" since those creatures might very well not be biologically human. Given significant enough changes in the natural world, organisms have few choices—flee, adapt, or die. Some of these possibilities are discussed in later chapters of this book; however, the point here is that at this juncture of natural history, human nature can be found supervening upon a cluster of properties that are instantiated to the highest degree in the biological species, human being. Since those properties, like the ones that define the species itself, are homeostatic, their instantiation is self-perserving, and this means that it is more likely than not that in the future where human nature is to be found, these properties upon which human nature supervenes will also be found in the same biological species. However, as the argument in this chapter has shown (and as the arguments in later chapters confirm), the instantiation of many of those properties in the cluster of properties upon which human nature supervenes is the result of human beings interacting with a certain natural environment. If that natural environment were to change drastically enough, it is quite possible that those properties would also change drastically enough that (like pepper moths changing their color) the causal nexus created by the cluster of properties would be destroyed and human nature would be lost.

Exactly what those changes might be and just how drastically the natural environment would have to change before those changes would destroy human nature are, at the moment, still the purview of science fiction writers; however, it is time that they become the concern of biologists and philosophers. Since the HNAP delimits the circumstances in which human nature might exist more narrowly than does HAP, the point is to imagine circumstances in which creatures who are biologically human exist (by whatever criteria biologists agree upon) but whose nature is so different that it would no longer be regarded as *human* nature. I do not intend to pursue this point further here except to consider one possibility. Consider the fact, which may seem too obvious to some people and too unimportant to others, that human beings are not alone in this natural world and have not evolved into the kind of creatures we now are in splendid isolation, i.e., as a biological species, human beings are simply one amongst a large number of living things. In other words, one of the features of the natural world with which human beings interact is that the natural world contains a large number of other living things. Arguably, the existence of some other living things is necessary to provide nourishment in order for human beings to survive; however, in fact, many more living things now exist on Earth than are necessary for human survival. In addition, it is easy to imagine a possible natural world in which human biology could be tweaked slightly so that we would require less nourishment and be less dependent upon other living things for survival. So, even if the existence of some other living things is necessary for human existence, of what importance or value are the many "extra" living things to human existence or human thriving? And what is the importance of our relationship to the other living things in the universe upon which we are not dependent for survival? There is the ecological perspective to answering these questions. Scientists emphasizing the importance of bio-diversity have argued for some time that a significant variety of different living things—plants and animals alike—are necessary for a healthy planet, which, in turn, provides a healthy natural environment for human existence and thriving. Additionally, some moral philosophers have claimed that we have moral responsibilities to the environment and "Mother Earth" independently of any practical concerns about the effects of a healthy environment on human beings.

My main concern here, however, is with a more direct and immediate relationship between human nature and Mother Earth and other living things. Consider just the relationship of man to other animals. I have argued in detail in this chapter that an important part of what makes us fully human, i.e., biological human beings with a certain nature, is the ways in which we are acted upon by the natural world and the ways in which we are able to act upon that natural world reciprocally. Included in the ways in which we are acted upon by the natural world and in the ways we are able to act upon the natural world are the ways in which we relate to and interact with other living organisms, i.e., an *extra*, *supra*, or *meta* biological feature of our species. Of course, such a pattern has evolved and changed over many centuries just as has human nature. In the early history of man's relationship with other animals, we human beings were more prey than predator. However, whether prey or predator, the kind of creatures that we are is fundamentally interconnected with the existence of other living things and the patterns of our relationships with those other living things.

Imagine a human existence in a natural world in which there are few different species of animals and very few individual animals of each species. Imagine, for example, that human beings are the only mammals in that natural world. In a worse case scenario, global warming might eventually produce a result close to such a world. Imagine also that, by whatever technological means that are available, some sort of food is available so that human life can be sustained at its present level and in its present form in the sense that the rest of human existence is unchanged except for the non-existence of other animal species. What effect would such a change have on human beings? Presumably, it would not affect our biological nature, i.e., we would still manage to survive, and we would still be biologically human. However, the severe loss of most or all other animal life on Earth would have a dramatic and profound effect on human nature quite independently of the practical issue of nourishment necessary for sustaining human life.

While it is not easy to project exactly what the effects would be of such drastic changes in the natural environment upon human nature, it seems most likely that they would be profoundly chilling and extremely alienating. Though still biologically human, human beings would indeed become strangers in a strange land. Even though the cluster theory maintains that human beings occupy a unique position in the animal world, a position that is the result of significant differences in the degrees to which different properties are instantiated in humans compared to other animals, that position is the result of interaction with and a shared history with other living things. In other words, part of what makes human beings the kind of creatures that we are is that which distinguishes us from other living things, and what distinguishes us from other living things is the result of a shared natural history that contains differing patterns of interactions with the natural world. Protagoras had it wrong. It is not that man is the measure of all things. It is rather that other things and other living things are, at least in significant part, the measure of man.

It is often reported that survivors of a disaster establish bonds that then continue through the rest of their lives. For example, survivors of a plane crash or a major life-threatening storm or other significantly "life-altering" event often establish close, intimate personal relationships. The claim here is that human beings are dependent upon other living things—especially other living mammals—even though the recognition of that dependency does not rise to the level of consciousness in most people. The totality of the natural history of the evolution and survival of living things on planet Earth, is the greatest natural disaster imaginable excepting the sudden and complete destruction of the planet. Too frequently overlooked in Darwin's account of the role of natural selection is the fact that the present state of affairs in the animal world is the result of a brutal and merciless process that has resulted in the extinction of numerous species of animals and countless hundreds of millions of individual living things. The living things that remain alive today are survivors of a subtle series of natural disasters of near-cataclysmic proportions. This is, in fact, what biological evolution is. The reason why many human beings do not feel the kinship with other living things is that there are still so many survivors left. As the surviving species and numbers of individuals become fewer and fewer, the recognition of the shared history and destiny will become greater and greater.

The cluster theory maintains that human nature is a function of many natural processes that result in various properties of human beings and a causal nexus that exists amongst those properties. As such, human nature is thus dynamic and changes along with the changes that occur in the cluster of properties that change along with the changes in the natural processes and features that occur in the rest of the natural world. Frequently, to account for the uniqueness of human beings, social scientists recount that crucial part of the evolution of the human species, in the Pleistocene Period, some time between twenty-five thousand to two million years ago, when man developed tools, weapons, and language and learned to hunt, write, and use fire. Most of these developments will be discussed in later chapters of this book. The focus in this chapter has been upon the role of the natural world in which these developments took place. The claim is that these crucial developments took place, to some significant degree, *because* of the features of the natural world in which they took place, i.e., because of HNAP.

According to HAP, had the natural world in which human beings evolved been significantly different, the creatures that are now human beings would have been significantly different biologically, and according to HNAP, had the natural world in which human beings evolved been significantly different (but not *so different* that what are now biological human beings did not evolve), human beings would have a very different human nature. Just how different might the natural environment in which human beings exist be without destroying human nature? The answer to this question is one that has dominated much of the speculation of science fiction stories. It ought to dominate much of good social science and philosophical theories as well. What has been ignored to a great extent is the role that a changing natural environment has played in the evolutionary history of human beings and the role of that changing natural environment in the evolutionary history of human nature. Some concerns of social scientists about the effects of situations such as urban living and space travel focus more narrowly upon questions about human nature. Concerns about possible catastrophic future changes in the natural environment on Earth as the result of nuclear war, global warming, or some pandemic, usually focus on the survival of human beings as a biological species; however, significant and prolonged changes in the natural environment on Earth would undoubtedly have profound effects on human nature in those human beings who survive biologically. Changes that would result in drastic loss of animal life or would require extreme artificial isolation and protection from the natural environment or would otherwise seriously affect what have become normal patterns of physical and social interaction amongst human beings and between human beings and other animals and the natural environment would threaten (and perhaps destroy) the existence of human nature as it now exists. The same kind of concerns apply to fictional accounts or serious scientific plans for human beings to live permanently in significantly different hostile environments in outer space, under ground, or under water. The lesson of this chapter is that human beings are the *kind* of creatures that we are, i.e., we have the kind of human nature that we do have, as a function of, to a significant degree, the range of ways that we have been able to act upon and be acted upon by a *particular* natural environment. Just as biological traits became selected for only because of the interaction of organisms with their environment, i.e., the environment of evolutionary adaptation (EEA), likewise the properties in the cluster of properties upon which human nature supervenes developed and survived only because of the interaction of human beings with a particular natural environment.

Notes

1. See John Bowlby, *Charles Darwin: A New Life* (New York: Norton Publishing Company, 1991).
2. There are several different versions of AP, including what have become known as "weak" and "strong" versions. Much discussion of AP has been related to arguments for the existence of God, and some philosophers of religion have seized upon AP as scientific evidence of intelligent design. For discussion of the different versions of AP and their relationship to arguments for the existence of God, see James F. Harris, *Analytic Philosophy of Religion* (Dordrecht, The Netherlands: Kluwer Academic Publishers, 2002), 133-39.
3. I will not enter the disputes here about original sin or whether human beings are basically good or evil.
4. Charles Sanders Peirce, *Collected Papers*, edited by Charles Hartshorne, Paul Weiss, and Arthur Banks (Cambridge: Belknap Press of Harvard University Press, 1934), Vol I, Section 300ff.
5. John Dewey, *Experience and Nature* (New York, NY: Dover Publications, 1958), 121-22.
6. *Ibid.*, 370-71.
7. The cluster theory also embraces what is perhaps the more controversial claim that not every individual that possesses human nature must be biologically human; or, at least, the cluster theory recognizes the vagueness of what it means to be biologically human. See Chapter 4 for further discussion of this issue.
8. There are other significant differences as well: for example, human emotions in the Garden of Eden would be limited to a very narrow range with presumably no anger, no guilt, no remorse, no sexual passion, or lust.

4

Human Biology and Human Nature

According to the cluster theory of human nature, it is important to recognize and maintain the distinction between being biologically human and having human nature. While it is a contingent matter of fact in the natural world that the properties in the cluster of properties that forms the causal nexus upon which human nature supervenes is usually instantiated (and instantiated to greater degrees) in creatures that are biologically human, the relationship between being biologically human and having human nature is not clear at all. At best, the relationship is a contingent one, i.e., it is a relationship that is the result of certain matters of fact that happen to obtain in this actual world, or, perhaps more accurately and precisely, it is a relationship that is the result of certain matters of fact that happen to obtain in the particular little corner of this actual world called Earth. Furthermore, there is significant biological variation amongst the members of the human species that happen to exist on Earth, and there is a wide spectrum across which the properties that subvene human nature are spread even when the focus is restricted to Earth. Biologically speaking, it is important to determine which, if any, traits or properties are essential for human beings being classified as such. While the cluster theory maintains that there are no essential properties for human nature, still the various combinations of properties in the cluster must, based upon the best available scientific data currently available, be instantiated in *some kind* of living creature. Thus, it becomes important to explore the nature of that creature and how the properties in the cluster of human-making properties map unto the biological traits and features that make human beings biologically human. Since the cluster theory is an empirical, descriptive theory about human nature and since the properties in the cluster of properties upon which human nature supervenes are, for the most part and to the highest degree, instantiated in creatures that are biologically human, it is reasonable to expect that some of those properties will be biological in nature. This may seem like a trivial and obvious a point to make; however, the cluster theory does not maintain that it is analytically or tautologically true that only creatures that are biologically *Homo sapiens* possess human nature. Therefore, for the moment, it is left as an open question whether those properties in the cluster of properties upon which human nature supervenes might be instantiated in creatures that are not biologically human.

As a biological species, human beings are classified by biologists as the species, *Homo sapiens* in the Animal Kingdom, of the class Mammalia, the order Primate, the family Hominidae, and the genus *Homo*. Each added degree of specificity is the result of additional and more detailed features that, along with a unique evolutionary history, are identified by biologists as distinguishing human beings from other animals. Animals in the class Mammalia have body hair and milk secreting glands and maintain a constant body temperature. Amongst other features, primates have a large brain, manual dexterity, and binocular vision. Members of the family Hominidae have no tails and have developed bipedalism and erect posture. The genus *Homo*, which includes both early and modern man (*Homo erectus* and *Homo sapiens*), has members with even larger brains who make and use tools and who use language.

There are other features—both morphological and evolutionary—that have not been mentioned here. Some of these features will be discussed later in this book. For example, Desmond Morris famously seized upon the fact that *Homo sapiens* are the only primate with no (or very little) body hair in his controversial book, *The Naked Ape*.[1] The varying importance of different features is debatable as is the process of classification itself. There is nothing magical or inherently correct or incorrect about biological classification. The process is a conventional one that simply gives guidance to biologists in their work by providing ways of distinguishing one species from others. The distinguishing criteria for the different levels of classification have changed over the years as have the locations of different species in the classification scheme as well as the systems of classification themselves. The process of biological classification is one that is designed to capture the various relationships amongst different living organisms, and, as such, different systems of classification reflect the special interests and emphases of those who designed them. The earliest systems of biological classification were non-evolutionary, and even though most biologists today would agree that the process of classification should include the evolutionary histories of organisms, the situation for taxonomists gets very confusing. For example, in terms of the kind of traits and morphology used above to distinguish *Homo sapiens*, crocodilians are more similar to snakes and other reptiles than they are to birds, but the most recent and reliable fossil data have revealed that crocodilians and birds share a more recent common evolutionary ancestor. Evolutionary history represents a relatively recent criterion for biological classification, and given recent and projected developments in chemical analysis and computer modeling, it is reasonable to expect that taxonomists will be faced with introducing and using other new criteria in the near future.

If it is true that the process of biological classification is conventional and if it is also true that any results of scientific investigation are held tentatively and are subject to revision or falsification on the basis of additional data, then the classification of human beings as *Homo sapiens* described above is doubly vulnerable to change. On the one hand, biologists might discover that they have just been wrong about some of the claims made earlier about the biological characteristics of human beings. On the other hand, they might decide that even though they have not been mistaken about their earlier descriptions of the biological traits and characteristics of human beings, they have been mistaken about the importance of those particular traits and/or characteristics for the classification of human beings. Furthermore, it is possible that, over some period of time, human beings might continue to evolve in ways that involve either the loss or the gain of certain traits that would significantly alter the currently accepted classification. These possibilities make it important to explore just how closely our current understanding of human nature is tied to our current understanding of *Homo sapiens*.

The cluster theory maintains that even though it is true that the properties that subvene human nature are instantiated to a greater degree in *Homo sapiens* than in any other creature, this is a contingent matter of fact that just happens to be true on Earth during a particularly short period of time in a long, long history of geological and biological evolution. Just how short this period is is difficult for many to comprehend. Consider the following analogy: Suppose we take the entire 800 million years of life on Earth as a single year so that the earliest, single-celled organisms exist in January of that year. Multicelled organisms begin to exist in April and the first vertebrates in May. The first amphibians appear in August, and the first reptiles, in September. Dinosaurs exist in October and November. The first primates appear sometime in December. With about twelve hours left in the year, *Australopithecus* appears in Africa. With only a minute or two remaining, what we call the ancient human civilizations in Egypt, China, and South America appear. In the last few seconds before midnight, all of the modern cultural and technological developments of "modern man" occur.[2]

Somewhere along the way in this long history of the biological evolution of man, creatures that possess what we regard as human nature appeared. It is not the purpose here to attempt to pinpoint exactly when this occurred. It is the purpose to attempt to gain more clarity about the nature of whatever biological properties there might be in the cluster of properties upon which human nature supervenes. To repeat, it is important to keep in mind that, according to the cluster theory of human nature, an individual possesses human nature by instantiating *some* particular subset (but no one *specific* subset) of properties in a cluster of properties, which then creates a causal nexus upon which the individual's human nature supervenes. The immediate implication of this claim is that none of whatever specific biological properties there may be in that cluster is either sufficient or necessary for human nature.

Recognizing and maintaining the distinction between biological human beings and human nature has some significant consequences that are likely to be met with a great deal of resistance on either religious or moral grounds. Since the purpose here is simply to develop a clear and coherent philosophy of human nature, I will leave it to others to sort through the various religious and moral implications of the consequences of the cluster theory and to address the various religious and moral conundrums. One obvious consequence of maintaining the distinction between humans and human nature is that not all humans will possess human nature simply by being human. Being biologically human provides *some* of the properties in the cluster of properties that, according to the cluster theory, produces the causal nexus upon which human nature supervenes, but, again, this just happens to be true at this particular moment. So, it might initially appear that an individual's being biologically human is sufficient for that individual having human nature. However, although many of the properties in the cluster of properties upon which human nature supervenes are produced in this natural world by being biologically human, it is the nature of those properties and not their biological origin or basis that is important for a theory of human nature. It is undeniable that many biologically human individuals do not possess many, if any, of the properties in the cluster of properties amongst which the causal nexus is generated and upon which human nature supervenes. This means that there are individuals who are biologically human but who do not possess human nature. Since very few of the specific properties that are counted amongst the properties in the cluster that subvene human nature have been discussed, suffice it to say at the moment that amongst others, fetuses, very young infants, idiots, those in a permanent vegetative state, and those with severe personality disorders are individuals that are biologically human but who do not possess human nature to any significant degree at all. Distinguishing between an individual being biologically human and an individual having human nature provides a clear and explicit basis for describing such individuals as not being "really human," i.e., not being completely human in the sense of having human nature.

Even if being biologically human is not sufficient for one having human nature, one might think that an individual's being biologically human is necessary for that individual having human nature. After all, it is only humans that have human nature, is it not? One answer to this question is "Perhaps, but if it is so, it is only contingently and historically so." Indeed, much of this chapter will be devoted to arguing that the biological features that are used to distinguish human beings as a biological species, while causally productive of certain properties in the cluster of properties from which the causal nexus and human nature arise, are only contingently so related. In other words, it is possible at least that these properties might be the result of slightly different biological features or slightly different natural processes. Another part of the answer is that human nature is not an "all-or-nothing" property. Individuals may possess human nature to varying degrees.

It is true that, according to the Human Nature Anthropic Principle (HNAP), discussed in Chapter 3, that the range of possibilities in the natural world that might give rise to the cluster of properties upon which human nature supervenes is very narrow; however, it is not true that that very narrow range of possibilities is delimited to the actual set of states-of-affairs that exist and that have existed in this actual world. This observation means that the properties that have been instantiated in a fairly stable form over a somewhat lengthy period of time in members of the human species might well have been instantiated in, or might, in the future, be instantiated in members of a different biological species, including the possibility at least of an extra-terrestrial species. In other words, there might be non-humans that have human nature. This claim ought not to be terribly shocking or controversial since, according to folk wisdom and common usage, people often say about their pets or farm animals that they are "almost human" or that they otherwise possess human-making qualities. Since the cluster theory of human nature does not maintain that there is a definitive set of specific properties necessary to produce the causal nexus upon which human nature supervenes, it would not be necessary for members of a non-human species to possess the exact same biological features that human beings possess; however, it would be necessary for whatever biological features those creatures possess to produce enough of the *properties* in the cluster to generate the causal nexus that then allows human nature to arise. While this claim remains very general and vague at the moment, the discussion of some of the specific possibilities later in this chapter will hopefully add some specificity and clarity. The main point is that being biologically human is neither necessary nor sufficient for having human nature.

It must be admitted that there is a certain vagueness and perhaps a deeply-seated indeterminacy about what it means to be biologically human. There has been keen interest in and speculation about the matter since antiquity. Ancient literature, folklore, and even religious traditions are rich with stories about situations involving individuals whose biological status is highly ambiguous. Descriptions of creatures that are part human and part some other animal abound in both ancient fables and modern fantasies. Exactly where the line is to be drawn between those who are "fully" human or "really" human and those who are "almost" human is not clear in these cases, and the ambiguity has fueled the focus of a continuing genre of literature through the ages. More recently, some philosophical literature and much of science fiction have had the same subject matter. While many of these stories simply have entertainment value, if any at all, or have value in the study of the mythology of ancient cultures, subtly embedded in some of them are important and troubling questions about human nature, how human nature is related to being biologically human, and what it means to be "fully" human.

One might think initially that it would be a simple matter to determine what is "fully" human if that description is limited to what it means to be fully human biologically. It might seem that one must simply decide what the necessary and sufficient conditions are for *Homo sapiens* and then apply those criteria. However, as already indicated above, the matter is not so simple. In the first place, there has never been complete unanimity, even amongst biologists, about those criteria. More importantly, however, for the purposes here, recent revolutionary discoveries and developments in what is perhaps most generically called "the life sciences," require a complete reconsideration of what it means to be fully human. Focusing upon the importance of these startling developments for our understanding of what it means to be fully human is one avenue by which we can arrive at a more complete understanding of human nature. Much of this chapter, therefore, focuses upon detailed examinations of some of those cases from ancient folklore and modern fiction, which are usually dismissed as pure fantasy, in light of recent, empirical evidence from the human sciences. As the modalities are stretched, philosophical considerations concerning human nature emerge—the net result of which is to further separate human nature from any necessary or sufficient biological conditions. To get clear about what, if any, relationship exists between being biologically human and having human nature, it is necessary "to push biology to its limits," "to divide biology at its joints," and "to explore biology at its margins."

Many of the most philosophically challenging cases involve creatures that are part human, in some vague, traditional, commonly accepted sense, and part non-human. Examples of such creatures from ancient literature are numerous, including satyrs, centaurs, and the like. In these tales, such creatures are usually the result of some divinely produced "curse," or "spell" or some "hanky-panky" between various gods and human beings, a form of cross-species fertilization that produces aberrant offsprings, which are usually combinations of human beings with some other mammal. But not always. There are also tales of creatures that are human beings combined with birds or reptiles. More recent fiction, such as Franz Kafka's classic story, *Metamorphosis,* or George Langelaan's much celebrated, *The Fly,* tell stories in which human beings gradually metamorphize into insects. Modern pulp fiction continues the tradition with such figures as Superman, the Hulk, and Spiderman.[3] Then there are the metaphysical-blurring creatures such as zombies and vampires, who are sometimes described as the "unhuman" although they can "pass" for human some of the time.

It seems that humans beings have long been fascinated and continue to be fascinated with "pushing the envelope" about what it means to be human. What can bizarre stories about fanciful creatures and comic book characters reveal about human nature? The importance of these cases is that they force us to consider the possibilities and to face the issue of just how different might human beings be biologically and still be "fully human." The immediately revealing thing about these cases is that in their telling and in the general response to the images created by their telling, there is, in each case, a common acceptance of the fact that creatures can be fully human, or "almost human," or "human-like," without being *strictly* biologically human. In each case, whether the creature is depicted as a fully developed combination of two individually recognizable biological species, or as gradually changing into a different species, or as biologically human but with sporadic, transforming chemical episodes that produce a distinctly non-human result, or even an alien-born creature that adopts human culture, something of a core of human nature is present in each case. There is the suggestion of a lesson in this observation that informs the cluster theory of human nature. *Some* sets of physical or biological properties are necessary for producing the cluster of properties that subvene human nature, but given the wide range of biological differences in these cases, it is clear that there is no *single*, definite set of biological properties that underlie human nature. This point illustrates the complicated relationship between the Human Anthropic Principle (HAP) and the Human Nature Anthropic Principle (HNAP) discussed in the previous chapter. HAP delimits the conditions under which human beings as a biological species might develop, HNAP delimits the conditions under which human nature might develop. While it might seem initially that HNAP would identify a discrete sub-set of conditions identified by HAP, this is not the case since it is possible, according to the cluster theory of human nature, that creatures that are not human beings in a strict biological sense can still possess human nature.

However, all of these bizarre creatures are *fictional creatures*, the result of *fictional* stories and, one might claim, over-active imaginations–the stuff of late-night or camp-fire stories to amuse or scare children. So, one might wonder, just how informative ought such stories about such creatures be for a theory of human nature. Surely, a theory of human nature cannot be based upon comic book characters. Well, minimally, as already indicated, the consideration of such creatures helps to focus attention on the modalities. However, more importantly, since modern science has now caught up with ancient folklore and modern pulp fiction, the modalities have come closer to being realities and fiction closer to becoming non-fiction.

Ancient stories of creatures that are combinations of different familiar species of animals come to life in what are called, in modern medical biotechnology, *chimeras*. Named after the ancient, mythical creature with a lion's head, a goat's body, and a serpent's tail, a modern-day chimera is *formed* by combining two embryos with two sets of "parents" each from genetically distinct species. For example, the chimera, *geep*, which has four parents, is formed by combining a sheep embryo and a goat embryo. A chimera is not a true hybrid, since such a creature does not contain new, distinctive cells of its own, i.e., there are no distinctive, geep cells. The sheep cells and goat cells are distributed throughout the geep's body in discrete groupings such as organs, bones, skin, etc. The result is a patchwork of the two original parents, much like a quilt that is formed by combining original small pieces of material. The geep is a quilt that is the combination of various sheep-pieces and goat-pieces. So, in one sense there is no such biological species as a geep, while, on the other hand, whatever it is that a geep is, it does not fit the biological classification for either a sheep or a goat. There are no experimental data on how geeps behave. At the present time, they are fragile animals that tend to have short life spans. But, obviously, if the concern here were about such things as "sheep nature" or "goat nature," the existence of geeps would raise some serious complications. It should be noted that although chimeras are created from two genetically distinct species, they can only be created from two genetically *similar* species. For the moment at least, modern biotechnology cannot create a chimera from a mouse and a whale, or, at least, if the two embryos were to be combined the resulting chimera would not survive.

The crucial question, of course, is what about human beings? There are already documented cases of human/human chimeras, which occur naturally when two embryos of fraternal twins combine into one during pregnancy. In such cases, the individual winds up with double DNA's, i.e., two distinct DNA's, which indicate a close family resemblance to each other. Such a person could literally be his or her own twin. Just how many such individuals there might be walking about out there is unknown. So, there is not a theoretical or genetic barrier to human chimeras. But what of interspecies chimeras involving humans? Can chimeras be created by combing human embryos with those of other animals? The easy and definitive answer is "yes." In fact, human/rabbit combinations have already been successfully completed in the laboratory, and applications have already been made to the United States Patent Office for patents for chimeras that are part human and part some different animal. Examples to date include the humouse (a combination of human and mouse), the humanzee (a combination of human and chimpanzee), the humpig (a combination of human and pig), and humboon (a combination of human and baboon).[4] What the theoretical or scientific limits are concerning chimeras that are part human are not clear. One might think that if the *brain* of a chimera that is part human is a human brain, then human biology (and perhaps human nature) might be preserved; however, there is no greater scientific barrier to creating a humouse with a mouse brain than there is in creating one with a human brain. Even if the resulting chimera has a human brain, it might be in the position of the characters in Kakfa's *Metamorphosis* or Langelaan's *The Fly*, trying to think like a human being while in the body of a different animal. The dependency of the proper functioning of the brain upon normal sensory input would put a quick end to "human thinking" (if indeed, such activity could ever take place).

The biotechnological processes necessary to produce chimeras that are part human are evidently relatively simple and straightforward. The difficulty and ambiguity arise about how such chimeras that might be formed using human beings are to be regarded and treated. There are, of course, the obvious legal and moral questions about the status of such individuals; however, the importance of such questions notwithstanding, such concerns are not the focus of the present inquiry concerning human nature.

Whatever moral or theological outrage the prospects of part-human chimeras might generate, the reality is that we are already living in an age where human biology can be tweaked by biotechnicians in ways that challenge long-held, established views about human beings. The immediate lesson of these modern developments for a theory of human nature is that human nature must be regarded as distinct from human biology, as the cluster theory maintains. The existence of chimeras is just one of several modern developments in biology that drive home this point. As an emergent product of a causal nexus that results from a combination of a cluster of properties, human nature is not tied to any particular set of necessary and/or sufficient such properties. It may very well be the case that for a particular historical period and as the result of a particular evolutionary history, the properties upon which human nature supervenes have been instantiated to a greater degree in creatures that are biologically human; however, to repeat a point made earlier, even if this is true, it is simply a contingent fact about our immediate neighborhood of this little corner of the universe. Whether any of the properties in the cluster of properties upon which human nature supervenes must be the products of biological processes is a matter still to be investigated.

It may well be the case that to be "fully" human is not to be biologically human at all. There is, admittedly, something of a slippery slope issue here. Scientists who have completed a complete comparison of the genomes of humans and chimpanzees report that they are almost 99 percent identical, i.e., there is just slightly more than a 1 percent difference in human and chimpanzee DNA. Some scientists think that because of this close similarity, chimpanzees shared a common ancestor some millions of years ago and that chimpanzees should be included in the genus *Homo* along with human beings.[5] There is even recent evidence of interbreeding between humans and chimpanzees following their divergence from the common ancestor. However, human beings and chimpanzees are significantly different kinds of creatures. All of the significant differences between humans and chimpanzees then—including bipedalism, vocalism, and the significant differences in the ways in which members of the two different species think and interact with other members of their own species and with their environments—are accounted for in terms of minute genetic differences. Even the development of the cerebral cortex in human beings, which is triple the size of that in chimpanzees and home to the complex, abstract, mental processes responsible for everything from art and music to philosophy, language, and technology, may be the result of a single gene in the human genome.[6]

The possibility of chimeras that are part human is simply one of a growing number of recent startling discoveries and/or developments in modern biotechnology that indicate that it is a mistake to tie human nature too closely to human biology. Consider, for example, the whole field of cybernetics. Human physiology has already been changed by cybernetics to a point that modern man arguably is significantly different than our predecessors of just a few hundred years ago. Relatively "minor" changes to human physiology are now so routine (such as eyeglasses, hearing aids, organ transplants, and joint replacements) that they seem hardly worth mentioning. One might maintain that such devices and procedures simply restore human biology to its "normal," "natural," state. However, other biotechnological and cybernetic developments are far from routine and serve the purpose of transforming rather than restoring human biology. Modern science is now capable of altering human biology both on the individual level and on a grand scale in unprecedented ways that would have been unimaginable just a few decades ago. And even more extraordinary possibilities loom over the future. Such transformations are so extraordinary that the World Transhuman Association, founded in 1997 by philosopher Nick Bostrom, Director of Oxford University's Future of Humanity Institute, predicts a "post-human" era in which cyborgs, individuals who are part human and part advanced computer, replace human beings. The potential prospects are mind-boggling with computer chips replacing or enhancing human brains resulting in cyborgs, "human-robots," the high-tech, "hard-ware" equivalent of chimeras. In theory, cyborgs might "transcend" "normal" human beings by being vastly superior in terms of both physical abilities and intelligence. The potential prospect is that "transhuman" will become the standard for human while "human" becomes subhuman. While such possibilities may seem fanciful and too Frankensteinian to be worthy of comment, transhumanism and all of the potential changes that come with it have caught the attention of serious social and political commentators, including Francis Fukuyama, who has called transhumanism the "world's most dangerous idea."[7] The focus of Fukuyama's concern is moral and political, which is the kind of concern that most philosophers who are interested in such biotechnological possibilities as chimeras, cyborgs, clonning, and the like, have. This kind of focus is concerned with preserving the notion of human rights, the notion of human agency, and equality and fairness of opportunity and treatment.

While such concerns are very legitimate and very deserving of serious philosophical attention, they are not the main focus here. The prospect of cyborgs joining or replacing biological human beings serves to focus attention on the following question: What fundamental morphological, anatomical, or genetic features, if any, are necessary to produce the properties that allow human nature to emerge? Or, what physical or biological qualities, if any, subvene human nature? In many ways, these questions are already being asked on a practical, non-academic level, and it is time that philosophers catch up with the rest of society. In many ways, the future is now. For example, a major current controversy concerns the use of steroids by athletes and whether the performances of athletes who use steroids should be recognized and legitimized. A philosophical way of analyzing the debate over whether Barry Bonds' home run records in the game of American baseball, reportedly steroid enhanced, should be shown in the record books with an asterisk, is to take the suggested asterisk as a way of distinguishing between "human" and "transhuman" performance. However, the line between "natural" ways of altering the human body, such as diet and exercise, and "non-natural" ways is not so clear. What about eyeglasses, lens transplants in the eyes, lasik surgery, or other medical devices or procedures to enhance eyesight? What is the qualitative difference between caffeine and steroids? What about joint replacements? All such supplements and procedures are "performance enhancing" to some degree or other. Some runners have protested that fellow competitors, amputees with prosthetic legs, have an unfair advantage. It may not be nice to "mess around with Mother

Nature;" however, it is not clear where the "messing around" ends and the "helping hand" begins.

Where does all of this leave the cluster theory of human nature? Well, as the possibility (and eventual probability) of the existence of chimeras and cyborgs that are part human makes clear, the biology of human beings is far from being a settled matter. To the extent that such individuals might continue to think, sense, act, and feel, the biological changes notwithstanding, it seems reasonable to suppose that human nature in chimeras and cyborgs could easily remain unchanged. Therefore, the cluster theory shares this with transhumanism: *no* biological properties are necessarily included in the cluster of properties upon which human nature supervenes. The consequence is that, in the future, chimeras, cyborgs, or other animals might possess human nature to a greater or lesser extent than currently existing individuals who are biologically human! Since it has become common to think of man as superior to the other animals and since, for many, that superiority is be measured not in biological terms but in terms of human nature, the future might well see the decline or end of that supposed superiority. The prospect looms therefore that other species of animals, or species that are part human, or even cyborgs that are non-human biologically, may well be superior to biological human beings in that the properties upon which human nature supervenes are instantiated to a much greater degree in those creatures than in creatures that are biologically human. This means that other creatures may be more "human-like" or more "fully human" than are human beings.

Such a reality is not hard to imagine. Fictional accounts from popular culture, especially pulp fiction, often portray intelligent aliens as superior to man. Perhaps one of the more poignant portrayals is found in Jonathan Swift's *Gulliver's Travels* in his account of Gulliver's fourth and final voyage to the country of the Houyhnhnms. The Houyhnhnms are rational, civilized animals in the shape of horses, and they are served by an inferior race of humans (called Yahoos) who are ignorant, uncivilized, boorish, and crass.[8] Although Swift's satire is directed elsewhere, for the purposes here, it is easy to imagine that in such circumstances, it would be natural to attribute to the Houyhnhnms (to the humice, to the humanzees, to the humpigs, to the humboons?) a greater degree of human nature than to the Yahoos. If this result is not readily apparent, it is easy to tweak Swift's story to make the Yahoos less and less human-like in comparison with the Houyhnhnms although they remain biologically human. They can be made to have no language, to have no "civilized" traits of any kind, to be cannibals, etc. At some point in the process, even the most reluctant would eventually be forced to admit that the Yahoos are just not fully human while the Houyhnhnms are more "human-like." The circumstances can be made to parallel Wittgenstein's example of the speaking lion discussed earlier in Chapter 2. To understand this, it is necessary to imagine oneself a modern human observing the situation, i.e., a non-Yahoo human.

In Swift's story, the Houyhnhnms are "speaking" the Houyhnhnm language, presumably with distinctive and recognizable phonemes whose *meanings* are unknown to us human beings who are untutored in Houyhnhnm. Assuming that the Houyhnhnms speak at regular times and familiar circumstances (just as speaking lions might do), it would be a relatively short time before an intelligent observer, one perhaps with some training in anthropology and linguistics, would produce Houyhnhnm to Standard English (or some other modern language) translations and dictionaries. As I argued in Chapter 2, this situation would not be significantly different from a situation in which one human being encounters a *new*, i.e., hitherto unknown human language. Although Swift does not tell his story in such a way so as to invoke explicitly the more provocative and challenging philosophical puzzle of what one might say and how one might react if the Houyhnhnms spoke common English, it is clear that he does not intend that the Houyhnhnms be understood as simply speaking an inferior "animal" language with primitive whinnies and snorts.

To repeat the point made in Chapter 2: Wittgenstein's claim about the speaking lion is that it is impossible to bridge the conceptual chasm between attributing meaning, understanding, and intentionality to the speakers of human language and doing the same thing to the speakers of Lion. For Wittgenstein, this would be conceptually impossible because speaking a human language is part of a *form of life*. The uttering of a meaningful sentence in a human language is not something that occurs in isolation from other features or characteristics that we take to be salient features of a particular *form* of life, and we do not, according to Wittgenstein, recognize lions as possessing or sharing those salient characteristics that are necessary for attributing the requisite intentions for meaningful discourse. However, in Swift's story much has changed. It is not a situation where modern humans as we now know ourselves and modern lions as we now know them are attempting to converse. It is a Houyhnhnmian civilization with abundant evidence of Houyhnhnmian accomplishments and advances and equally abundant evidence of the lack of such accomplishments and advances by Yahoos. In other words, there is strong evidence that the Houyhnhnms instantiate many of the properties in the cluster of properties upon which human nature supervenes to a much greater degree than do the Yahoos. In this strong sense of "imagine," it is easy to imagine that one would say that the Houyhnhnms, even given their biological differences, are more fully human than the Yahoos. Again, the cluster theory of human nature is a dynamic, fluid theory of human nature with the possibility that the core cluster of properties and the causal relationships amongst those properties might fluctuate in an individual or amongst numbers of individuals in a general population over a period of time or in drastically changing environmental circumstances.

There are other recent, significant developments in biotechnology, on the margins of biology, that are particularly revealing about the relationship between human biology and human nature. Consider the process of cloning, which, of itself, threatens to split biology at its joints. Again, to date, the concern of philosophers about cloning has been almost exclusively focused upon the bioethics of the process. The philosophical focus here is more fundamental. The concern here is how cloning might affect our fundamental understanding of human nature.

To understand the importance of the prospect of the cloning of human beings (and the changes that cloning might precipitate) to the study of human nature and to the cluster theory of human nature, it is necessary to understand something about the importance of human sexual reproduction and human sexuality to the cluster theory of human nature.

It is helpful to begin by noting that Darwin regarded sexual selection as an influence on evolution that is distinct from natural selection. In *Origin of Species*, he says that sexual selection "depends, not on a struggle for existence in relation to other organic beings or to external conditions, but on the struggle between the individuals of one sex, generally the males, for the possession of the other sex."[9] Although Darwin further distinguished sexual selection from natural selection by noting that sexual selection is "less rigorous than natural selection" since its results are not survival or non-survival but simply more or less progeny,[10] modern biologists have subsumed sexual selection under the general rubric of natural selection. Much of great significance to any attempt to understand human nature is lost or, at best, obscured, in this move. Natural selection is a process that is the function of the interaction between a species and its environment and other species. Sexual selection is a process that is the function of the interaction between the sexes of a species. Often, the properties or behavior of an individual that are conducive to success in sexual selection (e.g., bright, distinctive plumage in male birds) are counterproductive to survival. Obviously, in order for sexual selection to take place in a species, there must be distinct sexes in that species. The same is not true of natural selection minus sexual selection.

As a biological species, *Homo sapiens* is a sexually dimorphous species. The biological classification, noted at the beginning of this chapter, presumes that sexual dimorphism. This means that human reproduction is sexual reproduction. The bases for the rest of the biological classification of *Homo sapiens* follow from this feature. What would the consequences be to the biology of human beings if human reproduction became completely asexual? What would it mean to human nature if individuals became completely asexual, i.e., biologically androgynous? The answers to these questions are revealing for the cluster theory of human nature, and these answers must be pursued across a range of different possible consequences of human cloning.

Of course, there is an impressive variety of different kinds of reproduction in the animal world, many involving asexual reproduction, which occurs in both single-celled and multi-celled organisms. Asexual reproduction, the result of mitosis (or the division of the nucleus of a cell) results in a progeny with identical genetic material as the original (parent) cell, i.e., the progeny is a *clone*; so, technically clones already exist in nature. In the case of asexual reproduction, i.e., cloning, the only variation in genetic material between a single parent and the progeny will be the result of relatively infrequently occurring mutations; otherwise, all individuals in an entire lineage, over many generations, would be genetically identical. On the other hand, sexual reproduction is the result of a mixture of genetic material from two different parents and therefore produces progeny who differ genetically both from their parents and, in most cases, from each other as well.

Asexual reproduction results in a population with a very homogenous gene pool while sexual reproduction results in a population with a very heterogenous gene pool. Of what consequence is this fact to human nature? Well, the answer in this case depends upon the degree to which cloning might come to replace sexual reproduction in human beings. To date, there has not been an accepted, documented case of a human clone, but undoubtedly, at some time in the future, there will be. As the much publicized case of Dolly, the first cloned sheep, attests, mammals have already been successfully cloned, and since Dolly, the cloning of horses, cows, dogs, pigs, goats, rabbits, mice, mules, rats, and oxen has been documented. Scientists have reportedly resorted to cloning to preserve some endangered species, including the gaur, Javan bantengs, and the ibex.

Here is a question that has not so far been addressed, to my knowledge, in the literature about human cloning: Will the first "human" clone be *human*? The progeny will be genetically human but will not be the result of sexual reproduction. Which biological criterion will be deemed more important and win out for the sake of biological classification? The answer, I believe, will be that the progeny will be regarded as biologically human because it is genetically human and whatever adjustments that will become necessary in the biological classification of *Homo sapiens* will be made. It is also easy to imagine that this individual is indistinguishable from other human beings in terms of ways of thinking, experiencing, behaving, etc., so that, in terms of the cluster theory of human nature, the progeny will also be regarded as "fully" human. But what of the second "human" clone? The tenth? The ten-thousandth? The ten-millionth?

What if there becomes a "race" of individuals that are genetically human but who practice asexual cloning exclusively? In some ways, this is not such a farfetched supposition since it easy to imagine that cloning might come to be the preferred method of reproduction since it offers the opportunity for genetic engineering, which might be used, given the progress on the Human Genome Project, to select desired genes and to avoid undesired ones. On such a large scale, both the biological identity of human beings as well as human nature would possibly become threatened. Why? Well, the answer here must be very general, somewhat speculative, and is deserving of much more detailed and in-depth attention from biologists and geneticists; however, it is possible to identify some of the kinds of changes that might occur that would result in drastic changes to human biology and human nature. For example, on a somewhat modest level, one might wonder what effects would such widespread cloning have on familial structures and relationships. Clones have only a single parent; so, the fundamental fabric of parenthood, of mother and father, of parents and offspring, and of the family unit, might be undermined in a society of genetic humans who reproduce exclusively by asexual cloning.

Furthermore, although the popular literature on cloning ignores this point completely, there is no reason to suppose that the individual from whom the original cell is taken must be an adult. It might be a child, an infant, or even a fetus. Given potential differences in growth rate during pregnancy (and future ways of influencing that rate), progeny might well be born before their "parent." Clearly, what sociologists have come to call "the nuclear family unit," regarded by most as the fundamental unit of all known human societies, would not be necessary in a race or society in which universal, asexual cloning is the method of reproduction. Without any biological basis for familial relationships, e.g., mate to mate, parent to child, sibling to sibling, and the associated emotions and values, it is difficult to see how what we now regard as human nature would survive. In some ways, cloned humans would be biologically human, but it is doubtful that they would be "fully" human. The effect of such fundamental changes upon human emotions and values must remain an open question, but given the kind of biological basis of emotions and values sketched in Chapter 9, which ties those emotions and values to the fundamental family unit, it is difficult to see how basic human emotions and values and, in turn, the foundation for human societies and human civilization could remain unchanged. If the basis for such emotions as human love and such virtues as courage is biological in nature, e.g., love for one's mate and courage in protecting one's children, then universal cloning would clearly threaten the basis for such emotions and virtues. If the basis for the fundamental structures and organizations of human societies is biological in nature, then universal human cloning would also clearly threaten human civilization as we now know it. There may be some way of preserving human familial relationships, emotions, and values and human civilization in a "human" cloning society, but it is not clear at all how this could work. The prospects should keep biologists, sociologists, psychologists, and philosophers busy for decades to come.

Exactly what the other long-term repercussions might be of universal cloning on human biology and human nature are not clear. On a significantly more basic level, one might wonder what effects universal cloning would have on sexual dimorphism in *Homo sapiens*. Other animals have evolved from sexual reproduction to asexual reproduction; so, might not the same thing happen with human beings? If this did happen, what would then happen to the sexes? In discussions of possible human cloning, the question is often asked, "Are men really necessary?" Well, the short answer is that in the case of asexual reproduction by cloning, they are not. However, it is not clear that women are necessary either. Admittedly, there must be some way of nourishing the cloned cell while it replicates itself, and the human female anatomy and the possession of a uterus, placenta, and umbilical cord presently provide the only way that is currently available for doing this; however, there is no reason to suppose, particularly given the dramatic potential of biotechnology, that women will always provide the only way of doing this. There are all kinds of possibilities. The females of other species of animals, chimeras, cyborgs, or special "birthing laboratories" may do as good or better job of nourishing the fetus, and, given the inconvenience, pain, health threats, and loss to the labor force, of pregnancy and child birth, it is easy to imagine that most women might come to prefer other methods of producing progeny, especially if there is no father or sexual intercourse involved. It is possible then that women would not know or be able to recognize their progeny to any greater degree than would men. So, perhaps neither men nor women would be necessary for universal, asexual cloning.[11]

It is not clear what the long-term consequences (and by "long-term" I mean tens of thousands of years) of evolutionary development of cloned humans on sexual dimorphism might be.[12] It is not even clear how the evolutionary process and natural selection would continue to operate on the human level; however, it is clear that sexual selection, which Darwin regarded as a separate but equal influence on evolution, would no longer operate. Without sexual selection would sexual dimorphism persist in humans? The cloned progeny would presumably still have all of their respective sex hormones, the resulting secondary sex characteristics, and the respective male and female sex genitalia. However, if none of these was of any biological significance over a long period of evolutionary change, e.g., producing eggs or sperm, recognizing and/or attracting a mate, or sexual intercourse for reproduction, then, presuming that natural selection would still operate as it does now, it is difficult to see how any of these features would be selected for and continue to exist. Human genitalia might well become like the human appendix, i.e., functionless, or they might atrophy or disappear altogether. Whatever differences there might continue to be between men and women would then be biologically insignificant, and sexual dimorphism nonexistent. Such a society would become truly androgynous with no biological distinctions between male and female. Neither the current biological classification of *Homo sapiens* nor our current understanding of human nature would survive such significant changes, but, as noted at the beginning of this chapter, biological classification can and has changed. For example, *Homo sapiens* may no longer be of the class Mammalia if mammary glands atrophy, but such a reclassification will simply be a minor inconvenience for future students of biology. It is human nature that would suffer more, possibly irreparable, harm.

For the cluster theory of human nature, it is not simply sexual reproduction but sexual desire and sexual passion, i.e., human sexuality, that are important. It is easy to imagine a large number of humans that do not reproduce sexually. In fact, in modern American culture, many individuals make the choice not to have children, and practicing homosexuals do not produce children. While some people might regard those who choose to be childless as "unnatural" and as missing something, e.g., parenthood, that is important to human nature and to being "fully human," this reproach is misplaced. It is not simply parenthood but human sexuality that is important to human nature. This is why the important question that cloning poses for theories of human nature is not simply about the status of cloned progeny but rather about the long-term effects on sexual dimorphism and human sexuality.

The supposed connection of human sexuality with reproduction appears to be the result of confusions in both biology and theology. Much of the confusion in biology arises from subsuming sexual selection under natural selection. The case can be made that human sexuality and sexual selection in humans not only operate independently of natural selection, as Darwin supposed and as modern biologists ignore, but that they also operate *contra* natural selection. Aristotle and Freud were both right: man is a rational and a sexual animal. The designation, *Homo sapiens* (the wise man), follows Aristotle and results from the recognition of the importance of the development of an enlarged cranium, allowing for brain development; however, modern man could also easily be designated as *Homo sexus* (the sexual man), resulting from the recognition of the uniqueness of human sexuality.

In biology, the received, standard view is represented by the claims made popular by Richard Dawkins in *The Selfish Gene*. He claims that human sexuality, like all sexual activity in the animal kingdom, is explained by the biological drive to reproduce and produce progeny and that humans are simply sexual slaves to our genes, "the Replicators," which are able to produce exact copies of themselves (lacking mutation). So, according to Dawkins, humans are genetically determined to have sex since we are "blindly programmed to preserve the selfish...genes."[13] Human sexuality, on this view, is simply the battle ground on which genes fight for survival. The claim here, contra Dawkins, is that humans are driven to have sex but not to produce progeny. It is the fact that human sexuality and human sexual passion and human sexual desire can be separated from procreation that is distinctly human.

There are many features about human sexuality that make it unique in the animal world and provide evidence of a disconnect between human sexuality and reproduction. The claim that humans are *Homo sexus* is based on this disconnect. If human sexuality is understood only as the product of an evolutionary process designed primarily for reproduction, the preservation of "the selfish gene," and the survival of the species, then it is a very inefficient mechanism, and the survival and the flourishing of *Homo sapiens* in the face of such inefficiency would be very difficult to explain. The biological features of human sexuality that must be understood minimally as inefficient and realistically as counterproductive to natural selection suggest strongly that there are other, more efficacious, explanations for human sexual activity. In the first place, the adult, human female is continually receptive to sexual intercourse. Unlike most other mammals and all other primates, human female receptivity is not the result of estrus, which itself has been reduced in humans to the point that it is not even recognized by most biological text books as existing in female *Homo sapiens*. And, perhaps most importantly, nor is it recognized by adult human males who might be interested in sex. There are admittedly subtle biological changes that occur in women during ovulation, but with all of the discussion of pheromones and changes in body temperature notwithstanding, men seem particularly ill-suited to detect such "signals." Human sexuality seems to be one area where being sight-dominant is a handicap since men seem to be seriously restricted, again unlike other animals, in using other senses such as smell in their "pursuit" of the female. It is a well-known phenomenon amongst people who have regular contact with animals that other animals, particularly horses and dogs, can detect the subtle body odors of women that are indicative of different stages in the menstrual cycle about which men are utterly clueless. In terms of the biological and anatomical changes associated with fertility, in contrast to the females of other primates, who display their often brightly-colored genitals prominently during estrus, human females *hide* rather than advertise their receptivity.

Similarly, men's penises have not evolved the bright purple, red, and yellow coloration that allows for the visual displays used by the males of some other primates to attract females. So, understood strictly in terms of reproduction and the production of progeny for replicating the selfish gene, human sexuality is very inefficient and very understated—apparently ill-equipped for such purposes. It is not clear how such traits could have been selected for in terms of natural selection. Sexual selection must then operate on a different scale and with different priorities than natural selection. Just the existence and prevalent use of birth control amongst large numbers of human beings puts sexual selection at odds with natural selection.

At the same time, human sexuality seems *overly* designed for mere reproduction. Consider, for example, the male penis in humans. What men's penises lack when compared to those of some other primates and monkeys in terms of coloration and visual appearance, they certainly make up for in terms of size. While the size of a male's penis might be a delicate subject for many to consider, there is a very serious point to be made here. If the human penis is understood merely in terms of natural selection for reproduction, it is difficult to explain why men are so over-equipped for the job. The average human penis is over five inches when erect compared with less than two inches for gorillas and orangutans, and, on average, it is also much thicker than the pencil-thin penises of other primates. One might think, based solely on natural selection, that so long as a penis is long enough to deliver the sperm to impregnate the female, that *smaller* penises would be selected for since they would be less cumbersome and restrictive allowing their owners to be more agile and thus to avoid predators better. Merely for purposes of sexual reproduction, very little in the way of size is necessary since the only purely sexual function of the penis is to deliver sperm. The most likely explanation for the unusually large size of the human penis, particularly given the absence of brightly-colored visual display, would seem to be related to pleasure during sexual intercourse—for both the man and the woman.

Also, while the existence and importance of the female orgasm was undeniably ignored or denied in patriarchal societies for a long time, biologists now think that human females are unique amongst the females of primates in reaching orgasm during sexual intercourse. This is another feature of human sexuality that is unnecessary for simple reproduction and difficult to explain solely on the grounds of natural selection. As any casual observer of animal reproduction is aware, sex does not have to be enjoyable or pleasurable to be effective. Thus it seems, the sexual physiology and behavior of both male and female humans cannot be accounted for solely in terms of sexual reproduction and natural selection. Sexual selection, pleasure, and human choice and preference all apparently play important roles as well.

There are other characteristics of human biology and anatomy directly related to human sexual behavior and human sexuality that also deserve careful attention. As Desmond Morris points out in *The Naked*

Ape, while one might initially claim that human sexuality is largely culturally determined, realistically it is more likely that "the advance of civilization has not so much moulded modern sexual behavior, as that sexual behavior has moulded the shape of civilization."[14] This claim is entirely in line with the bottom-up, naturalistic cluster theory of human nature. Both the amount of sexual behavior and the intensity of sexuality in *Homo sexus* makes human beings the sexiest primate that exists. As Morris documents, the long period of female receptivity, lengthy courtships, prolonged pair-bonding, extended foreplay, lengthy copulation, and female orgasm are all missing in other primates.[15]

There is little doubt that these features of human sexuality are the result of evolutionary changes that took place over a long period of time that also saw the other changes associated with the hunter-gatherer ancestors of modern man (namely, the development of a larger brain, bipedalism, and cooperative behavior); however, none of these features is necessary for mere reproduction. Most of the biological, anatomical, and behavioral characteristics of human sexuality are excessive and unnecessary for mere reproduction and actually simply make sex "sexier," i.e., more pleasurable and enjoyable for both men and women. The continual receptivity of the woman, which promotes greater sexual contact, "naked" skins, which are more sensitive to tactile stimulation, more erogenous zones with more nerve endings, which result in greater pleasure, and even enlarged brains, which allow sexual fantasy all contribute to a significantly greater amount of pleasure and enjoyment from sex for human beings than is necessary for mere reproduction.[16]

Morris also maintains that many other human features such as the possession of earlobes, a protruding nose, facial musculature, lips, and protruding breasts in women all contribute to sex signals that promote frontal sexual approach, an increased emphasis on the identity of the sex partner, and face-to-face copulation—all of which, in turn, help to promote pair-bonding and cement long-term relationships.[17] All of this means that human sexuality is closely tied with human culture and that some aspects of human biology are to be included in the cluster of properties that form the causal nexus upon which human nature supervenes. Exactly which properties those might be is not clear and whether entire societies of chimeras, cyborgs, or robots could have those properties is an empirical question that can only be answered by examining the anatomy and the sexuality of the individuals. A very detailed story would have to be told. It is easy to imagine creatures, which are significantly different biologically and anatomically, that still have something closely resem-

bling human sexuality. This situation might very well exist with intelligent extra-terrestrial beings. However, it is difficult to imagine anything
like human sexuality existing in creatures in which there is no sexual
dimorphism. Admittedly, there is now frequently significant overlap in
the physical characteristics that account for differences between men
and women, and there is also frequently significant ambiguity in those
physical characteristics. Such overlap and ambiguity have led some to
claim that sexual dimorphism is consequently culturally determined. That
culture plays some role in sexual dimorphism is undeniable; however,
it is difficult to imagine how such a fundamental distinction could be
completely cultural where there are no recognizable biological differences between men and women. Hence, it is difficult to imagine how
human nature (as we now understand it) could survive in creatures that
are biologically asexual even in recognition of significant cultural differences in attitudes towards sex and understandings of human sexuality.

The debate concerning human sexuality in Christian theology is an
old and persistent one. Christians, it seems have just had a very difficult
time coming to grips with the fact that human beings are sexual animals.
One of the primary theological reasons for this difficulty concerns the
status of Jesus who was, according to mainstream Christian theology,
both fully human and fully divine. If human sexuality is completely
natural and a part of human nature, then Christians would be faced with
the prospect that Jesus himself was a sexual being and engaged in sexual
behavior including masturbation as an adolescent and sexual intercourse
as an adult, or, at least, experiencing sexual desire.

Faced with such a choice, many early Christian theologians simply
denied that human sexuality is natural. Connected with this denial is a
host of related theological claims and historical developments including
the doctrine of the virgin birth, which served to completely isolate Jesus
from any human sexual activity, the doctrine of original sin, which served
to account for human sexuality as something base and sinful and part of
God's punishment and the "Fall" of man, and the treatment of women
and everything feminine by the early Christian church, which served to
eliminate the threat of sexuality represented by the feminine.[18]

Detailed records of the earliest Christian theological concerns with
human sexuality date to the debate in the fifth century between Augustine on the one hand and Pelagius and Julian on the other about whether
death and sexual desire are to be regarded as a part of nature (Pelagius
and Julian) or whether they are to be regarded as antithetical to human
nature and imposed on man by God as punishment for Adam's sin (Au-

gustine). Augustine's view of original sin eventually won the debate, and the doctrine of original sin has been an official theological doctrine of the Roman Catholic Church ever since.[19] According to Augustine, Adam and Eve had sex, but they did not have sexual desire and thus no human sexuality. In the case of Adam, apparently he did not achieve an erection because of sexual excitement or sexual desire but by volition, i.e., as an exercise of his *will*, something akin to raising his arm. Presumably, there could have been no sense of pleasure that comes from the satisfaction of sexual desire. If human beings have sexual desire and die, not as a natural part of some inherent nature, but only because we are sinful, then this would explain why Jesus, since according to Christian theology he was not sinful, neither died nor had sexual desire.

Separating human sexuality from human nature separates human nature from man's animal nature and the natural world at the most fundamental level and thus helps buttress the Christian, top-down, essentialist view of human nature, according to which the possession of a spiritual soul is what uniquely characterizes human beings and sets human beings off from the rest of the natural world. For a religious believer, separating death and sex from man's "true" nature can also help explain how human beings are made "in the image of God" and how human beings can have a unique spiritual relationship with God by overcoming this sinful (and unnatural) condition. Overcoming what is regarded as the depraved, sinful condition of human beings would also provide a rationale for the need of a hierarchical church to shepherd man out of this situation. The suppression of sexual desire and the vow of celibacy on the part of some monks, priests, and ascetics result from the view that sex is unnatural, sinful, and distracting from one's true spiritual nature. On the cluster view of human nature, it is the suppression of human sexuality and celibacy that is unnatural since such suppression denies the natural consequences of the long, evolutionary development of the biological species, *Homo sapiens* (*Homo sexus*). The Augustinian view of sex in the Garden of Eden, which was sex without sexual desire or human sexuality, is distinctly non-human sex. On a bottom-up view of human nature, human sexuality is one of several properties in the cluster of properties that has developed slowly and naturally and in conjunction with other such properties to produce a causal nexus from which human nature emerges. This does not mean that human sexuality is an *essential* property of human nature, but it does mean that asexual individuals are missing something that is an important part of what it means to be "fully" human. This does not mean that such individuals are not human or that they have *no* human nature, but it does mean that they are missing something that is an important element of human nature.

To use a metaphor introduced earlier, the situation is like hearing a familiar melody with a few wrong notes or that is slightly off-key or like hearing a familiar symphony being played by an orchestra that is missing an entire section of instruments. The melody or theme is recognizable, but something is missing, out-of-tune, or incomplete. Might human beings evolve in the future to the point where sexuality no longer characterizes the species in the ways in which it does now? Certainly such developments might occur, but with such significant changes would come changes in human nature itself. Would this mean that human beings are no longer mammals? So long as the rest of the natural world and animal kingdom remains unchanged or relatively unchanged, human beings cannot become completely asexual and remain "fully human," *Homo sapiens* with our present human nature, since being *Homo sexus* contributes to that nature so significantly. Future biologists and/or philosophers might say about such creatures something such as, "these creatures were characterized by a certain *nature*, at a much earlier time—a nature characterized, in part, by a peculiar kind of human sexuality that has since been lost."

To complete this examination of the relationship between human biology and human nature, let us examine the significance of the occurrence of extreme anomalies in human biology and the consequences of those anomalies for the cluster theory of human nature. These cases constitute another "seam" in biology or biology "at the fringes" and another soft place to split biology and separate it from human nature. Consider, first of all, the discovery of the skeleton remains of a species of "tiny" humans on the remote island of Flores in Indonesia—what has since been named *Homo floresiensis* and is now better known as "Flores Man" (and nicknamed by some, "the Hobbit"). The remains of Flores Man, found in 2005, date to less than 20,000 years ago and provide strong evidence that anthropologists may very well have to rethink both the evolutionary history and the definition of *Homo sapiens*. While sharing most of the biological, anatomical, and cultural characteristics with *Homo sapiens*, Flores Man was barely three feet tall with a correspondingly small, but perhaps very advanced and sophisticated, brain. One line of speculation about the origin and development of Flores Man is that the species is the result of the process of "dwarfing" during which *Homo sapiens*, who were stranded on a remote, isolated island with very limited resources gradually reduced in size, over several generations, in order to survive on food resources that were inadequate to support "normal-sized" human beings.

There is presently wide-spread disagreement amongst scientists over the significance of these skeleton remains, and it is likely to take decades for anthropologists to sort through the complications and implications of Flores Man. However, the possibility of a significantly smaller species of human beings that are otherwise nearly identical to modern man, both biologically and culturally, poses an interesting thought experiment that is revealing about the relationship between human biology and anatomy and human nature. We might call this thought experiment *the experiment of the incredible shrinking man*. Just *how small* (or large) might human beings be? And just *how small* (or large) might human beings be and still have what we now regard as human nature? Alternatively, does *size* really matter after all? If this question is about the *body* size of human beings, then the answer is in the affirmative, i.e, a certain *range* of body size seems important to human beings being the kind of creatures that we are and having the particular human nature that we do given the characteristics of the natural world in which we live. While there is admittedly a wide range of differences in size amongst *Homo sapiens*, there are also limits to that range. The possibility of a species of humans merely two inches tall, for example, stretches the imagination beyond the breaking point. To gain some insight into the implications for the cluster theory of human nature of this thought experiment prompted by the case of Flores Man, it is important to ask whether it is strong or weak imagination that is called for in the thought experiment. In the case of weak imagination, where one imagines the size of human beings being significantly smaller but the rest of the natural world remaining as it is, the implications would seem to be dramatic. If humans were unchanged biologically and anatomically except for being reduced to being two inches tall, the range of different ways in which we might interact with and appropriate our natural environment would be drastically altered. Few, if any, of the major accomplishments of human development would have emerged. Also, if humans were the natural prey of practically every other carnivore in the natural world from the size of mice and up, it is difficult to imagine what we regard as human civilization ever emerging. If it is strong imagination that is called, where perhaps everything else in the natural world changes in exact proportion to the change in the size of humans, then obviously the changes would affect nothing at all about human nature or anything else (except perhaps the speed of light). It is not the absolute size of human beings that is important, but it is the relative size of the members of the biological species in relation to the natural world that affects the ability to experience, interact with, and to appropriate different parts of the natural world conditioned in the way in which we have known it to exist—all of which is discussed in the next chapter.

There are also extreme anomalies of biology that occur during the processes of human pregnancy and birth that pose serious questions challenging any attempt to align human nature with human biology in any essentialist way. Consider the cases known as *fetus in fetu*, i.e., a fetus *inside* a fetus. These rare circumstances occur when there is originally a pair of identical twins in the mother's womb, and, during pregnancy, one of the fetuses develops normally but encircles and envelops the other one so that the second fetus does not develop normally but becomes a *parasite* within the abdominal cavity of the normal (host) fetus. This may happen with male or female fetuses. The result is known medically as a "vanishing twin," where one of the fetuses, detected by sonogram early in a pregnancy, "disappears" into the body cavity of the normal (host) fetus and becomes a parasite, nourished by a surrounding embryonic sac fed by the blood supply of the "normal" twin. The parasitic twin is not viable since it does not develop internal organs and is as grotesque as anything dreamt of by any author of science fiction novel or horror tale. At least one young boy has lived until the age of eight with such a parasitic twin living inside his abdominal cavity!

A second case of an extreme anomaly that has occurred during human pregnancy and child birth involves a case described as *cranial para parasititus*. Only ten cases of such a condition have been medically documented and only three fetuses have survived to the point of live birth; so this is one of the rarest anomalies of human development. This condition involves an otherwise normal fetus that develops a second *parasitic* head. The parasitic head shares a single brain with the normal fetus and has a face with all of the normal features of a human face, but otherwise has no other body parts or internal organs. Where such a condition manages to survive until birth, the result is literally a child with two heads. Although there have been more recent and better documented cases, the most publicized case, which occurred at the end of the eighteenth century, involved the child who became known as The Boy of Bengal. This child was displayed as part of a traveling "freak show" until he was killed tragically by a snake bite at the age of four. While the existence of Siamese twins raises many of the same issues, this child managed to single-handedly extend the range of credulity of the biological variations under which human beings might survive. In the case of Siamese twins, two complete individuals (sometimes sharing some vital organs) are attached to one another while in the case of "the boy with two heads," there is a single individual with two distinct heads with one parasitic head living off of the "host body."

While it may be politically incorrect to acknowledge the fact, in both of these cases, the *fetus in fetu* and *cranial para parasititus*, the individuals are struggling not only with an extreme medical, biological condition but with a condition that threatens their very humanity. With any reasonable sense of "normalcy," it is difficult to imagine these individuals living anything approaching a normal life, and whatever degree of normalcy they might achieve comes only through enormous efforts from other "normal" human beings. If these medical conditions are corrected through radical surgery, not only is the medical condition addressed but issues related to what it means to be "fully human" are addressed as well. If the parasitic fetus or head is successfully removed, one wants to say not only has something been taken away but something has also been *restored*.

One's reactions to these extreme anomalies of child birth demonstrate that while still being perhaps genetically human, the effects of these children's deformities extend far beyond the medical condition itself. Before the advent of modern medicine, these individuals would probably never have survived, but even modern medicine cannot bestow human nature upon a two-headed child or upon a young boy with a parasitic fetus growing in his abdomen. To extend the *concept* so radically, i.e., to suppose that large numbers of such individuals might fall under the same rubric of human nature, is to extend the concept beyond the breaking point.

While there is some flexibility in the way in which human nature is related to human biology and while it is a mistake to equate human nature with human biology, what this chapter demonstrates is that the present concept of human nature cannot survive the division of biology at its seams, i.e., at its most fundamental levels. The biological properties that belong in the cluster of properties upon which human nature supervenes consist of a *range* of properties that conjointly represent something like a range of biological normalcy within which human nature can survive and thrive. This range may be a wide one, and there is obviously room for misunderstanding and abuse of what this means on sexual, racial, or ethnic grounds, but the issue here involves biology *at its joints and at its fringes*. The issues about the relationship between human biology and human nature raised by chimeras, cyborgs, cloning, the Flores Man, and extreme anomalies of biology have nothing to do with sex, race, or ethnicity. The properties in the cluster of properties which create the causal nexus upon which human nature then supervenes must be instantiated in some kind of creature. It may be simply a contingent matter of evolutionary fact that the kind of creature in which those properties are currently most optimally instantiated is a particular biological species called *Homo sapiens*, a biological species that is classified by biologists in the ways indicated at the beginning of this chapter. To some extent, it is possible to imagine that human biology might change and that the biological classification of *Homo sapiens* might change. However, the possible changes addressed in this chapter belie the old adage that the more things change the more they remain the same. *Drastic* changes in human biology (splitting biology at its joints) portend the twilight of human nature and perhaps the end of the age of human nature as we have come to regard it.

Notes

1. Desmond Morris, *The Naked Ape* (New York: McGraw-Hill Book Company, 1967).
2. This time line is borrowed from Peter Farb, *Human Kind* (Boston, MA: Houghton Mifflin Company, 1978), 9.
3. The inclusion of Superman at this point, perhaps the best-known pulp fiction hero raises unique issues since, according to the story, Superman is an alien, born on another planet. He is raised in a human family and, in his Clarke Kent "disguise," "passes" as human. Similar cases are discussed later in this chapter and in the next.
4. "Humpig" and "humboon" are my neologisms. It is doubtful that these part-human chimeras have actually been created, and the reason for the patent applications from members of the Council for Responsible Genetics is probably to block others from receiving such patents and to discourage genetic engineering.
5. For further exploration of this issue see Jonathan Marks, *What It Means to Be 98% Chimpanzee: Apes, People, and Their Genes* (Berkeley, CA: University of California Press, 2002).
6. The gene is called HAR1F. See *Nature*, August 17, 2006.
7. Francis Fukuyama, "Transhumanism," *Foreign Policy*, 144, Sept.-Oct., 2004. 42-43.
8. This story, of course, is responsible for the introduction of the word, "Yahoo," into common English to denote a person with such characteristics, which were, for Swift, decidedly too commonly found in human beings.
9. Charles Darwin, *Origin of Species* (Garden City, NY: Doubleday & Company, Inc., 1859), 95.
10. *Ibid.*
11. On a different note, which promises to decidedly favor women over men, researchers have managed to produce mice from mice eggs from a female without fertilization by a male. Since this process uses an unfertilized egg, it is not cloning but *parthenogenesis*, the unassisted production of female progeny from female parents.

12. There is admittedly some ambiguity about sexual dimorphism that occurs in nature when there is lack of agreement between individuals' chromosomes and their genitalia.
13. Richard Dawkins, *The Selfish Gene* (Oxford: Oxford University Press, 1976), v. To be fair to Dawkins, he holds out some hope that, through cooperation and altruism, humans might resist the pernicious consequences of our selfish genes (but only because cooperation and altruism have some evolutionary advantage).
14. Desmond Morris, *The Naked Ape* (New York: McGraw-Hill Book Company, 1967), 50.
15. *Ibid.*, 62-63.
16. See *ibid.*, 66ff.
17. See *ibid.*, 70ff.
18. These topics are currently receiving much attention and are the subjects of a large number of books, articles, and news accounts focusing on the relationship between Jesus and Mary Magdalene as well as the roles of other women in early Christianity.
19. A detailed account of this debate can be found in Elaine Pagels, *Adam, Eve, and the Serpent* (New York: Vintage Books, 1988), Chapter VI.

5

Human Experience and Human Nature

In Chapter 3, I argued that rational human agency and practical reason can best be explained as results of a pattern of efficacious adaptation over a long period of evolutionary change to dramatically, and sometimes rapidly, changing natural environments. This pattern of interactions with those environments is one that is unique to human beings. Following Charles Peirce, I argued that it is the particular *haecceity* (the *thisness*), the *come-up-againstness*, presented by the natural world provides human beings with a particular physical environment within which actions can be fitted to circumstances in certain ways in order to attempt to bring about certain desired results. Therein lies the most fundamental basis for will, choice, and rationality. Without this *haecceity* and *come-up-againstness* presented by the natural world, I claimed, human will, choice, practical wisdom, and rational agency cannot be explained. However, the *haecceity* and *come-up-againstness* in the natural environment that is necessary for human agency and practical wisdom cannot be the entire story of human interaction with the natural world since human beings must somehow be able to become aware of, to *experience*, and then to *understand* (to make sense of) those immediate surroundings and that natural environment. The *haecceity* and *come-up-againstness* presented by the natural world cannot be so blunt and nondescript that it is impenetrable by human experience and understanding; otherwise, human beings would not be able to interact with that natural environment except by wild, undirected, and ultimately, irrational flailings. That *haecceity* and *come-up-againstness* must exhibit regularities and patterns of events, and these regularities and patterns must somehow be detected by human beings. Consequently, something about human experience and human understanding of the natural environment must be included in the core cluster of properties that subvene human nature. In this chapter, I distinguish and examine three kinds of human experience and their importance to the cluster theory of human nature. Following several others, for the sake of convenience, I will refer to the first two kinds of experience as primary experience and secondary experience, which are primarily, although not completely, forms of sense experience. The third kind of experience discussed in this chapter is experience of the self, i.e., self-awareness. I leave the experience of other human beings, which I take to be more a social experience, until Chapter 9.

I begin with human sense experience. There are several significantly different, and perhaps equally important, kinds of philosophical questions about human sense experience: one involves the issue concerning which part of sense experience is attributable to "bare" experience and which part is the result of "innate" qualities, structures, or categories of the human mind; another involves issues about the varying phenomenological aspects of different kinds of sense experience; and, the third involves the nature of the relationship between human sense experience and human nature. Philosophers have examined the first two kinds of questions *ad infinitum* (and some might say, *ad nauseam*). For the most part, for whatever reasons, the third kind of question has been left to psychologists and psychiatrists or ignored completely. I will have little to say about the first two kinds of questions except about the ways in which the answers to those questions are related to the third. Contra Plato and Descartes and other rationalists (who maintained that human beings know the true "substance" of things in the surrounding natural world only through unaided reason), everything that modern science and human biology have revealed about the natural world and human biology supports the claim that whatever information human beings are able to gather about the natural world begins with sense experience. This is not to say, however, that such sense experience is the complete story of how human beings come to understand the natural world or that such sense experience is somehow "naive," "bare," or "pure." I will return to this issue later in this chapter.

To reexamine the nature of the interaction between human beings and the natural world and the ways in which human beings gather information about the natural world requires some further comments about human biology. In the previous chapter, while discussing the relationship between human biology and human nature, I deliberately avoided any mention of the various sense organs that are a part of human biology and sense experience arising from the function of those sense organs.

While everyone may be vaguely familiar with "the five senses," some details about the proper functioning of those senses and the limits of the ranges of those senses are revealing about what it means to be "fully human." While philosophers have long debated the nature of and the importance of sense experience for human knowledge, little attention has been given to the importance of *the nature* of human sense experience and how whatever it is that constitutes human knowledge is based upon that unique range of sense experience. So, what is needed is some exploration of the nature, range, and limits of human sense experience, an understanding of the importance of human sense experience for human understanding of the natural environment in which human beings have lived, developed, and flourished, and the relationship between human sense experience and human nature.

There is perhaps greater variation amongst different living creatures in how they experience their environments than there is in any other biological feature found in the animal kingdom. Ignoring this diversity and the sticky, biological details that explain this diversity, philosophers have too often talked about human sense experience as a single, non-individuated phenomenon with little or no attention given to the biological differences amongst the five senses or the differences between the human senses and those of other animals. Some examination of both of these relationships is importantly revealing about the nature of human sense experience and its relationship to human nature.

Different species of animals have different ranges of sense experience that are unique to each species. Different species of insects, fish, birds, and mammals, for example, all experience their natural surroundings in significantly different ways. Different senses are dominant in different species. Different *ranges* of experience for different senses exist in different species, and, in some species, some senses do not exist at all. I will call the unique collective range of sense experiences, across all senses, and the interconnected set of relationships amongst the different senses, that exist in a particular species, the *species-sense* for that species. The claim here is that the unique *species-sense* that is the *Homo sapiens species-sense* is a major contributor to the properties in the cluster of properties that creates the causal nexus upon which human nature supervenes.

It is common knowledge that *Homo sapiens* is a vision-dominant species; so, one should expect that part of what makes the *Homo sapiens species-sense* unique to human beings is the role of vision in the ways in which human beings are able to interact with the natural world.

Generally, in the animal kingdom, the closer members of a species live with their heads to the ground the less dependent they are on sight and the more dependent they are on other senses for information about their immediately surrounding environment.

Consider some comparisons between human beings and other animals, which is very revealing about the importance of the particular range of sense experience enjoyed by members of *Homo sapiens* for the cluster theory of human nature. Voles, moles, most snakes, and other creatures, for example, that live mostly in holes or boroughs in the ground have very poor eyesight, or, in some cases, no eyesight at all, and no sense of hearing, no means of detecting sound that travels through the air. However, some of their other senses are very highly developed. Some snakes have a very keen sense of smell and a very unique sense of *chemoreception*, aided in large part by their much-maligned forked tongues and the special Jacobson's organ, for detecting prey and for gathering information about the odors and presence of chemicals in their immediate surroundings. Other snakes, called "pit vipers," have special, highly-sensitive, heat-detecting organs on their heads for gathering information about the subtle differences in temperatures of different surfaces in their immediate surroundings. Some snakes might be said then literally to smell their way around in the world. What does this information about the sense experience of snakes have to do with the cluster theory of human nature? Well, it helps to think about this as a variation of the well-worn question, what is it like to be a bat? What is it like to be a snake? That is, what sort of *nature* might snakes have? To the extent that any sort of *species-nature* is partially a function of how members of that species interact with their natural environment, a claim argued for at length in Chapter 3, the answer for snakes must be—not much. On the one hand, when compared with snakes (and dogs and even other primates), human beings are extremely limited in the olfactory department with a very poorly developed sense of smell. On the other hand, when compared with snakes on a more general level of how members of the two species are able to experience and understand their natural surroundings, human beings are far superior. Snakes never experience or "understand" (to the point of being able to interact with) anything about their natural environment to any point beyond just a few feet from their bodies. Their universe is a very limited one.

The particular way in which this universe is structured, i.e., the *specific* way in which *haecceity* and *come-up-againstness* is presented by this natural world, means that snakes are extremely limited in the information that they can gather about their natural environment through sense experience while human beings are not. Consider how what are called the respective "standing" physical conditions in the world necessary for vision and smell differ. Light travels great distances very quickly (since it is the fastest thing in the known universe) and transmits information almost instantaneously from those great distances. The minuscule chemical particles that stimulate the olfactory receptors in the nostrils and mouth to produce the sense of smell are, by comparison, slow-moving, air-borne, and fast-dissipating and provide information from only very close distances away from the sensing subject. Members of species that are smell-dominant do not and cannot have a very keen sense of "the big picture" or their place in the universe. Their ability to interact with, to influence, and to appropriate their natural environment is similarly, extremely limited.

Snakes are interesting, even fascinating animals, but they will never develop a culture or civilization. Why is such an obvious observation significant? The answer is that the existence of snakes, like so many other animals, is too much a function of their immediate surrounding conditions, their lives are too much a function of reactions to immediate stimuli, and their survival is too much a function of *reacting to* rather than controlling or even influencing those conditions and stimuli.[1] In other words, the *species-sense* of snakes, in this particular, actual world at least (given its physical laws), is extremely limiting. In comparison, as noted in Chapter 3, human beings are able to achieve some distance, both temporally and spatially, from immediate stimuli and immediate natural surroundings, primarily because the unique range of normal sense experiences that characterizes members of *Homo sapiens* (*Homo sapiens species-sense*) allows for an equally unique range of adaptation to and appropriation of the natural world. Comparisons between the *species-sense* of human beings with the *species-senses* of other animals can be both fascinating and revealing, but this is a task that I will abandon now and leave to others. The main point is clear: the place of a species in the world and whatever nature it might have are, to a significant extent, a function of its particular range of available sense experiences—its *species-sense*. The range of ways in which members of a species are able to interact with, respond to, and appropriate their natural surroundings is a direct function of their *species-sense*. Obviously, different animals have different ranges of possible sense experience, different *species-senses*, and consequently, different ranges of possible ways of interacting with their environments. The focus here turns to an examination of the particular nature of human sense experience, i.e., the *Homo sapiens species-sense*, the resulting range of ways in which members of *Homo sapiens* can interact with the natural environment, and the importance of the relationship between the *Homo sapiens species-sense* and human nature.

The relatively highly developed sense of vision in human beings is unique amongst primates, and makes humans more similar in this regard to birds than to other mammals. Undeniably, birds, which live with their heads higher above the Earth's surface than do human beings, generally have a more highly developed sense of vision, which is sharper, revealing of more details, and operates at greater distances and in lower light conditions. Hawks and eagles have several times the visual acuity as do humans. Consider the Great Horned Owl, which is alleged to be able to see as well by moon light or even star light on a clear night as human beings do in bright sunlight. One might be envious of such a highly developed sense of vision, but the *species-sense* of great horned owls leaves much to be desired since they have no olfactory sense at all (which helps to explain why one of their favorite foods is the skunk). Other animals sense extreme regions of the electromagnetic spectrum whereas human vision is limited to a very narrow band of visible light. For example, on one end of the spectrum fruitflies sense ultraviolet light, and, on the other end, pit vipers, as noted earlier, sense infrared radiation (heat); however, the *species-senses* of fruitflies and pit vipers are severely more limited and limiting than the *species-sense* of *Homo sapiens*. Similarly, whales can hear sounds (detect sonic waves) over vast distances of oceans, but they have no sense of smell at all.

Human beings not only have a unique *species-sense* because of the number and range of the five different senses but also because of their locations. Consider the senses of smell and taste, which, while distinct senses, are closely associated with one another. Human beings have certain ranges of sensitivity for smell and taste, i.e., the chemical stimuli have to be of a certain strength to be detectable. The ranges of sensitivity for these and the other senses as well (and hence the ranges of resulting sense experiences) are commonly known to vary widely amongst different species in the animal kingdom. For example, pigs and rabbits have roughly double the number of taste buds as do humans. However, perhaps more important for a theory of human nature is the fact that the olfactory sensors are located in the nasal cavity while the taste buds are located in the mouth. This arrangement is not true of all animals. For example, common flies and butterflies have their chemical sensors on the bottoms of their feet while fish and earthworms have them distributed along their skins. Human beings have a variety of different mechanosensors distributed along the skin and just beneath the skin, which account for the sense of touch in its varying degrees from itches, tickles, light touches, and temperature changes to pressure and pain.

Again, there is great diversity in how different animals sense touch, and some surprising variations that are known to exist amongst human beings, discussed below, pose serious questions about how a significant deviation from the norm of a single sense can affect the *species-sense*. The sense of hearing in human beings not only accounts for the detection of sounds but also for a sense of equilibrium, i.e., the recognition of the relative position of the body to the direction of gravity. The outer ear directs sound waves into the auditory canal where they are amplified by the tympanic membrane and passed on through the cochlea to the auditory nerve and finally, to the brain. The sense of hearing is similar to the sense of touch in that it is a sense that arises from *physical* stimuli from the "outside" world since sound waves are actually *pressure waves* that travel through air; whereas the senses of smell and taste result from chemical stimulation and vision results from light reception, touch and hearing result from the respective mechanosensors being impacted *mechanically* or *physically*. Thus, hearing and touch are responsible for a different kind of contact with the physical environment, a different kind of orientation of the individual to the external, physical world, and a different kind of phenomenological experience of being causally impacted by that external, physical world. Again, in the animal world, the sense of hearing in humans is nothing really special since the audible range is 20-20 kHz compared to up to 50kHz in dogs, 90kHz in rats, and 100kHz in bats!

Finally, the sense of vision in humans is accounted for in terms of photosensitivity. While in simpler forms of life photosensitivity simply allows for a very general orientation toward the sun, in humans it provides for the most detailed information about the surrounding sensory environment, and it does this instantaneously. When stimulated by light, photosensors in the eyes (made photosensitive by a molecule called *rhodopsin*) release a neurotransmitter that then passes along the visual pathway and along the optic nerve to the brain. All of this is very standard and routine. Measured against the rest of the animal world, human vision is really nothing special. Measured against other primates, it is very special. Its contribution to the *species-sense* of human beings is immeasurable, and largely accounts for the superiority of the *species-sense* of humans compared with those of other animals.

These details about the *species-sense* of *Homo sapiens* bring to mind again the complaints that David Hume voices in his *Dialogues Concerning Natural Religion* through the character of Philo about the way in which humans are constructed. Philo seems to suggest that human beings are ill-equipped to experience and interact with the natural world when compared with other animals since other species of animals see, hear, or smell better. However, as noted earlier, when one sense in a particular species is more highly developed, e. g., vision in hawks and eagles, other senses are less highly developed or completely missing, e.g., smell. When it is not individual senses but *species-senses* that are compared, humans beings compare very favorably with other animals and are arguably, superior. Hume was wrong then in suggesting that human beings are sensory deficient when compared to other animals. The proper point of comparison is not a single sense but the *species-sense*, and the human *species-sense* is far superior to that found in any other animal. It is this *species-sense* that allows human to act upon and be acted upon by our natural environment in ways that are significantly more complex and sophisticated than those found in other animals.

The most important and salient philosophical consequence of the particular nature of the *species-sense* of *Homo sapiens* is the particular position it puts human beings in vis-à-vis the external world and the natural environment. Through a unique set of sense experiences resulting from the unique *species-sense*, human beings are able to experience the natural world to a much greater cumulative extent and with a much greater variety and complexity than any other animal known to exist or to have existed. The result is what I call the *species-orientation* of a species. As I first hinted in Chapter 2, the *species-orientation* of a species is the causal consequence of a complex set of interrelationships that exist between members of that species and their environment. Those interrelationships include the relationships to other members of their own species, the relationships to other living and non-living things, the ways in which they both act upon and are acted upon by their environment, and the ways in which they experience different parts of their environment. In the present context, it is important to recognize that an important aspect of a particular species' *species-orientation* is the sensory perspectival position in which members of a species stand in relationship to their surrounding sensory environment as a result of their *species-sense*; thus, an individual's *species-orientation* is the immediate and direct consequence of that individual's *species-sense*, which he or she has as a member of a particular species.

The *species-orientation* of *Homo sapiens* is responsible for produc-ing properties in the cluster of properties upon which human nature supervenes in two important ways. First, it is the *species-orientation* of human beings vis-à-vis the immediately surrounding sensory environ-ment that accounts for the notions of agency, rationality, and practical wisdom explained in Chapter 3. In other words, it is only because of our *species-orientation* to the natural world, accounted for by our unique *spe-cies-sense*, that we come to be in a position to act in whatever particular ways it is that we take to be the proper ways to bring about certain inten-tions or to satisfy certain desires. Secondly, whatever moral, aesthetic, or linguistic sensibilities human beings might have are, to a significant extent, a function of the unique *species-orientation* resulting from *Homo sapiens species-sense* and the unique set of phenomenological experi-ences that are produced by this *species-sense*. This claim is explained and defended in Chapter 9.

Although there is what might be described as the "normal" ranges for the different senses in human beings that allow for the characteriza-tion of a *species-sense* at all, there is, admittedly, a wide range of sense experiences amongst members of a species. Clearly, people vary greatly in their abilities to see, hear, smell, taste, or touch for a number of dif-ferent reasons. Particular senses may be developed to a greater or lesser extent in some people because of genetic differences; some senses may be developed in some people to a greater or lesser extent through train-ing and education; and some senses may be developed in some people to a greater or lesser extent through aging and/or disease. Wine tasters possess more highly developed senses of smell and taste than do most people, and musicians have a more highly developed sense of hearing than the average person. Other examples of individuals who have a more highly developed particular sense are plentiful. Even given such variations, however, it is possible to specify "normal" ranges for the five different senses and to arrive at a fairly clear notion of a *species-sense* for humans beings. For the moment, I will leave such biological and physiological specifications to the scientists.

While the variations amongst some individuals regarding a particular sense might be startling, they are not the cause of substantive recategori-zation or biological reclassification. It is not clear just how much variation could be tolerated in the *species-sense* of *Homo sapiens* without major changes in the biological classification. However, given the amount of variation that already exists, it appears that biology can tolerate a sig-nificant amount of variation in the *species-sense* of members of *Homo sapiens* since other biological features, which are held constant, might very well compensate for the differences. On the other hand, extreme variations in members of the species *Homo sapiens* regarding our *species-sense* would be the cause of serious concern about possible substantive effects on human nature if those changes resulted in extreme variations regarding the *species-orientation* for *Homo sapiens*, and it seems likely that this would usually be the case.

Consider again the example first discussed in Chapter 2 of the conceptual "exercise" of redesigning human anatomy by placing a third eye somewhere on the human body. This is a change that it is easily possible to imagine that biology might tolerate. In fact, it is easy to imagine that such a change might be selected for by natural selection over a long period of time. It is much more difficult to imagine that human nature could tolerate such a change without significant alteration since it seems that such an alternation would significantly affect the *species-orientation* of *Homo sapiens*. On the cluster theory of human nature, one of the properties in the cluster that produces the causal nexus upon which human nature supervenes is the *species sense* of *Homo sapiens*. While the integrity of this causal nexus might tolerate certain variations or changes in individual senses, changes that are significant enough to threaten the *species-sense* and the resulting *species-orientation* also threaten that causal nexus. Intuitions might differ about how adding a third eye to the human anatomy might affect human nature, but my own reaction is similar to the one expressed in the preceding chapter in the discussion of *The Fly* and *Metamorphosis*. At some point, significant anatomical changes, in particular changes that substantially affect sense experience, can undermine what it means to be "fully human" by undermining the human *species-sense* and *species-orientation*. What this means is that even though an individual undergoing such changes might still be "fully biologically human," such an individual might either have the phenomenological nature of sense experience distorted so significantly or have the pattern and range of ways of interacting with his or her natural environment distorted so significantly that the properties that subvene human nature are no longer instantiated to an optimal degree or perhaps, even to a minimal degree.

Leaving examples of provocative fictions and modalities aside for the moment, what is to be said of the *actual* significant variations both in individual senses and in *species-sense* that are known to exist amongst human beings? And just how significant can the variation be in a single sense be before the *species-sense* and then the *species-orientation* change as a result? Consider, for example, the situation of people that suffer from major sensory deprivation of one kind or another, the loss of an entire sense or even the loss of two entire senses.

Perhaps the best known, best documented, and most poignant cases of such instances involve the loss of both vision and hearing in Laura Bridgman and Helen Keller. Some detailed analysis of the particular deficiencies of these two women—the details of their respective "education," and the professional assessments of their respective, eventual developments— provides some important clues for assessing the role of the *species-sense* in producing the properties and the resulting causal nexus amongst properties upon which the cluster theory of human nature depends. Since these two cases provide insight into two different aspects of the role that the *species-sense* plays in making one "fully human," I will discuss the importance of Laura Bridgman's case here, and the case of Helen Keller in Chapter 9. Given the extremely well-documented nature of these cases and their relevance and poignancy to fundamental philosophical issues having to do with the philosophy of mind, sense experience, moral theory, and human nature, it is inexplicable why they have been almost completely ignored by contemporary philosophers. Epistemologists, it seems, should discuss Bridgman and Keller as frequently as moral philosophers discuss the Holocaust. As it appears, with rare exceptions, William James was the last major philosopher to take a keen interest in the kind of empirical data provided by such cases.

Laura Bridgman was born in New Hampshire in 1829 and, although a sickly child, appeared to live a fairly normal life until age two when she was stricken with scarlet fever, which completely destroyed her senses of vision and hearing. At age seven, she became a patient and student of Dr. Samuel Gridley Howe, a Harvard trained physician and Director of the Perkins Institution for the Blind in Boston, the first school for the blind in the United States. Thereafter, the story of Laura Bridgman and her "education" attracted the world's attention and was widely recounted in news accounts, professional journals, and even children's story books. In fact, both Bridgman and Howe became major celebrities of a sort. Both her predicament and her eventual successful adaptation to the then-new "mechanical language" taught by Howe were surrounded by cultural, political, and theological issues that were cause for great public debate at the time.[2]

There were those in Boston, which was a center of Calvinism at the time, who interpreted Bridgman's illness and her resulting disabilities as the result of Original Sin and as evidence of God's punishment for what they took to be the fundamental corruption of human nature and the predestination of human souls. This understanding of human nature, easily traced to New England Puritanism, is clearly a "top-down," dualistic theory, as described in Chapter 1. The alleged corruption of human nature is supposedly the result of a punishment imposed by God, from a distinct metaphysical realm, and it extends to everything that is *human* about human nature, including the human senses, human reason, and, as I argued in the last chapter, human sexuality. Against this view, Howe stood as a "liberal Christian," a defender of Enlightenment science, a proponent of "progressive" education, and a follower of the Scottish School of Common Sense. He rejected the view that human nature is fundamentally corrupt along with John Locke's view that the mind is a passive *tabula rasa* in favor of the view credited to Thomas Reid that the mind has certain faculties that perform certain *actions* through which the external world is experienced.[3] Such views were, of course, considered to be nothing short of heretical by the Calvinists. Laura Bridgman and the techniques Howe used for her "education" thus became one of the battlegrounds over which struggles concerning many of the same issues presently under discussion, having to do with human nature, were conducted in mid-nineteenth-century America.

Initially, Howe was convinced that Bridgman possessed "pure," natural, and untainted "mental faculties," including a faculty for moral sense, for religious sense, etc., as well as a faculty that was especially designated for sensing the external world. The negative effects of non-functioning physical senses could be theoretically "bypassed" by education and scientific control of her environment in order to provide the crucial data necessary for that faculty to interpret and understand her natural environment. This approach reflected the Enlightenment view of the perfectibility of human nature shared by Thomas Jefferson and other promoters of liberal democracy and progressive education in the United States. By educating Laura Bridgman, Howe could demonstrate the egalitarianism of democracy and how education could reach even the most unfortunate and disabled.

In the end, with a sense of disappointment and frustration growing out of his treatment of Bridgman, Howe gradually began to abandon this view. On one level, Howe's treatment of Bridgman was certainly a success. She learned the mechanical language, indeed she was the first blind/deaf person to do so; thus, she learned to communicate with others. She developed some other mechanical skills and became a seamstress, making many of her own clothes. But, in other areas, there were major disappointments. Laura Bridgman evidently was a very difficult person with major character flaws her entire life. She was frequently uncooperative, volatile, and deceitful and sometimes violent and harmful to others and their property—in Howe's view, somewhat "deranged." While it is not entirely clear, evidently, Howe eventually came to the point that he decided (still operating within the limited framework of phrenology), whatever "pure" and natural faculties there might be in the brain, they need sensory data not only to interpret but to *develop* and *operate* properly. Because Laura Bridgman's mental faculties had been robbed of sensory input from vision and hearing, Howe finally concluded, they had failed to develop properly and had atrophied, just as unused muscles do. Now no amount of education or training could correct that deficiency or restore the proper mental, moral, and sensory development.

The story of Laura Bridgman is heart-rending, challenging, and illuminating. How might one analyze her case using the cluster theory of human nature? Well, the first thing to observe is that Laura Bridgman's loss of vision and hearing were serious enough that they apparently destroyed her *species-sense* and hence, her *species-orientation* to her surrounding environment. While Howe lacked the proper scientific and theoretical framework within which to express his changed orientation, he obviously had discovered the importance of what early childhood developmental psychology has since established as the importance of the early developmental stages of sensory, cognitive, and conative development. The aphorism, "use it, or lose it," is most frequently used to describe the condition of the faculties of the aging, but it applies, perhaps even more accurately, to infants. While trying to avoid metaphysical issues and disputes in the philosophy of mind—whether it is "the mind," mental faculties, or neuron pathways in the brain—atrophy and crippled development result from malnourishment, under-stimulation, and sensory deprivation. The senses provide the necessary nourishment and stimulation for the proper development and functioning of that part of the mind (or the brain or human cognitive psychology) that accounts for human *species-sense* and the resulting *species-orientation*. When interruptions or disruptions occur to a person's *species-orientation* that are significant enough, then that individual is no longer "fully human" even though that person might be biologically human. Death is a major such disruption. A corpse is still biologically human, but its *species-orientation* has changed so dramatically that no one would want to say that *it* instantiates the properties responsible for human nature. Neither does a person in a deep coma. Such a person is a *living* human being but does not possess human nature to any significant degree.

Political incorrectness notwithstanding, something similar must be said of Laura Bridgman. Her early, misfortunate loss of vision and hearing prevented her from instantiating, to any significant degree, many of the properties upon which human nature supervenes. This is because her *species-sense* and her *species-orientation* were permanently disabled to such an extent that she was never able to orient herself to her environment in anything like a human-way. She was able to survive, even on the most elementary level, only because of an enormous investment of time, energy (and the best scientific knowledge and techniques available at the time) on the part of individuals with a "normal" human *species-sense*. Even with all of these resources and even after mastering the mechanical language, she was never able to mature and develop fully. The degree of abstraction and generality with which she understood the nature of the external world, a major component of human *species-orientation*, was extremely limited. It is also doubtful—given that both her phenomenological experience and her *species-orientation* were extremely limited—but difficult to determine, if she understood or possessed moral or aesthetic values. Even her understanding of familial relationships had to be clouded by her lack of understanding of human sexuality. Thus, in the end, we must conclude that on the grand spectrum of human nature, Laura Bridgman instantiated very few of the properties that create the causal nexus upon which human nature supervenes to a minimal degree and consequently, was not "fully human."

This may be taken as a harsh, even cruel judgment (one that leaves the cluster theory open to abuses and possible charges of sexism, racism, or encouraging eugenics), but the claim here is not that Laura Bridgman was not a human being or not a person or not deserving of the full rights and privileges of every other human being. The claim is that even being biologically human, it is extremely doubtful that she instantiated to a minimal degree enough of the properties in the cluster of properties for the causal nexus amongst those properties to develop and thus for human nature to develop. On the cluster theory, even a human infant with a normal *species-sense* does not have very much human nature since it does not instantiate enough of those properties which are required for the causal nexus amongst the properties, upon which human nature supervenes, to develop. This explains why parents might say at some point in their child's development, when little Johnny or Suzie begins to walk and talk and understand and respond to verbal stimulation, "He or

She is becoming a *real* person." What they mean, of course, is that little Johnny or Suzie is finally developing enough of those latent properties for the causal nexus to emerge, which, in turn, allows for human nature to emerge. In this sense, it is difficult to imagine that anyone would have said of Laura Bridgman, "Ah, finally, she is a *real* person," meaning that she had finally instantiated enough of the properties to allow human nature to emerge. The case of Helen Keller, discussed in Chapter 9, provides a counterpoint.

As Samuel Howe came to realize in the case of Laura Bridgman, sense experience alone is not adequate for a person developing a normal *species-sense* and *species-orientation*. In Bridgman's case, she was missing two major avenues of sensory input but, evidently, she also was missing fully developed or properly functioning mental faculties for processing whatever sensory input she did receive. Even the most radical empiricists have now abandoned the notion that "bare" or "raw" sense data can account for sense experience. For sensory input to rise to the level of sensory *experience*, it must meet with a friendly reception in the experiencing subject.

What is needed is some understanding of how human experience advances from John Dewey's primary experience to secondary experience or how human experience manages to become refined, organized, collected, related, structured, categorized, reliable, and rational from what would otherwise simply be a confused and unrelated collection of events, i.e., what William James called "one great booming, buzzing, confusion." How human beings are able to do this has been the battle ground through the centuries for philosophers to wage philosophical war—usually rationalists against empiricists. I earlier claimed that the interaction between man and environment is a reciprocal one, and I have emphasized, to this point, the role of the environment in that interaction. It is now time to examine the nature of the reciprocity of that interaction between man and environment and what it is that man contributes to it.

What human beings contribute is the process that is responsible for the multitude of sensory data from the individual senses being culled and organized in a way that is rational, i.e., it is the process by which the data of sensory input are processed, organized, systematized, collated, integrated, and recorded in ways that make them available for conscious recognition and later recall. I will call this process the *sensory-integration process* or perhaps simply *sensory-integration*. Whether this process is spelled out in terms of Kantian *a priori* categories, or in terms of patterns of neuron firings in the brain, or in terms of the proper functioning of mental faculties, it is what is responsible for the particular nature of the *species-sense* of human beings. Compare the *species-sense* of human beings to a photograph. The visual depiction of content in the photograph, the arrangement of objects, the colors, etc., are the result of stimuli that are comparable to those relative to the different individual senses. However, it is the light sensitivity of the paper and the exposure to the proper chemicals that are responsible for the synthesis and integration of all of the conditions and stimuli into a Gestalt whole that produce the picture.

Sensory-integration obviously takes place in different ways for different species; so, I will refer to the species-specific process of *sensory-integration* as the *species-sensory-integration process* or perhaps simply *species-sensory-integration*. *Species-sensory-integration* is the process that produces the human *species-sense* that then allows for human *species-orientation*. It is also the process about which epistemologists and philosophers of mind and, more recently, cognitive psychologists have been in the most disagreement and about which we know the least.

The process of *species-sensory-integration* is also the process about which we understand the least in other animals. Consider one of the most puzzling forms of animal behavior—what is called "flock behavior" in birds or "school behavior" in fish. Hundreds or thousands of birds or fish, moving in a particular direction and at a certain speed, can then change both directions and speed *instantaneously* as a single organism. Astoundingly, both birds and fish are able to do this without bumping into one another or pushing one another about. There is nothing about any single sense of birds or fish that explains such behavior, but their respective processes of *species-sensory-integration* and their respective *species-orientations* somehow permit a behavior that is impossible for humans to duplicate.

Consideration here of just two cases of people with rather unusual neurological problems serves to illustrate both the necessity of the process of *species-sensory-integration* and the important role that it plays in the *species-orientation* of human beings. I attempt to provide no diagnosis or medical account for these cases since even the leading neurologists are unable to do so. I also do not intend that the point about the vital importance of *species-sensory-integration* can only be explained by such extreme cases, but the point is made more clearly and more poignantly by the cases that are at the borders of modern medical science. I simply emphasize the importance of these cases for helping to understand the notion of *species-sensory-integration* and the role that *species-sensory-integration* plays in *species-orientation*.

The first case involves a man with extreme visual agnosia, popularized by Oliver Sacks as "The Man who Mistook His Wife for a Hat." This patient, a musician, had lost the ability to recognize familiar objects of his visual perception, including objects such as shoes and hats, the faces of members of his family, and even his own face and body. Apparently gifted with normal eyesight, he could recognize certain *features* of objects or faces, such as the color, size, or shape, but could not put those features together into a recognizable, Gestalt whole. When handed a red rose to identify, for example, this patient said, "About six inches in length...a convoluted red form with a linear green attachment."[4] This man managed to get along in the world only with the help of his wife and by humming or singing different tunes to himself to structure and organize his activities. Somehow music replaced the normal process of visual integration and produced a minimally workable process of *sensory-integration*, but certainly not one even closely resembling a human *species-sensory-integration*. Consequently, his *species-sense* and *species-orientation* were also significantly distorted. He could manage to get along in the music world, but fared very poorly in the world of objects and people. With such a permanent condition, one would have to say that this poor man was missing an important element of what it means to be "fully human" because, although his individual senses were apparently normal, his *species-sense* was not. Because of the inability to organize and integrate those different senses into a coherent and sensible whole, his understanding of his surrounding sensory environment, his place in it, and his relationship to that environment were compromised to the point that they resulted in a situation that deviated significantly from normal human *species-sense* and *species-orientation*. It is difficult to imagine the kind of existence that an entire race of biologically human beings, suffering from the same kind of agnosia, might have, but it would certainly not be a *human* existence since the *species-sense* and the *species-orientation* would be completely different.

A more particularized and generally less debilitating form of agnosia is prosopagnosia, face-blindness, a condition, the most severe form of which prohibits a person from recognizing and remembering familiar faces, *even one's own*. Again, people suffering from prosopagnosia have normal eyesight and can "see" another person's eyes or nose, but cannot put the different features together into a Gestalt whole. Face recognition is currently thought by neurologists to be the result of a broadly based brain function in which the temporal and occipital lobes play a prominent role, and, although the details are not yet forthcoming, prosopagnosia results from some malfunctions in those areas of the brain. Exactly what the specific malfunctions are in the pathology of face-blindness is still not clear, but Noble Prize winners Torsten Hubel and David Wiesel have provided some good clues. Some of the details of Hubel and Wiesel's discovery are both intriguing and informative. They demonstrated that a single cell in the cortical area of the brain responds not to a point of light, as individual cells do in the retina, but to a *line* of light. How can a *single* cell respond to what amounts to a multiplicity of stimuli? Hubel and Wiesel explained this phenomenon by showing that there is a hierarchy of cortical cells with each higher order of cells more complex than the last. Information from *simple* cortical cells is passed to a single *complex* cortical cell, and information from complex cortical cells is passed on to a single *hyper-complex* cell. At each step in the process, as information flows "up" the neural pathway, the information converges and is integrated in the higher-level cell so that increasingly more specific response properties result. The theoretical consequence of Hubel and Wiesel's hierarchical model is that there is a single neuron in the cortical area of a person's brain that fires only with the visual stimulation of a particular individual's face. If something goes wrong along the pathway as visual information flows up the hierarchy of cells, then the "face-recognition cell," higher up the hierarchy, does not fire, and the person is "face-blind."[5]

Even if one does not accept this hierarchical model, it is commonly accepted by neurologists that visual, conscious experience is the result of a process with several discrete stages. Clearly then, the *species-sensory-integration* of human beings is a process that essentially involves a neurological component in the brain that is responsible for processing and bringing some sense, order, convergence, and integration to the otherwise "great blooming, buzzing, confusion" of the raw data in the stream of visual information that is fed to the brain. The pathology of prosopagnosia is just one illustration of how things might go wrong in the process of *species-sensory-integration* that must take place successfully for people to live normal lives.[6]

Without successful *species-sensory-integration* across a wide spectrum of sense experiences, an individual's *species-orientation* will be seriously altered to the point where that individual is no longer "fully human," i.e., that individual does not instantiate an optimal or even minimal number of the properties in the cluster of properties that conjointly subvene human nature. In the particular case of people suffering from acute prosopagnosia, it is difficult to imagine how such people can engage in social, familial, or interpersonal relationships (discussed in Chapter 9) when every person's face is that of a stranger and loved ones can only be identified visually by some artificial means such as some special clothing that they might wear or some unique special feature such as a scar or eyeglasses. The only alternative is to rely upon non-visual information such as the voice or posture or gait while walking. One wants to say that these may be ways of being orientated to one's environment, but these are not *human* ways, i.e., these are not ways that are congruent with a distinctly human *species-orientation*.

In *On Certainty*, Wittgenstein says, when talking about those things of which one is most certain, the "rock bottom" of one's convictions, that having two hands (in normal circumstances) is one of those things. He also says this:

> If someone said to me that he doubted whether he had a body I should take him to be a half-wit. But I shouldn't know what it would mean to try and convince him that he had one. And if I had said something, and that had removed his doubt, I should not know how or why.[7]

Yet, there is documented evidence of cases of people who suffer from a loss of *proprioception* (the sense that one's body is one's own), not having a "sense of body," not being able to "feel" one's body, and feeling disembodied altogether.[8] In one such case, the patient was diagnosed as suffering from acute sensory polyneuritis, an inflammation of spinal fluid that had damaged the spinal and cranial nerves throughout her nervous system, and, in the process, had destroyed her proprioceptive sense of her own body. So, Wittgenstein was right if he intends that the disclaimer "in normal circumstances" is meant to apply to being certain of one's body also. Normally, certainly, as a part of one's *species-orientation*, a human being must have a sense of one's own body to have a sense of one's place in one's environment and one's relationship to that environment. What allows for that orientation is one's own *species-sense,* which, in turn, requires the particular *species-sensory-integration* belonging to one's species. Whatever the particular neurological causes, this woman's *species-sensory-integration* had malfunctioned to the point that her *species-sense* and her *species-orientation* were both undermined. This poor woman was not certain of her own body, nor of her place in her environment, nor of how to interact with that environment. She was able to adapt partially by using her vision to locate parts of her body, i.e., she could look at a part of her body, her arm or her leg, and make it move and thus receive a form of sensory proprioception, which, given the original meaning of the term, is an oxymoron. Her condition is indeed tragic and made all the more so in that, in having her *species-sensory integration* and her resulting *species-orientation* so seriously compromised, she was robbed of much of her human nature.

The intuitive truth of Wittgenstein's claim about the "rock-bottom" nature of the knowledge of the existence of one's own body is explained by the vital role that that knowledge plays in understanding and explaining *species-orientation*. In this natural world at least, the only way to understand and explain the notion of *species-orientation*, the relationship of oneself to one's immediate environment, is by some form of *perspectivalism*. I am *here*. This is *me* and *mine*. *That* is not me. *That* is something or someone else. *I* am over *here* doing *this* to or with *that*. Without such fundamental distinctions between self and non-self, a normal, *human species-orientation* is impossible.[9] Perhaps some other animals have such self-awareness. Undoubtedly, not all other animals do. Without such a distinction between self and non-self resulting from a properly developed and distinctly human *species-orientation*, the notion of agency (discussed in Chapter 3), wherein one understands oneself as *acting* in a particular way to bring about a particular desire or intention, would be impossible. Even "normal" individual senses, which fall somewhere within the average or normal ranges, cannot result in a normal *species-sense* and a normal *species-orientation* without a successful and normal *species-sensory-integration*. Whatever one's metaphysics turn out to be, i.e., whether one appeals to the mind or mental events as opposed to neurological processes, some account must be given of the process of sensory-integration to explain the notion of human nature adequately. As a naturalistic, bottom-up theory of human nature, the cluster theory embraces the latest and best results from neuroscience as the best that we can do in explaining this process. Admittedly, there is still quite a bit of black in the box of neuroscience, but there is less opaqueness in that scientific box than there was just two decades ago, which is more than can be said for the progress made in illuminating the spiritual or mental metaphysical view over the past two millennia.

Another important aspect of *species-sensory-integration* and the resulting *species-orientation* is the role played by memory. Just as one must have a successful *species-sensory-integration* to provide a sense of perspectivalism in one's physical environment, one must also have the integration of sensory experiences *over time* to provide a sense of

perspective in and continuity over one's successions of temporal environments and one's conscious experiences. A normally functioning memory
does exactly this by allowing a person to think I am *here (in time)*. This
collection of experiences (including those experienced earlier in time)
are *mine* and *this* experience is after *that* one that *I* just had. *Those*
experiences, reported by other people, are not *mine*. *Those* experiences
must belong to something or someone else since *I* do not remember ever
experiencing *those*. *I* am here *now* doing *this* to or with *that*, and *earlier*
I was doing *that* to or with *this*. Such fundamental distinctions provided
for by a normal functioning memory allow for a normal, *human species-
orientation* vis-à-vis time and one's experiences.

A person might have a sense experience without memory, but one
cannot have normal *sensory-integration* without memory. Part of what
allows for a uniquely human *species-sensory-integration* is a uniquely
human memory. It is not possible to give a complete, detailed treatment
of human memory here; however, in order to explain the importance
of memory to human *species-sensory-integration*, it is necessary to
explain the roles of what are now customarily classified as *declarative
episodic memory* and *declarative semantic memory*. These are forms
of long-term memory and are also sometimes called forms of *explicit*
memory. Declarative episodic memory is that function of memory that
is that ability to recall (at the right time, in the right circumstances, and
under conscious control) some specific event(s) or circumstance(s). For
example, I can now recall getting out of bed this morning, letting the
dog out, seeing the Great Blue Heron fly by, making the morning pot of
coffee, feeding the dog, sitting down at the computer and beginning to
write this chapter of this book. Declarative semantic memory provides me
with a wealth of general, "background," knowledge that I bring to bear
during such experiences as those just described. For example, semantic
memory allows me to recognize what a bed is, a door, a dog, a Great
Blue Heron, a pot, coffee, a computer, a chair, etc. It also provides me
with the semantic relationships amongst concepts. For example, semantic memory provides me with the information that my dog, Casey, is a
Dalmatian, and that a Dalmatian is a dog, and that a dog is a mammal,
that a mammal is an animal, etc. Similarly, I am able to understand that
a Great Blue Heron is a bird, that a bird is not a mammal, but that a bird
is an animal. That both episodic and semantic memory are declarative,
i.e., that they are under the control of the conscious will, is evidenced
by the fact that I just consciously used them to explain these examples
of their functioning.

Perhaps other animals have declarative episodic memory and declarative semantic memory and perhaps they do not. How this question is answered depends to a great extent upon how much conscious control of mental activities one is willing to attribute to other animals. For various reasons, having to do mainly with theology and anthropocentric concerns, most biologists have been reluctant to attribute conscious control of memory to other animals, even in the face of compelling *prima facie* behavioral evidence to the contrary. Abundant animal behavior indicates that they are able to "remember" migratory routes, distinguish members of their own species from other animals, "remember" and distinguish home from the vet's office, and "remember" and distinguish friend from foe. The cluster theory of human nature has no difficulty in attributing specific animal memories to various different species of animals. In each case, those species-specific memories would play a similar function in accounting for the process of *species-sensory-integration* for the members of that species.

Perhaps some of those species-specific memories in other animals are declarative, under the control of a conscious will, and perhaps they are not. In any case, it is clear that no other species of animal is known to have a declarative episodic memory or declarative semantic memory with anything like the range, degree, detail, or complexity of human beings. This is most easily demonstrated with episodic semantic memory. While researchers have demonstrated that some other primates are able to remember and recall the difference between colors and shapes, this is a degree of declarative semantic memory equivalent to a human infant. Human declarative and semantic memory explain the uniquely human *species-sensory-integration* and resulting *species-orientation* by allowing human beings to experience and understand our surrounding sensory environment *and beyond* (to molecules, atoms, electrons, protons, and quarks or to the sun, the planets, and distant stars and galaxies) to a degree and complexity unequaled by other known living creatures.

When things go wrong with either declarative episodic memory or declarative semantic memory, human nature is undermined. Exactly just how much human nature is undermined depends upon exactly what goes wrong, to what degree, with what duration, and with what effect. Most of us have had minor breakdowns of declarative episodic memory on occasions for various reasons, but when either serious injury or illness causes a major breakdown in either declarative episodic memory or declarative semantic memory a person's *species-sensory-integration* also breaks down. Unfortunately, this is tragically true of those individuals who suffer from severe Alzheimer's disease. A great deal of detail or elaboration seems unnecessary to explain or justify this claim.

Without a properly functioning human memory, which means a memory that functions within some reasonable limitations of a "normal" human range, the continuity and integration of sense experience that characterizes human *species-sensory-integration* is lost. Thus, to a significant degree, uniquely human *species-sensory-integration* and the resulting *species-orientation* are functions of uniquely human declarative episodic memory and declarative semantic memory. These forms of memory are thus to be counted by the cluster theory amongst the properties that subvene human nature since it is so obvious and indisputable that they contribute in significant ways to what is unique about human *species-sensory-integration*. There may be other forms of memory that are also to be included in the cluster of properties upon which human nature supervenes. For example, some may count the verbal form of short-term memory in that cluster; however, at this point, since I have provided here the theoretical framework within which such a consideration might take place, I will leave this issue to the neuroscientists and philosophers of mind and move on to a consideration of a final important factor that is responsible for a uniquely human *species-sensory-integration* that eventually allows for the emergence of human nature.

Earlier in this chapter, I noted in connection with the discussion of the case of Laura Bridgman that Dr. Samuel Gridley Howe, the Harvard trained physician and Director of the Perkins Institution for the Blind in Boston where she was treated, rejected Locke's view that the mind is a passive *tabula rasa* upon which sense experience imprints. Howe's reasons for rejecting Locke's *tabula rasa* claim have already been noted; however, there are more compelling and obvious reasons for rejecting this view. It is impossible, on Locke's *tabula rasa* view, to explain how human beings have a uniquely human *species-sensory-integration*. If the human mind were, as Locke describes it, a completely "blank tablet," this would mean that the *species-sensory-integration* of human beings would have to be accounted for completely in terms of the unique characteristics of human sense organs; however, this is impossible as the earlier considerations of this chapter have made clear. The mind, or in the naturalistic view of the cluster theory of human nature, the human *brain*, is a major contributing factor to both *species-sensory-integration* and the resulting *species-orientation*. Modern neuroscience has made clear that the brain is far from being a blank tablet in the Lockean sense. It is more similar to a highly and complexly structured and multi-faceted honeycomb with numerous compartments and "pigeonholes" into which sense experiences are distributed, sorted, and fitted and thereby, organized, structured, and categorized. Through these processes, sense experience becomes *integrated*, the final result of which is *species-sensory-integration*. The different ways in which different species are endowed with differently constructed honeycombs, i.e., the different ways in which different species are endowed with different neurological or "mental" processes (along with the various factors noted earlier), are major factors in explaining the differences of *species-sensory-integration* amongst species.

Exactly how the "pigeonholes" of the "mind" are to be explained is the subject of enormous philosophical controversy of long-standing and are the subject of Chapter 8. The range of possible explanations runs from the innate ideas of the early rationalists, such as Descartes, to Kant's *a priori* categories of the pure understanding, to Hume's psychological expectations. Currently, the debate continues over how many of these "categories" are hard-wired and how many are socially constructed, a modern variation on the nature/nurture controversy. The philosophical disagreement about the nature of what it is that the brain (or, for some, the *mind*) contributes to *species-sensory-integration* is one that will not be resolved here.

Since the cluster theory of human nature is a naturalistic theory, it has no need of or sympathy with claims regarding metaphysically distinct mental events; however, whether it is the brain or the mind that makes this final contribution to species-sensory-integration will not be addressed here since, in an important respect, the claim is independent of the metaphysical dispute. Certain minimum claims seem clear. Although Kant may have been wrong about many things, modern neuroscience has proven him right about this much: in Kantian terms, concepts without percepts are empty and percepts without concepts are blind. In other words, sense experiences with no pigeonholes into which they are placed never rise above the level of a "great booming, buzzing, confusion," which never registers with the conscious mind. Concepts, categories, or operations with no sensory content, no data, are simply empty pigeonholes waiting to be filled. What happens in between is still the subject of philosophical speculation and neurological research. Modern neuroscience has revealed that when the pigeonholes of the brain are stimulated by sensory input they spring into action performing the necessary "operations" on the sensory data to produce human, sensory experience.

It is indisputable that the brains and the central nervous systems of different species are structured differently and that the operations performed by those differently structured brains and nervous systems are also different. This means that each species has a unique neurological component to its *species-sensory-integration*, and thus, there is a uniquely human neurological component to human *species-sensory-integration*. In addition to the particular characteristics of the different sensory apparatuses of different species, it is the unique nature of this neurological component in each species that explains the species-specificity of a species' *species-sensory-integration*. There is, undoubtedly, some acceptable variation amongst different members of a particular species concerning the neurological component of that particular *species-sensory-integration*. It is equally obvious, however, that if the neurological processes necessary for *species-sensory-integration* fail to operate properly for an individual member of a species within some range of normalcy for that species, then *species-sensory-integration* will breakdown for that individual as will that individual's *species-orientation*. The pathological result is captured by the metaphor of "the deer in the headlights." Just as deer are blinded by bright lights and unable to interpret properly or react properly to the stimulus they are receiving, any member of any species will be "blinded" and unable to interpret properly or respond properly to stimuli when *species-sensory-integration* breaks down.

The immediate consequence of *species-sensory-integration breakdown* is a similar breakdown in *species-orientation*. As demonstrated in the various cases of anomalies discussed above, when an individual does not or cannot process sensory data normally to produce a reasonably integrated result, then that individual cannot interact with his or her environment, respond to external stimuli, or act upon that environment in characteristically human ways. When *species-orientation* breakdown occurs, the unique pattern of interactions with the environments, which is unique to human beings, is lost. I have shown how the particular *haecceity* (the *thisness*), the *come-up-againstness*, presented by the natural world provide human beings with an immediate environment within which human actions can be controlled and suited to different circumstances in that environment in order to attempt to bring about desired ends. If an individual suffers from severe agnosia and cannot distinguish his wife and his hat, then that individual suffers from a severe inability to form his different senses into a coherent and sensible whole. The result is a breakdown in the process that results in a particularly human understanding of the surrounding sensory environment and a particularly human relationship to that environment, including a particularly human pattern of interacting with that environment. The same is true of those who suffer from prosopagnosia. Other diseases and injuries that result in the loss of declarative episodic memory or declarative semantic memory can similarly undermine the range, degree, detail, and complexity of the *species-sensory integration* and *species-orientation* of human beings.

I have claimed earlier that it is the uniquely human configuration of individual and environment, human *species-orientation*, that explains human will, choice, practical wisdom, and rational agency. In this chapter, I have shown how the various factors that contribute to the uniqueness of human experience, the *species-sense* and the *species-sensory-integration* of human beings, produce a uniquely human *species-orientation*. On the cluster theory of human nature, two of the most important properties in that cluster of properties upon which human nature supervenes are the *species-sensory-integration* and the resulting *species-orientation* that allow human understanding of and interaction with the *haecceity* and *come-up-againstness* present in the natural world.

Notes

1. Not all of these limitations are completely a function of snakes' particular range of sense-experience. Their particular anatomy and their cold-bloodied nature as reptiles are also limiting factors.
2. See, for example, Maud Howe and Florence Howe Hall, *Laura Bridgman: Dr. Howe's Famous Pupil and What He Taught Her* (Boston: Little, Brown, and Company, 1903) and Ernest Freeberg, *The Education of Laura Bridgman: The First Deaf and Blind Person to Learn Language* (Cambridge, MA: Cambridge University Press, 2001). Much of the following discussion of Howe's treatment of Bridgman is based on these two sources.
3. To complicate matters, Howe also was a practitioner of phrenology, a failed science. Evidently, he took phrenology to provide the physical and scientific basis for the psychology of distinct mental faculties.
4. Oliver Sacks, *The Man Who Mistook His Wife for a Hat and Other Clinical Tales* (New York, NY: Touchstone, 1970), 13.
5. This description of Hubel and Wiesel's hierarchical model closely follows the account in Todd Feinberg, *Altered Egos: How the Brain Creates the Self* (Oxford: Oxford University Press, 2001), 112-13.
6. There are many other pathologies that demonstrate the same point. Not addressed here, but more commonly discussed, are problems generated by bisected brains and multiple personalities.
7. Ludwig Wittgenstein, *On Certainty* (New York, NY: Harper Torchbooks, 1969), 257. Also see 248 and 250.
8. The description of this case is drawn from Sacks, *ibid.*, 43ff.
9. The role of such perspectivalism in *species-orientation* also undermines what would seem to be the possible implications of a top-down, essentialist, spiritual view of human nature, according to which *I* could occupy another body or no body at all.

6

"Supernatural" Experience and Human Nature

In the previous chapter, I argued that human beings enjoy a unique *species-sense* and a unique *species-sensory-integration* that result in a unique *species-orientation*, i.e., a unique pattern of ways of acting in and being acted upon by the natural world. While maintaining a position of metaphysical neutrality, these positions were developed with a firm commitment to methodological naturalism. Some thinkers have maintained that human experience extends beyond the kind of sensory experience from which the notions of *species-sense, species-sensory-integration*, and *species-orientation* are developed. Specifically, some religious thinkers have maintained that human experience includes a unique kind of experience, which is described by various figures as *religious experience* or experience of the *holy*, the *sacred*, or the *supernatural*. This kind of claim is frequently made by those defending a top-down, essentialist view of human nature where the essential ingredient is a metaphysically distinct soul. The general claim is that human beings have a unique nature because of our ability to have experiences of a metaphysically distinct kind that are qualitatively different from our experiences of the natural world, e.g., religious experiences or experiences of God, angels, or disembodied spirits. Some think that human beings have a special "religious sense" to allow such experiences. If indeed human beings have such a distinct nature, then *Homo sapiens* might be equally regarded as *Homo religiosus*. The claim is not that *all* human beings actually have such experiences of the supernatural. Indeed, some theists claim that the lives of non-theists are disadvantaged in certain ways since non-believers do not have such experiences. For example, those who defend the Divine Command Theory maintain that non-theists are disadvantaged when it comes to making normative moral judgments, and those who defend religious experience maintain that non-theists are deprived experientially. Some theists have also maintained that non-theists are deprived in terms of the phenomenological feelings that accompany certain experiences. While the accompanying phenomenological feeling of an experience is closely related to the notion of a religious experience itself; however, it is a separate matter of determining whether qualitatively distinct phenomenological feelings accompanying certain experiences can give rise to one's notions of the holy or the sacred.

The notions of *species-sense, species-sensory-integration,* and *species-orientation,* which partially account for our notion of human nature, are based upon a consideration of the full range of sensory experiences that are characteristically human. Creatures otherwise very similar or even otherwise identical to human beings with a significantly different range or set of sensory experiences, I have argued, would have a very different nature from what we now regard as human nature. Similarly, since *species-orientation* is a function of the interaction of members of a species with a natural world that presents a particular *haecceity* (the *thisness,* an *come-up-againstness),* human *species-orientation* would be quite different given a significantly different sensory environment. The present issue is whether the sensory experiences that have been used to characterize the human *species-sense* exhaust the full range of human experience or whether there is also a range of non-sensory experiences that is uniquely human and whether there is a special, additional sense that allows such experiences. For example, some theists claim that human beings can "see" God or otherwise experience things that are spiritual or holy. If this claim is true and if the ability to have such experiences is unique to human beings, then it seems that such an ability ought to be counted in the cluster of properties upon which human nature supervenes. It is not clear how the cluster theory might accommodate what would amount to a significantly expanded view of *species-sense.* A range of human experience expanded to include experience of a different metaphysical realm would appear to undermine the notions of *species-sense, species-sensory-integration,* and *species-orientation* developed earlier in favor or some sort of top-down essentialist theory of human nature. Consequently, the cluster theory of human nature is threatened unless such experiences are explicable within a naturalistic methodology. This chapter is devoted to a consideration of the claims made by theists that human beings are *Homo religiosus* since some human beings have experiences that are qualitatively different from "normal" sense experiences and that these experiences can only be explained as experiences of the supernatural. The cluster theory embraces the first claim and denies the second.

Understanding and exploring this particular claim about human nature (and then further considering whether the ability to have non-sensory experience that is qualitatively different from sensory experience ought to be included in the cluster of properties upon which human nature supervenes) require some preliminary considerations about certain aspects of theism and claims about "the holy" and "the sacred." Eventually, I will return to the consideration of what the business about alleged experiences of the sacred or the holy has to do with the cluster theory of human nature.

There is a curious tension in theism, or, perhaps it is more accurate to say a curious tension in mainstream Christian theology, between the secular and the sacred. I call it a "curious tension" because, on the one hand, ordinary material objects in the natural world, i.e., the "secular" world, are devalued and sometimes even regarded as corrupt and corrupting. In this regard, mainstream Christian theology still reflects the view of the natural world found in the Neo-Platonists, according to which the natural world exerts a pernicious influence upon the spiritual soul. Natural appetites, desires, and some forms of the kind of sensory experience discussed in the previous chapter are seen as evil or are, at least, in competition with spiritual purity, and the influence of the sensory, secular world must be countered or somehow "overcome" in order for the spiritual soul to become godly and receive salvation. Blood, sweat, tears, and theological ink have been spilt for centuries over disputes about exactly how this process is supposed to work. The tension is created because, on the other hand (although according to this view, the natural, secular world is not valued *in general,* in and of itself), *particular* material objects or places in the natural, secular world are sometimes viewed as sacred and valued extremely highly, *upon certain occasions and under special circumstances.*

Evidence of the devaluing of the natural world in Christian theology abounds in both scripture and religious tradition. Thus, the various elements of the natural, secular world are often regarded as having little or no value in and of themselves since the natural world, in and of itself, has little or no value. Whatever value the natural world might have wanes in significance when compared to the sacred since worldly concerns and interests, whatever they may be, represent obstacles to the salvation of one's immortal soul.

On this view, some things are presumably sacred *simpliciter,* in and of themselves. So, for example, the throne of God or the Godhead itself might be regarded as sacred; however, places and things in the natural world are not sacred *simpliciter* but become sacred through a certain process. One finds this view not only in Christian theology but in Judaism and Islam as well. For instance, God tells Moses when he appears to him in the burning bush, "put off your shoes from your feet, for the place on which you are standing is holy ground." (Exodus 3:5) Consider as well the way in which Jews regard the Ark of the Covenant, which housed the tablets containing the Ten Commandments given Moses by God, and the way in which some Christians regard the Shroud of Turin, which supposedly laid upon the dead body of Jesus. Muslims regard the Kaaba, the large stone structure in Mecca, as holy, and a pilgrimage is required of all Muslims to this holy place. Millions of devout Muslims travel there during Hajj every year. Examples of religious relics and places of worship that are considered sacred by different religious believers can easily be multiplied.

According to this account of the sacred, *particular* objects and/or places are set apart from the rest of the secular world and *transformed* or *elevated* to the status of *holy* or *sacred* by contact with the divine and/or an infusion of the supernatural into the natural world. This view of the sacred is thus what I call a *value-added* theory according to which ordinary materials, objects, or places in the natural world take on a special, additional value brought about by the combination of the supernatural with the natural.[1] This same view of the nature of the sacred provides the theoretical framework within which the Roman Catholic Church accounts for the belief in transubstantiation, or, perhaps, more fundamentally, it provides the general metaphysical framework within which Christians account for the belief in the incarnation. In both cases it is believed, ordinary material objects—wine and bread or flesh and blood—are transformed into something holy by an infusion of or action by the divine. Furthermore, the value that is added is not understood as simply the result of qualitative changes in the sensible, material properties of the material object. That is, the sacredness of the place of thing is not the result of something that is red becoming green or something that is cold becoming hot. On some occasions, there might indeed be such qualitative changes in the sensible properties of the material object, but, on other occasions, there might not be such changes. However, according to this view, the special, added value of a sacred place or thing is understood as being capable of being experienced by human beings.

There are thus special accounts of how human beings are supposed to be able to experience the holy or the sacred.

This theistic view of the sacred presupposes some interesting and puzzling metaphysics to which the cluster theory avoids commitment. It is a metaphysics that is dualistic since it presupposes a metaphysical distinction between the natural and the supernatural. In many ways, this view of the sacred is simply a refinement of primitive animism that regarded various parts (or, in some cases, all) of nature as embodying supernatural spirits. Metaphysically, there is little or no difference between a forest, river, or mountain being highly valued because of the belief that it possesses some kind of spirit and a religious relic or place of worship being highly valued because of some special contact with the spiritual. The belief that a mountain has a spirit in it might be regarded as primitive by some modern theists while the belief that a mosque, synagogue, or cathedral has the Spirit of God in it is commonly accepted as non-problematic.

The refinement added by modern theism comes in the additional belief that the spirit in question is able to detach itself from its physical location to reappear in a different physical location or exist independently of any physical location at all; however, the basic metaphysics is the same in each case. Again, while the belief that sticking a voodoo doll with a pin can marshal supernatural forces to affect changes in the natural world might be regarded by most theists as primitive and simply superstitious, the belief that supernatural forces can be invoked during the Eucharist to change the material substances of bread and wine into the body and blood of Christ is commonly accepted by some theists. Again, the metaphysics appear to be the same. (The same seems true of *consubstantiation* as well.)

Some variation of this dualistic metaphysics is presupposed by most forms of top-down theories of human nature, but trying to explain or explore the complications of this underlying metaphysics is not the primary focus here. The seemingly intractable problems of such a metaphysics, for example, of how the two metaphysically distinct kinds of substances can be understood to interact or be related at all, are well-known and widely discussed. It suffices to say at this point that naturalism extends the same initial skepticism and perplexity that many theists might feel at talk of the spirit of the mountain to talk about the Holy Spirit of the Eucharist. Whether a suitable theory of this underlying, theistic metaphysics can ever be worked out is debatable and a project for another occasion and not the concern of the cluster theory. It is clear, however, that mainstream theistic claims about the alleged "supernatural experiences" of the holy and the sacred *presuppose* this dualistic metaphysics. Perhaps, it is even tautological within the mainstream of theism that the holy or the sacred is supernatural.

Leaving the metaphysical questions and problems aside, the main purpose here is to show how it might be possible to develop a theory of the sacred without such metaphysical presuppositions. If it is possible to account for human, non-sensory experience within a commitment to a completely naturalistic methodology, it then becomes possible to demonstrate further how the claim that *Homo sapiens* is also *Homo religiosus* is related to the cluster theory of human nature. Also, understanding how spirituality and the sacred can permeate "ordinary" existence and everyday life, i.e., how spirituality and sacredness can be found in metaphysically naturalistic experiences, allows one to understand better the connection between contemporary religious beliefs and practices and such practices of animism and totemism in what are commonly called "primitive" cultures. It is reasonable to believe that contemporary theistic religious beliefs and practices (with an emphasis on the notion of a supernatural sacred) are extrapolations from naturalistic understandings of the sacred resulting from modern theism's incorporation of the Aristotelian "two-world-view." "Primitive" peoples may be thus understood as equally *Homo religiosus* but as more "primitive"(i.e., "restrained") in their metaphysics, which, in terms of the commitment of the cluster theory of human nature to methodological naturalism, makes them more in tune with the most recent and sophisticated theories from the natural and social sciences.

In the history of philosophy and religious thought, many thinkers who have championed top-down views of human nature have claimed that human beings are unique because of what have been generically described as "religious experiences." I do not intend to trace an account of different historical figures that have made such claims here; however, it is valuable and illustrative to examine closely one celebrated, contemporary example of such a claim. Consider the well-known and highly influential treatment of the sacred and the holy developed by Rudolf Otto.[2] Otto's treatment of the holy is framed by his attempt to capture that part of religion that is not captured and that cannot be captured by rational or moral categories. That is not to say that Otto denies that there are rational and moral aspects to religion. He does not. He does, however, think that religion has been dominated by the rational at the neglect of the non-rational. The unique value of the holy or sacred, minus any rational or moral consideration whatsoever, is what he terms the *numinous*. The *numinous* is that additional part of the Holy that transcends all moral and rational categorization. For Otto, one's experience of the *numinous* and the *numinous* as a category of value is *sui generis* and not explicable in terms of or reducible to any other experience or category. Such an experience of the holy, which Otto takes to be "the deepest and most fundamental element" of religion, is a form of religious *feeling* that is captured by his now well-know phrase, *mysterium tremendum*. This is the unique phenomenological feeling sometimes elicited in such situations as those involving solemn religious rites and rituals and by such places as religious temples and churches. Although Otto frequently describes such situations as producing "the *numinous* feeling" (*das numinose Gefühl*), he does not intend that this feeling be understood as a purely subjective one, but he rather clearly intends that this feeling be understood as a feeling *of* the *numinous*, i.e., it is a unique phenomenological feeling that is intentional in that it takes the objectively existing *numinous* as its object.

If Otto is correct, then it would appear that the uniqueness of human beings may be accounted for by a special nature that allows us to have the unique phenomenological feeling of *mysterium tremendum* produced by an experience of the *numinous*. Although Otto himself does not attempt to develop a theory of human nature based upon his notion of the *numinous* and the *mysterium tremendum,* it seems obvious that his views support an essentialist theory of human nature that easily could be developed according to which having such unique experiences and phenomenological feelings is taken to be an essential feature of human nature. For example, according to Augustine's view, human beings exist in order to gain a beatific vision of God. Thus, human beings are what we are because, on a very fundamental level, we are able to experience God or commune with "the holy," or "the spiritual." Similarly, Calvin and some of his more recent followers such as Alvin Plantinga claim that human beings have a special *sensus divinitatis*—a uniquely human propensity to believe in God—that, when stimulated by certain kinds of experiences of the variety under discussion, leads one to believe in the existence of God or to believe that one has been in God's presence or the presence of something holy. Thus, *mysterium tremendum* experiences (or simply, more generally, "religious experiences") are taken by these theists as evidence of God's existence.

According to Otto, the *mysterium tremendum* is something that is so alien, inexplicable, and incomprehensible on the level of ordinary, sense experience, so "wholly other," that it strikes one dumb and puts one into a state of *stupor* by overpowering one's rational mind and filling one with complete awe, wonder, and astonishment. The modifier, *tremendum*, is intended to capture the elements of "awfulness," "overpoweringness," and "urgency" in the *mysterium*. According to Otto's phenomenological account of the *numinous* feeling then, when having such a feeling a person is aware of the presence of a frightening, overpowering, vibrant, mysterious "wholly other" that completely fills one with awe, fear, dread, and a feeling of complete dependence and an awareness of one's "creaturehood," i.e., an awareness of one's insignificance and the insignificance of other creatures.[3]

Otto claims repeatedly that "the natural man," (the non-religious person) can not experience such feelings of *mysterium tremendum*. According to Otto, the non-religious person not only cannot experience *mysterium tremendum* but is further limited in such a way that he is unable to "shudder," feel absolute horror, in the true sense of the word, since such feelings are provoked only by an experience of *numinous* value that "has no place in the everyday natural world of ordinary experience...." Such feelings of absolute horror are possible, according to Otto, only in the religious person in whom a special spiritual faculty with special capacities for a special quality of feeling have been awakened. It thus seems that Otto's claims about the feeling of *mysterium tremendum* should be understood as an example of a top-down view of human nature, which is dependent upon a metaphysical view that includes a non-naturalistic dimension of some sort. According to this view, a religious person experiences the world qualitatively differently than does the secular person, i.e., with a greater depth of feeling, for example, with feelings of "true" horror. The seat of such unique feelings is a special faculty, presumably unique to human beings, which is awakened in the religious person. It follows that only religious believers who experience the *numinous* through an experience of *mysterium tremendum* can experience the feeling of an awful and overpowering, a daunting and fascinating mystery that completely fills one with awe, fear, dread, and a feeling of complete helplessness and dependence. These experiences and their accompanying phenomenological feelings are the result, according to Otto, of the awakening—the stimulation in some manner—of a special, spiritual faculty in man, and human nature then is importantly, or perhaps essentially, characterized by this special, spiritual faculty which allows human beings to have religious experiences.

There are many poignant questions posed by theistic treatments of the sacred: Do human beings, in fact, have such experiences and feelings as Otto describes? Do human beings have a special *sensus divinitatis* as Plantinga claims? And if human beings do have such experiences, must one then invoke a metaphysically distinct realm of the non-natural, spiritual *numinous* to account for such experiences and feelings? Or must one also invoke a special *sensus divinitatis* to explain their occurrence? Can the occurrence of such experiences be explained without additional metaphysical commitments and admission of an essentialist and top-down view of human nature?

Consider how a naturalist account for what Augustine, Otto, and Plantinga describe as religious experience might be developed. Such an account requires a brief detour through some phenomenology and the philosophy of language—particularly, some observations about denotation. The first thing to note is that Augustine, Otto, and Plantinga load their metaphysics at the front end. Each begins with a commitment to the existence of a metaphysically-distinct realm and then simply describes or defines religious experience in such a way that it is nothing more than the form in which one supposedly experiences some aspect of that metaphyscially-distinct realm. Consequently, for example, the feeling of *mysterium tremendum* involving experience of the *numinous* is tautological for Otto. He makes no *argument* for this claim. He simply defines *mysterium tremendum* in a way so that it is tautologically true. The metaphysics thus drives the phenomenology. It follows from the presumed metaphysics that naturalism cannot give an account of what is supposed to be the theist's qualitatively superior, religious experiences since naturalism does not accept the metaphysics and the ontology upon which the claim for the qualitative difference is based. However, to give a genuine phenomenological account of *mysterium tremendum*, one needs to begin with the *experience*—with the *feeling, mysterium tremendum*—and then see what it is like and what intentional object, if any, it really takes and what ontology it requires.

The whole purpose of a phenomenological account of experience is to do so with as few initial commitments as possible to get as close to the "raw" experience as possible. In Otto's account of the sacred, the supernatural metaphysics is front-loaded into the theories of sacred and holy events and objects, and through a kind of trickle-down effect, one winds up with *the* sacred or *the* holy, which is a manifestation or revelation of the supernatural. The consequences for a theory of human nature based upon a special faculty that produces feelings of *mysterium tremendum* follow from front-loading the metaphysics. *Homo religiosus*, on these terms, presupposes the supernatural.

Before considering some possible examples of experiences of sacred events and objects that might be explained completely within a naturalistic metaphysics, consider two significant points from the philosophy of language: First, according to the *OED*, the dominant meaning of the word "sacred" is found in its adjectival form. As J. L. Austin pointed out about the word "real," the word "sacred" is "substantive-hungry." Thus, whenever we find the description "the sacred," it is always appropriate to ask, "The sacred *what*?" Common usage indicates that there are sacred objects and events but using "sacred" as a noun as in the definite description "*the* sacred" starts the long slippery slide into reifying the sacred as a distinct metaphysical entity. After all, since proper names and definite descriptions are commonly taken to be referring expressions, simply using the definite description, "*the* sacred," starts the search for a referent. In common usage, as a noun, "sacred" takes its meaning from the sacred items used in acts of worship, sacrifice, or consecration; so, "the sacreds" might be used to refer to those sacred items. "*The* sacred" appears to be a theistic neologism used only by theologians and philosophers or religion of a certain persuasion. The use of "*the* sacred" thus prejudices any treatment of sacred or holy events or objects towards the theistic account. To keep the door open at least for a naturalistic understanding of sacred events and objects, one should use the word "sacred" only in its adjectival form. Secondly, what is regarded as sacred is relative to time and culture. One person's sacred is another person's secular, and which is which appears to be largely a function of one's knowledge and understanding of certain natural phenomena. Thus, solar and lunar eclipses and natural events such as volcanoes and thunderstorms were regarded as sacred by some peoples of earlier times, but are not so regarded by most people in modern, Western cultures today. So, one should expect that different people will give different accounts of sacred events and objects, and "sacred" should be defined in a way that allows for this possibility.

The secular meaning of "sacred" simply means being dedicated, set apart, or otherwise appropriated for some special purpose or with some special value. Of course, the number of different uses with different meanings of these words is of no real importance in this argument. The case here does not turn on ordinary language usage but upon phenomenological analysis. The issue is whether there is a legitimate secular use of the notion of a sacred event or object and whether it is possible to give a phenomenological account of the feelings that accompany the non-sensory experiences of such events or objects within a completely naturalistic metaphysics. Then, it must be determined if such experiences and the feelings that accompany them should be included in the cluster of properties upon which human nature supervenes.

It is an indisputable empirically-given fact that human experiences differ significantly from one another; so the relevant questions become something like these: are some human experiences so significantly different from others that they can legitimately be regarded as producing the kinds of phenomenological feelings that are claimed to accompany experiences of the sacred or the holy without invoking a metaphysics of the supernatural? And ought the ability to have such "supernatural" experiences be included in the cluster of properties upon which human nature supervenes? Can human beings have experiences of transcendence (and hence have legitimate claims to *Homo religiosus*) that are completely naturalistic? The cluster theory maintains that the answers to these questions are in the affirmative. The point is not that all human beings have such experiences or that only human beings have such experiences, but rather, the point is that the ability to have such experiences is one of the properties that is to be included in the causal nexus of properties upon which human nature supervenes. If it is possible to give an account of what some people describe as religious experiences or supernatural experiences appealing only to a naturalistic methodology without appealing to a special *sensus divinitatis* or the like, then it becomes possible to add a bit of thickness to the otherwise thin cluster theory of human nature. *Homo sapiens* and *Homo sexus* are also equally *Homo religiosus*. Whether such experiences with their accompanying phenomenological feelings are uniquely human is an issue that will be addressed momentarily.

To consider possible candidates for such experiences, one must engage in some thought experiments. The concern *here* is not with claims about reputed religious experiences that are ostensibly experientially supernatural such as being appeared to by disembodied spirits or having the dead raised. The experiences themselves are taken to be metaphysically naturalistic, but they produce the qualitatively unique *feeling* of *mysterium tremendum*, of the sacred or the holy. At the same time, these experiences are significantly different enough from ordinary sense experiences in ways so that they stand out, command our attention, and are highly valued. The following examples fall into four categories of such experiences, which represent something of the full spectrum of the kinds of feelings described by others as religious or supernatural experiences.

Perhaps the most common kind of experience that might qualify on completely naturalistic grounds as *mysterium tremendum* experiences are aesthetic experiences. A salient feature of aesthetic experiences for the present discussion is that there are generally taken to be different kinds of aesthetic experiences. Some are very cognitive in nature such as when a person considers or analyzes an art object or an experience and forms some kind of judgment. This is not the kind of aesthetic experience in which I am currently interested. There is a different kind of aesthetic experience, a non-cognitive one, during which a person is simply emotionally overwhelmed by the experience. These are experiences that are difficult or impossible to categorize or explain but which have a dramatically different phenomenological nature from ordinary experience. Some philosophers have taken such experiences to be so significantly different from ordinary sense experience that they have been taken as the distinguishing feature of *Homo sapiens*. For example, John Dewey describes such experiences as the stirring into action of deep resonances of dispositions of a person which are developed primitively and which are inexpressive and unattainable in ordinary sense experience. During these experiences, a person experiences meanings and values that have "depth," i.e., meanings and values that transcend ordinary ones and that might be regarded as "ideal" or "spiritual."[4] Such a view is captured by John Keats at the end of his "Ode on a Grecian Urn," when he says,

> "Beauty is truth, truth, beauty,"—that is all
> Ye know on earth, and all ye need to know.

The truth of which Keats speaks is not propositional truth of some assertion or other. He means something more vague, subtle—something of a "spiritual" value, which one detects only rarely and upon only extraordinary occasions. Of course, different people see the kind of beauty, which ravishes one into admiration, in different things. Some may see it in a Grecian urn. Some may see it in a painting. On rare occasions, eating and drinking might rise to this level for some people. Some never see it at all. I find such beauty in such music as Mahler's *First Symphony*, Mozart's *Requiem*, and the second movement of Beethoven's *Fifth Piano Concerto*. Just recently, friends related an account of their experience of seeing the Southern Cross while sailing in the South Pacific Ocean for the first time. They practically swooned as they described the fierce and total darkness of the night sky and the impact of the bright stars against

that black canopy. It was like nothing else they had ever previously experienced on Earth, they said, and, for them, this experience was clearly
spiritual though secular. An experience of *Homo religiosus*.

On this account, aesthetic experiences are occasions of sense experience but not just normal, everyday sense experience, but rather,
qualitatively different, *heightened* or *elevated* sense experience—sense
experience that produces reactions and feelings that are *qualitatively
different* from those produced by ordinary, common sense experience.
Thus, what Keats and Dewey called "ethereal" values, i.e., what some
people call spiritual, eternal, or universal values, can be found in the
experience of nature itself. We might say that, on occasion, since human
reason has its limitations, it ultimately fails to provide us with access to
some of what we take to be the most valuable and fundamental values.
Where reason fails, religious persons insert religious experiences and
a supernatural metaphysics to explain how human beings access those
values, while the cluster theory maintains that it is possible to appeal to
aesthetic experiences within a completely naturalistic metaphysics to
account for access to those same values.

Consider next what I call instances of *kinesthetic immersion*. As we
have seen, the *species-orientation* of human beings means that as living
organisms in the natural world, we are constantly engaged with and in
interaction with our environment in a unique range of ways. Important
though they are, most of these connections and interactions are relatively
mundane and ordinary and become so familiar, routine, and habitual
that they command very little of our attention and deserve very little
mention. In other words, we become so habituated on the basis of our
species-sense through the process of *species-sensory-integration* to our
"normal" *species-orientation*, that we fail to notice or appreciate the
importance of the role of *species-orientation* until there is a significant
departure from the norm. In the preceding chapter, I explored some of
the ways in what various pathologies can affect human species-orientation and the usually deleterious effects of those pathologies.

However, some of the departures from the normal range of acting
upon and being acted upon by our environment are not pathological at
all. Occasionally, there are rare moments when those connections and
interactions between an individual and his or her environment are so
extraordinarily different with accompanying phenomenological feelings
that are so qualitatively distinct that they become regarded as spiritual
or religious experiences. These are moments when, to invoke a bit of
poetic license, the planets align and every blinding rushing atom in the

universe momentarily falls obligingly into its proper place—golden moments—frozen forever in an infinitude of time. Moments of the confluence of unknown forces and events. Frequently, examples of these moments involve some kind of physical performance. Athletes sometimes call the experience of such moments as "being in a zone"—being able to perform, for whatever brief period of time, certain physical feats perfectly, seemingly without effort and without fear of failure. Hitting a thrown ball with a wooden bat might be such a moment. These are not moments that are rational in the sense that they lend themselves to categorization or interpretation in familiar terms. The experience of such a moment is the experience of a synergetic, kinesthetic immersion of one's self into one's immediate environment and a blurring or loss of the conscious distinction between self and non-self.

In one religious account of such moments, Zen Buddhist monks are described as being able to perform uncanny and inexplicable feats of archery while blindfolded or in darkened rooms by "emptying" themselves and merging with the One.[5] But some people report experiencing such moments of perfect oneness with one's immediate environment with no explanation in terms of any supernatural, metaphysical underpinnings at all.

Sometimes experiences of just a few seconds duration are so qualitatively distinct and sublime that they are still registered indelibly in people's memories decades later. Some have called such experiences "peak" experiences or "optimal" experiences. There is some similarity between what I call experiences of kinesthetic immersion and the kind of experiences that result from what psychologist Mihaly Csikszentmihalyi has called activities of *flow*.[6]

Since whatever limited athletic performances I ever had personally are now in the distant past, I must draw upon other kinds of activity for any kind of first-hand account of kinesthetic immersion. I did have such an experience a few years ago while building a fence. I was driving case-hardened nails into seasoned, black locus fence posts. Seasoned black locus is one of the densest woods known, and attempting to drive a nail into a black locus post is much like attempting to drive one into a steel beam. On a good day, with a lot of care and practice, I could usually drive two or three nails out of ten into the posts without bending them. But on this particular day, when the planets and the stars happened to align for a few brief moments, I slipped into a zone. I drove nail after nail straight and true into post after post. The shrill ringing of hammer on nail was like the sound of a blacksmith's hammer striking an anvil.

I was astonished. I said to the person working with me, "This is incredible. I'll bet I can do this with my eyes closed." And I did! I could start a nail and then close my eyes and swing the hammer and drive the nail perfectly without looking at it. It was like being in a trance. I did not think about hitting the nail or concentrate more carefully on hitting it. I just slipped into a perfect rhythm and motion and repeated it over and over again until my arm became weary and weak and the moment slipped away. For those brief moments, driving the nails was a unique *feeling* of ergonomic comfort like scratching an itch, and, at the same time, the experience had something of a spiritual quality about it. I was definitely "in the flow."

Musicians sometimes report similar experiences of practicing and practicing and struggling with a piece of very difficult music and then finally "getting it" when they become so engrossed in the music that they play it perfectly without any conscious effort or struggle. Long distance runners sometimes report having what is called a "runner's high" when the endorphins in the brain produce a state of euphoria, which allows for highly accelerated performance with little or no effort or pain. Running then takes on an ethereal and spiritual-like quality. The claim here is that certain physical activities may sometimes deviate so significantly from the normal range of activities captured by the notion of species-orientation that they produce experiences that are spiritual but metaphysically naturalistic—experiences that qualify easily as experiences of *Homo religiosus*.

The third example of experiences that are ontologically naturalistic but which might be taken as experiences of *mysterium tremendum* involve what I will call horrific/heinous experiences. Contrary to Otto's claim that the only experiences of true horror are experiences of the supernatural *numinous*, there are, unfortunately, examples of experiences that are completely naturalistic to which one can appeal that are experiences of true horror. Since appeals to the holocaust by philosophers are too common, I will consider other examples of experiences that might produce feelings of pure horror and monstrous evil that are completely overwhelming. Consider two such examples based upon actual events. Imagine yourself to be a young man, eighteen or nineteen, staring out across the battle field of Antietam, on September 17, 1862. This day has proven to be, to the present, what some historians have called the deadliest day in the history of the United States with at least 6,000 men killed in just a few hours and twice that number seriously wounded.[7] The battle is waged by the most awesome concentration of cannon and fire power one could ever imagine at the time. The sulfur of gunpowder hangs heavy in the air. The cries and screams of wounded men and horses pierce your mind. The stench of blood and human waste is so overpowering that you retch and vomit involuntarily. The noise of the gunfire and cannons is so deafening you cannot hear yourself think. Your body shakes uncontrollably from the concussions produced by the explosions. It is as if every earthquake and thunderstorm since the beginning of time have all been gathered into one place at one time. It is a scene from the inner circles of Dante's *Inferno*—a scene so terrible that witnesses thought the horror to be beyond what any tongue could tell, any mind conceive, or any pen portray. While you are struggling to maintain your sanity and composure, your commanding officer says, "Let's go, boys." And you realize that you are about to make your way into that moment of Hell through and over the dead bodies, bloody viscera, human and animal waste, and indistinguishable human and animal body parts to almost certain death.

Again, imagine yourself a young man of twenty or so in Belgium in January, 1945. You are one of only 60-odd GIs out of over 900 that have managed to survive two weeks of fighting German tiger tanks with M1 rifles in the Battle of the Bulge. As the Germans are finally pushed back, you are put in charge of the burial detail by your commanding officer. It is bitterly cold. It has not been above the freezing point for days, and you are charged with putting the corpses of those men who were your friends and comrades—now frozen into grotesque positions—into standard-issue, U. S. Army body-bags. Imagine yourself wrestling with those bodies–pushing, pulling, forcing, breaking, and ultimately, mutilating those bodies to get them into the body bags—dozens of them, *hundreds* of them—day after day.

Surely these are examples of a kind of experience of such monstrous horror that is so qualitatively different from anything found in ordinary, everyday experience that we might wonder just how much more horrible a feeling of "true" horror (that Otto insists must be an experience of the *numinous*) might be. The experiences described here are ones that frequently produce the kind of involuntary physiological reactions never associated with "standard-issue religious experiences" such as panic, paralysis, nausea, incontinence, and loss of bowel control—sure signs of feelings of terror and horror. When William T. Sherman said, "War is hell," considering such scenes as those described here, he can easily be understood as speaking literally and not simply metaphorically since such places produce a kind of uncontrollable, visceral sense of horror and revulsion that no contemplation of a theological promise of Hell ever produces.

Nor need one appeal to the extreme circumstances that occur in war for examples of such experiences. Imagine yourself as a caring, loving parent having to watch your child die slowly over months or years in excruciating pain from incurable cancer. Or, place yourself in the position of a caring, loving parent like tens of thousands of parents in various parts of the world who have watched their children's eyes and stomachs swell as they slowly die of starvation. These are completely naturalistic experiences that easily and naturally produce the feelings of helplessness, complete dependence, and creaturehood, which Otto reserves for *mysterium tremendum* experiences. However, these are completely naturalistic experiences that can be explained with no appeal to a special *sensus divinitatis* . Such experiences explain how *Homo sapiens* might also be regarded as *Homo religiosus* within the cluster theory.

The last category of experiences considered here that might provoke the same kind of feelings as do *mysterium tremendum* experiences are those that occur in some interpersonal relationships. Romantic love has been given short shrift by most philosophers and theologians alike; so a brief apology for a certain form of romantic love might be in order. Describing these intimate experiences as involving simply feelings of love seems inadequate for the kind of experiences in intimate relationships that might be comparable to experiences that others describe as experiences of the holy or the sacred. Psychologists sometimes characterize such relationships as involving incidents of *enmeshment,* i.e., the entanglement or mixture of identities. Perhaps such relationships are uncommon—few and far between—but so are *mysterium tremendum* experiences. These relationships may be better understood in comparison with what Martin Buber called "I-Thou" relationships.[8] In such relationships, the I becomes completely vulnerable and exposed to the Thou, with no pretensions or safeguards. It is a fully committed relationship, which involves a qualitative change from the relationships found in the ordinary, "I-It," relationships. Such relationships involve commitment and vulnerability on the high wire of life with no safety net. For Buber, "I-Thou" relationships are the contemporary, secular source of the divine in human existence.

Now it is not clear that all personal relationships that are characterized by extreme, intense intimacy are healthy. They are intense and volatile relationships, which sometimes end tragically when they are not reciprocal. These are probably not the kind of relationships in which people marry, have children, and remain happily married for many years since such relationships are characterized by intense, sometimes even compulsive passion and intimacy instead of long-term commitment and normalcy. However, during such relationships, people sometimes describe having epiphanies of emotion during times of intimacy that are so powerful that the descriptions of them rival anything attributed to experiences of *mysterium tremendum*. Some of these experiences reportedly occur during times of sexual intimacy while others do not. These are experiences during which a person feels oneself struggling to preserve one's very identity, and people report such experiences to be intensely terrifying and prompting extreme physiological reactions which go far beyond simple orgasmic climax. These are experiences with no boundaries, safeguards, or precautions. These are experiences during which one finds oneself completely and helplessly vulnerable to the other person. On the other hand, some people report feeling "complete" or "fulfilled" for the only times in their lives during such experiences, and people sometimes report still being affected by such experiences decades later after being separated from the other person. Such experiences with another person give a new ironic twist to Sartre's notion of the Other. It is not simply that one sees oneself as the Other sees one or that one comes to understand oneself as being experienced by the Other; it is rather that one feels oneself *becoming* the Other or feels the Other actually *enmeshing* or *intertwining* with oneself. Contrary to Sartre, one comes to feel that one's identity is *threatened* by the Other. Consider this chillingly poignant description: "You willingly stretch yourself out completely naked, alone, and defenseless on the Alter of Love, close your eyes, and hand the Other the knife." One thus finds oneself completely at the mercy of the Other.

Now one might well have something of an immediate feeling of creaturehood and dependency upon an omnipotent God by contemplating the vastness of the starry heavens, but that phenomenological feeling of helplessness and dependency is nothing when compared to the realization that the imperfect and flawed beloved that you are holding or who is holding you has the power to destroy you and everything you value completely—the power to squash you like the insignificant little insect that you are. Now *that* is the kind of person that one approaches with fear and trembling! *That* is the immediate feeling of being on the back of a tiger that might turn on you unpredictably and devour you at any instant, an overwhelming feeling of helplessness and dependency. The feelings that are produced by such relationships and the moments of extreme intimacy that accompany them are so qualitatively different from the feelings that accompany what we might call "normal" or "ordinary" intimate experiences that they give some credence to Aristophanes' suggestion in Plato's *Symposium* that human beings are originally split in half. Perhaps each of us has another half to ourselves with whom we seek to reunite. Such experiences of extreme intimacy give rise to phenomenological feelings of transcendence that give a completely different meaning to the notion of "seeing God." Reverence for the same kind of extreme intimacy might well lie behind other ancient rituals that elevated sexual union to spiritual union and thus to religious status.

These examples are representative cases of the various kinds of non-sensory experiences, which are explained completely in terms of a naturalistic metaphysics, but which might plausibly produce the kinds of phenomenological feelings that Otto maintains are *mysterium tremendum* experiences—experiences of the holy or the sacred. The feelings accompanying these experiences apparently satisfy the full spectrum of descriptions offered by Otto. Some of these feelings might very well be "thrillingly vibrant and resonant" while others might well "burst in sudden eruption up from the depths of the soul with spasms and convulsions." Others may take more "wild and demonic forms" and lead to a state of "intoxicated frenzy" or "ecstasy." Surely some are feelings of "grisly horror" while others may be "beautiful and pure and glorious," and still others are feelings of complete vulnerability and insignificant creaturehood. Strictly phenomenological accounts of these different feelings might well reveal that there are intentional objects of these feelings, but there are no phenomenological grounds upon which to base a sensible judgment that these feelings are feelings produced by any object or thing or person that is metaphysically distinct from the material objects of the experiences themselves. Thus, one might describe one's experience of *the music* as producing feelings that are beautiful or glorious, or one might describe one's experience of *hammering* as producing feelings that are thrillingly vibrant, or one might describe *a battle or its aftermath* as producing feelings that are horrific, or one might describe an instant of extreme intimacy with *another person* as producing feelings of complete creaturehood and dependence.

Having such experiences that produce such feelings that rise above the dull, ordinary, everyday sense experience give a vibrance, vitality and exalted sense of being to human existence—a sense of transcendence. The occurrence of such experiences with their accompanying feelings provide the basis for regarding human beings as *Homo religiosus*.

While the ability to have experiences that produce such a heightened sense of being might be counted along with the other properties in the cluster of properties upon which human nature supervenes, having such experiences is certainly not essential for characterizing human nature. Individuals who do have such experiences simply have a somewhat "thicker" human nature than those who do not. Even given the full range of sense experiences discussed in the previous chapter, a person who *never* experiences *any* heightened form of sense experience such as those discussed here or the accompanying phenomenological feelings of such heightened experiences is certainly missing an important aspect of human nature.

Those given to a theist account of human nature account for such distinctive experiences and unusual feelings in terms of a metaphysically distinct sacred or holy realm and a special *sensus divinitatis*. What I have shown is that it is possible to account for "special," heightened kinds of experiences that human beings report having on occasions that produce unique phenomenological feelings without resorting to theological dogma or ad hoc religious faith in something like the *sensus divinitatis*. The claim that *Homo sapiens* is also *Homo religiosus* thus does not necessitate a commitment to special, additional metaphysical claims or the notion of a *sensus divinitatis*.

There may well be some unique features of the human brain and its chemistry that may, at some point in the future, be used to explain why human beings have optimal or peak experiences. Neurophysiologists are beginning to discover the neurological functions in the brain that are responsible for the phenomenological feelings produced by such experiences and those which are called experiences of the sacred or the holy by religious believers. In particular, one commonly shared feeling is one of helpless disorientation, a feeling of being outside oneself or of losing oneself, a feeling of being "swept away" into a different reality. Increasing evidence associates such feelings with the excitation of the posterior superior parietal lobe of the brain, which is responsible for a person's understanding of the distinction between self and non-self and one's physical orientation in space. The disorientation of this part of the brain, which is responsible for the proper physical orientation of the self, can be triggered by the repetitious, rhythmic actions found in religious rituals as well as in such secular "rituals" such as reciting a pledge or engaging in familiar ceremonies. The prolonged exposure to the quiescent effects of music or sex can exert an inhibition on neural activity in the brain producing the same kind of differentiation in the posterior superior parietal lobe, which then results in the phenomenological feelings of the loss of self, unreality, and even transcendence. Perhaps the repetitious nature of hammering can do the same.

Further evidence that spirituality is biologically based comes from the study of genetics, which suggests that some individuals have a strong, heritable predisposition that is genetically based that inclines those individuals towards spirituality and the belief in some higher, metaphysically distinctly power. There may be, in fact, a "God Gene," which is responsible, in part, at least, for explaining why some people have a strong religious faith while others do not and why some people see the hand or act of God in certain events or circumstances while others do not.[9] In other words, *Homo religiosus* may be genetically based. Using studies conducted on twins who have identical genetic makeups and a scale to measure spirituality, some have argued that spirituality is partially the result of a person's genetic makeup and that, furthermore, spirituality might have been selected for by natural selection by reducing stress, promoting a sense of purpose, and producing a happier, more optimistic (and hence, healthier) life for the spiritual/religious person. Thus, there is evidence from both neurophysiology and genetics to support the claim that what some people describe as spiritual experiences are the result of neural-chemical activity in the brain (mainly through the actions of monoamines such as adrenaline, dopamine, and serotonin, which control emotions), which may be the result, in significant part, to a genetic encoding. Therefore, what some have called the *sensus divinitatis* may be what others have called the God Gene.

I have argued thus far in this chapter that there are some human experiences that are so unique and different that they give rise to phenomenological feelings in some people that are qualitatively different from those accompanying ordinary experiences, and I have maintained that the potential for such non-sensory experiences and the phenomenological feelings that accompany them should be included in the cluster of properties upon which human nature supervenes (although, again, it is not essential). I have further argued that these experiences can be explained on completely naturalistic grounds and that there is no need or reason to describe these feelings as "value-added" experiences, which are explained only by presupposing a metaphysical dualism and by an infusion of the supernatural into the natural world.

Instead of describing these as "value-added" experiences of a different metaphysical ilk, they should be described as experiences that are qualitatively enriched by the *emergence* of highly increased value.

The phenomenological feelings that accompany our experiences of sacred or holy places, objects, or events can be explained as emergent properties that occur in certain unique combinations of circumstances and conditions. Spiritual experiences of sacred or holy places or things are not the result of a value that is inserted *into* the natural world but a value that grows out of the natural world. In certain situations, ordinary material objects and/or events, which are ontologically naturalistic, take on extraordinary value, which is felt in a fashion that is qualitatively different phenomenologically from what is produced by "ordinary" experience. When oxygen and hydrogen are combined, the liquidity of water is not "added;" it simply appears or emerges. Sacred or holy qualities also simply *appear*. Sacred or holy experiences are those that produce certain phenomenological qualities that supervene upon and emerge from completely natural properties. Such experiences occur in certain places and at certain times and in certain circumstances (and maybe with certain people) when conditions are just right for those experiences to occur, and the phenomenological qualities of those experiences are extraordinarily and qualitatively different from those of ordinary experiences. The cluster theory of human nature accounts for such extraordinary experiences by appealing to nothing but a completely naturalistic metaphysics. Some examples are aesthetic experiences, or experiences of kinesthetic immersion, grisly horror, or personal enmeshment. Some top-down theories of human nature call the feelings produced by such experiences, *mysterium tremendum* and take them to be manifestations of the supernatural detected by a special *sensus divinitatis*. The account given here demonstrates that such a metaphysical account of sacred or holy events and objects is neither necessary nor warranted.

Nothing that has been argued thus far has addressed the question of whether the non-sensory experiences of the holy or sacred and the qualitatively different phenomenological feelings that accompany them are uniquely human or whether other animals have such non-sensory experiences and feelings. Since the cluster theory of human nature is a thin theory, it is necessary to explain if and how human beings differ from non-human animals in this regard. The kinds of experiences that philosophers have attributed to other animals are spread across a wide spectrum. At one extreme, Descartes, of course, denied that other animals are even sentient beings, and his resulting notion of human nature must be regarded as one of the thickest in the history of philosophy. Attributing heightened sensory experiences of the holy or the sacred to other animals (with the kind of accompanying phenomenological feelings described above) would certainly be at the other extreme end of the spectrum. When philosophers have considered what it might be like to be a different animal, e.g., a bat, the focus of philosophical speculation has been in terms of qualia. But the questions that need to be raised here are both more general and more fundamental and might be understood as distributed along a scale of increasing importance. Do other animals have aesthetic experiences? Do other animals have experiences of kinesthetic immersion? Or intimate relationships of emotional enmeshment with other living things? Or experiences of horror, revulsion, impending doom, helplessness, or their own mortality? Obviously the important question is not whether all animals or even a significant number of different animals have such experiences but whether any non-human animals have such experiences and what the differences are between human and non-human animals.

It is impossible to address all of these questions here, but it is possible to gain some insight into some of them. One might initially think that the suggestion that there is a "God Gene" that affects brain chemistry in human beings would mean that spirituality or the experience of God is uniquely human. However, there is no evidence that the human "God Gene," if there is one, is unique in the animal kingdom, and there is no reason to believe that the particular effect that monoamines have upon the brain is uniquely human. The "God Gene," again, if there is one, would explain *individual differences* amongst different individuals of a species, but it cannot be used to explain why human beings might be spiritual while other animals are not. So, whatever claim is made about the kind of spirituality that human beings have must be very limited. No one would probably seriously maintain that earthworms have religious experience or mollusks; however, one should not be very sanguine about the other primates or even Golden Retrievers or thoroughbred horses.

Are aesthetic experiences unique to human beings? Our anthropocentric bent would have us believe that they are; however, a careful consideration of certain animals provides some compelling evidence to the contrary. For example, Darwin attributes a sense of beauty to other animals and explicitly cites the appreciation that some female birds have for the displayed plumage of male birds and the ways in which bowerbirds and certain hummingbirds use ornaments to decorate their nests and passages as evidence that other animals appreciate beauty. He also thinks that female birds have an aesthetic appreciation for the melodious songs of male birds.[10] Darwin explicitly denies that the aesthetic appreciation of beauty is unique to human beings and even suggests that the aesthetic sense in certain other animals may be more highly developed than in those that he calls "[human] savages!"

Consider the experience of kinesthetic immersion. When philosophers have made pronouncements concerning human nature or moral psychology, they have long been accused of being "armchair psychologists." When comparing human beings to other animals, too frequently, philosophers are "armchair biologists," relying upon prejudices, speculation, limited or selected data, or anecdotal evidence. This is a case where philosophers need to get serious about considering what the empirical evidence has to say. As Wittgenstein might say, if one wants to know what it's like to be a bat or any other animal, one cannot sit in the comfort of one's study and speculate; one must establish a relationship with the animal and carry on a conversation with that animal—not necessarily literally, of course, but metaphorically. One must be engaged on an intimate level over some period of time with an animal. All of which means that philosophers still have a lot to learn from people who have life-long contact with animals, those who conduct serious animal studies, and those who work, play, and otherwise live closely with animals—farmers, biologists, veterinarians, and animal trainers. Philosophers need to talk to people in the circus.

As one who has spent most of my life around animals, I can certainly attest that one's philosophical theories need to be better informed by a certain overwhelming poignancy of certain experiences with animals. One becomes extremely reticent, as Darwin was, to reserve any single property exclusively for human beings. Consider, just for example, the following story: Some years ago, I owned and trained horses. I came to own a blind brood mare. Now owning a blind horse is a particularly challenging situation. The tooth and fang law of animal existence is exhibited in many ways. Horses tend to abuse and dominate the weak or seriously injured or sick. I could not keep the blind brood mare with other horses, but she had a fine blood line so I bred her. I had not, of course, anticipated the complications of having a new born filly with a blind dame. The filly was healthy, but she simply stood idly by her mother's side for days and days when she should have been running and romping across the pasture to build those muscles so essential for proper early development. So, I shut the blind mare in a stall and put a halter with a short lead on the filly and gently led her away from the barn and out into the pasture. I pulled and cajoled her to get her to run, but she resisted and stumbled and followed grudgingly and reluctantly. What should have been the most natural and easy motions simply would not come. And then, one day, as I was tugging her along the pasture, she broke into a trot and then into a slow canter, and then, as the English would say, "the penny dropped," or as Professor Higgins would say, suddenly, "she got it!" She broke from my grasp and began running at full gallop across the pasture tossing her head and whinnying and kicking her heels and farting (as young colts and fillies normally do as they run and frolic). It was a moment as poignant as any description of a human experience except that this situation involved a horse that had finally learned to control certain muscles and to engage in a certain physical activity. The sudden breakthrough was dramatic, and the filly, which would hardly move just moments earlier, ran circles and sprints back and forth from one end of the pasture to the other—tossing her head and whinnying—until she was completely lathered and exhausted. I could then lead her back to the barn and cool her down. It was an experience I would unhesitatingly describe as one of kinesthetic immersion. The filly was as much in her groove of physical activity as I was in my hammering, and her elation and elevated sense of enjoyment and engagement with her physical environment was as obvious to me at the time as my own was while hammering nails into black locust fence posts. It was obvious that this was a qualitatively different experience for the filly in the same way as human beings report instances of qualitatively different experiences that are then often taken as experiences of the holy or the sacred.

It is not too far fetched to imagine that the young horse was *feeling*, for the first time, its kinesthetic abilities and its place in its surrounding environment, and the effect on the observable behavior was dramatic. If we impose an anthropomorphic sense of self-consciousness on the horse, then the most likely thought process would be something like, "Wow, this is great! This *feels* fantastic." Just as walking upright might be taken as one of the properties in the cluster of properties upon which human nature supervenes, running might be taken as one of the properties of that cluster of properties that result in a thoroughbred horse being the kind of animal that it is with the kind of special nature that it has. In terms of the framework developed in this book, one would say that running is an important aspect of a horse's *species-orientation*. For those who say with some seriousness that thoroughbred horses are born to run, something like this is the intended meaning. It is not too far-fetched to imagine a horse feeling something like, "This is what I am—a thing that runs. *This* is what I do."

The treatment of experiences of the holy or the sacred in this chapter may lead some readers to wonder about the role of emotions in human nature. The role of emotions in the causal nexus of properties upon which human nature supervenes is treated in some detail in Chapter 9. The issues of how unique emotions are to human beings is also addressed there; however, it is possible to make two preliminary points about emotions here. While there are disagreements about exactly what the evidence might be to support the claim that other animals experience emotions or to undermine that claim, there is no good reason to deny that other animals experience emotions without a careful consideration of the evidence except as the result of either an anthropocentric bias or an argument from ignorance. The evidence and the disagreements about the evidence must be examined carefully. Secondly, to the degree that emotions are the result of or supervene upon neurochemical activities in the brain, then at least part of the basis for the answers to the questions about what emotions really are, the role that they play in human nature, and what kind of creatures have emotions must rely heavily upon information from biology and neuroscience. Some of this information is considered in Chapter 8. In the spirit of genuine inquiry, for the time being, these questions must remain open ones.

In the final analysis, it is of little importance to the cluster theory of human nature whether other animals have aesthetic experiences or experiences of kinesthetic immersion, horror, or interpersonal enmeshment because the ability to have such experiences is simply one of a cluster of experiences upon which human nature supervenes. Restricting such experiences to *Homo sapiens* and *Homo religiosus* may be important for theists or others who defend a metaphysically thick theory of human nature based upon some sort of top-down claim according to which the possession of a special *sensus divinitatis*, an immortal soul, or metaphysically distinct, immaterial mind is essential for human nature. We might say, for the moment at least, that there is some compelling evidence that other animals do have such experiences and that the evidence that they do is at least as compelling as the evidence that the experiences that human beings have require a top-down explanation of human nature and metaphysical and ontological commitments beyond the natural world.

Notes

1.   In the same sense, Divine Command Moral Theory is a value-added theory since moral value is regarded as originating from some contact with the supernatural or ontologically based upon the supernatural.

2.   Rudolf Otto, *The Idea of the Holy* (Oxford: Oxford University Press, 1923) and *Naturalism and Religion* (London: Williams & Norgate, Ltd., 1907).

3.   *Ibid., pp. 13-24, en passant.*

4. John Dewey, *Art as Experience* (New York, NY: Perigee Books, 1934), p. 29.
5. See *Zen in the Art of Archery*, Eugene Herrigel, translated by R. F. C. Hall (New York: Vintage Books, 1953).
6. See *Flow: The Psychology of Optimal Experience*, Mihaly Csikszentmihalyi (New York: Harper & Row, 1990).
7. The following description of the Battle of Antietam is based upon *Crossroads of Freedom: Antietam*, James M. McPherson (Oxford: Oxford University Press, 2002).
8. See Martin Buber, *I and Thou* (New York, NY: Touchstone, 1970).
9. See Dean Hamer, *The God Gene* (New York, NY: Doubleday, 2004).
10. From Charles Darwin, *The Descent of Man* in *Readings on Human Nature*, edited by Peter Loptson (Ontario, Canada: Broadview Press, 1998), 294.

7

Material Culture and Human Nature

In earlier chapters, I have explained how *species-orientation* consists in a range of ways in which members of a species are able to act upon and be acted upon by their natural environment. I have shown how a particular species' *species-orientation* is a function of that species' *species-sense* and *species-sensory-integration*. Furthermore, I have argued that the Human Nature Anthropic Principle (HNAP) delimits the features of the natural world in which human beings could have evolved into the kind of creatures that we are. The *haecceity*—the *thisness* or *come-up-againstness*—of the natural world provides a framework within which rational agency and practical knowledge can be explained and related to the range of ways in which human beings act upon and are acted upon by the natural world.

To this point, I have focused upon the sensory and more general or abstract aspects of *species-orientation*–perhaps, some will think with some justification, to the neglect of the more detailed, morphologically-based aspects of *species-orientation*. It may be well and good that human beings have experiences that produce feelings of the sacred and the holy, but what about what some people might regard as the more mundane and ordinary experiences such as making or using a computer or a can opener? The answer lies in examining the variety of different ways in which the *haecceity* (the *come-up-againstness*) of the natural world is presented to us. The claim regarding the importance of this *come-up-againstness* of the natural world has earlier been made in only the most general and vague fashion. To become the kind of creatures we are, human beings have needed the resistance of the natural world against which to act, but, as the HNAP implies, this resistance must come in a very particularized form. This world might have possibly offered resistance in the very nondescript and indecipherable form of the invisible box depicted in the routines of performing mimes. There are some such general and "invisible" aspects to the *haecceity* of the natural world, e.g., the force of gravity or the speed of sound or light. There are close approximations between the role of gravity in the *thisness* or *come-up-againstness* of the natural world and the invisible box of the mime. Both are responsible for severe restrictions or limitations on the nature of the *species-orientation* of human beings, and neither is material or physical in the sense of being directly or publicly observable. In both cases, we might say, we only observe the effects of the existence of the invisible box or gravity. Such aspects also are ways in which the *come-up-againstness* of the natural world acts upon individuals or prescribes the limitations within which individuals can act upon the natural world. These are features of the *thisness* or *come-up-againstness* of the natural world that are "hard-wired," i.e., these are features that create a framework *within which* all human behavior (and all other animal behavior and events for that matter) takes place but which are unaffected by that behavior. These aspects of the *come-up-againstness* of the natural world thus capture the *fixed* ways in which the natural world acts upon us and affects us. These natural laws or forces are unalterable and confining and regulatory in nature, and I will refer to these aspects of the *haecceity* or *come-up-againstness* of the natural world as collectively comprising the *fixed haecceity* of the natural world.

The focus of attention here, however, is upon the very *particularized* ways in which *haecceity* of the natural world is presented to us and the ways in which and the degrees to which human beings can *act upon* these aspects of the natural world and *affect them.* For example, when, as a part of our general *species-orientation,* we human beings use our *species-sense* to identify certain features of our immediately surrounding environment, to *act* in a particular way, those actions are always characterized by a certain specificity. It is *this* rock, *this* tree, *this* river, or *this* mountain towards which one's actions are directed. In terms of locomotion, for example, *walking* requires directing one's conscious attention to maneuvering about in or traversing over *this* ground with *these* rocks or *these roots.* The specificity with which individuals confront the *come-up-againstness* of the natural world thus provides the opportunity for a range of actions, which is restricted by those aspects of the *fixed haecceity* of the natural world that provide a framework or a backdrop within which actions take place. Actions are therefore delimited or regulated by that *fixed haecceity*, but those fixed aspects of *haecceity* do not require that they be objects of one's attention. However, acclimation and habituation to the *fixed* abstract laws or forces of *come-up-againstness* are necessary to survive.

On the other hand, a large number of specific events or material objects encountered in the natural world are, at least to some extent, malleable and can be affected by human actions. There is a variety of different ways in which an individual might interact with those *material* aspects of the natural world that can be influenced by those actions. Members of all species of animals have a range of possible ways in which this may be done. The important observation for the cluster theory of human nature is that there is a unique range of ways in which human beings are able to interact with those malleable, material aspects of the natural world in order to influence them causally. One might act upon those things in order to acquire or consume them. All living things must do this in some fashion in order to be nourished and survive. Acquisition, appropriation, or consumption of some sort of material substance in some fashion or other for sustenance is necessary for all living things. Hunting and gathering are both activities that are acquisition-oriented, and whatever it might be that is acquired through hunting or gathering is acquired for consumption. Consumption occurs with little or no modification of the acquired good in question, and whatever modification does take place is for the purpose of easier, more efficient, or more pleasurable consumption.

In contrast to simple acquisition, the focus here, however, is upon those ways in which an individual might act upon the material aspects of the *come-up-againstness* of the natural world in order to affect, shape, or change those material things in order to combine or configure them differently enough or to alter them significantly enough that "new" material things are produced. The products of this activity are intended to be preserved for some reason or other rather than to be used for immediate consumption. While some animals other than humans engage in this activity, not very many do, and no other animal modifies, combines, or reconfigures the malleable, material aspects of the natural world to produce new products to any degree or in any complexity approaching the ways in which human beings do. The "new" things or objects are *products* of human interaction with the plastic, material aspect of the *come-up-againstness* of the natural world.

There are obviously ways in which living organisms interact with the natural world by using the acquired substances necessary for sustenance and altering them through digestion and elimination to produce waste products. Animals produce CO2 (and other waste products) while plants produce O2 (and other waste products). This is not the kind of "alteration" or "reconfiguration" that is the focus of concern here. Arguably, such "manufacture" or "production" of "new" products is the result of biological processes and not deliberate actions. The kind of reconfiguration or manufacture that is significant for the cluster theory of human nature is the result of deliberate, conscious, intelligent *techne*.

The notion of *techne* (and the more contemporary related notion of technology) has been the object of attention by philosophers since ancient times. Aristotle, for example, who may be taken as representative of the Greek attitude towards *techne*, famously held *techne* in very low regard and treated it as less than "real" or "proper" knowledge, *episteme*, the highest form of which was *theoretical* knowledge. *Techne*, or *practical* knowledge, was the purview of the craftsmen, the blue-collar, working class, while *theoretical* knowledge was the purview of the philosophers. *Theoretical* knowledge, for Aristotle, was knowledge "for its own sake," while *techne*, practical knowledge, is always for the sake of something else. When Aristotle said that man is a rational animal and that man, by nature, desires to know, he was thinking of theoretical knowledge, *episteme*, and not *techne* because he took the abstract, speculative kind of epistemological inquiry as distinctive of human beings and not the practical, productive form of knowledge captured by *techne*. Whether this ranking of different forms of knowledge by Aristotle was completely the result of his philosophy or whether it was affected by considerations of class and politics remains a matter of some controversy amongst Greek scholars. In either case, so far as the cluster theory of human nature is concerned, Aristotle missed the boat by failing to recognize or appreciate the significance of *techne* for making human beings the kind of creatures that we are. In other words, he failed to appreciate the importance of *techne* to the cluster of properties upon which human nature supervenes—an importance that is at least equal to that of abstract, general, theoretical knowledge. The same failing has persisted amongst philosophers who have generally been bewitched by the ethereal and immaterial and by the theoretical and abstract. The practical and *techne* have generally been denigrated by philosophers while the theoretical and *episteme* have generally been exalted—with some exceptions, including Henri Bergson, Martin Heidegger, and John Dewey.

Emphasizing the theoretical and eschewing the practical reinforce top-down, thick theories of human nature. The cluster theory embraces *techne* as capturing a fundamental aspect of the ways in which human beings are grounded in the natural world and a fundamental way in which human beings are engaged with the natural world. Generally, social scientists—anthropologists, archeologists, and sociologists—have shown much more interest in *techne* than have philosophers. In particular, archeologists have developed the sophisticated study of *material culture* by which they attempt to determine what the less permanent aspects of ancient human cultures were like (such as patterns of living or social institutions or practices) by studying the more permanent physical objects produced by those cultures, preserved through the years, and discovered by researchers. In contrast with the concerns of the social scientists, the focus here is not upon a particular form or pattern of material culture or any particular human society. The concern is a much more general one that focuses upon the relationship between human beings and the malleable, material world and the import of that relationship for understanding the *kind* of creatures that we are.

Generally, when other philosophers have focused upon the relationship between human beings and material objects, it has usually been within a context where the primary concern is really some broader social, historical, economic, or political theory. It is useful, however, to compare what some philosophers have said about the importance of material culture for understanding human beings to the claims made here about the importance of human *techne*. Perhaps the most obvious example of how the nature of man's relationship with the material world is considered primarily within a broader historical or cultural context can be found in the work of Karl Marx. Marx develops his historical materialism by arguing that the capitalistic economic and political framework which has controlled the production of "the material means of existence" by laborers in recent centuries is responsible for the misery and alienation of the masses. He claims that the historical dialectic eventually leads to a collapse of capitalistic control of the material goods of labor and the establishment of a socialized state in which the value of the products of one's labor is not determined by the wages paid to the laborer or the price the product might bring in a capitalistic economy. Thus, Marx's main concerns are political and economic rather that philosophical.

In Martin Heidegger's well-known treatment of Being and the nature of human existence, he uses the notion of "Daesin," to focus explicitly upon the existence of human beings in relationship to other things. Daesin is "being-there," and human beings are "there" by being grounded ontologically in the world; human existence is explicable only in terms of "Being-in-the-world." "Facticity" is the term that Heidegger uses to capture the particular factual world into which individual human beings are "thrown." The "throwness" of an individual's being includes the historical, geographical, political, cultural, and personal particulars of the situation in which one finds oneself, and it is within this facticity of one's Being that one then acts, according to Heidegger, either authentically or inauthentically. While it may seem initially that Heidegger's notion of facticity is similar to the notion of *species-orientation*, its focus is much more narrow and limited. Heidegger is concerned with how specific individuals are faced with differing historical, geographical, cultural, political, and personal milieus and how being thrown into those different milieus affects an individual's ontological situation. For example, the Being of a slave in Rome in 100 BC is a different sort of "Being-in-the-world" than would be the Being of an aristocrat in seventeenth-century France. The focus of the notion of *species-orientation* is on the more fundamental species level, and it is an attempt to capture the relationship that human beings have as a species to the natural world that then allows for the creation or development of the cultural and political aspects of Heidegger's facticity. Significant contributions to the factical milieu into which an individual is "thrown" are literally man-made and are the results of the unique range of ways in which human beings are able to act upon and be acted upon by the natural environment, i.e., including human *techne*.

William James is another example of the more rare philosopher who focused some attention upon the importance of human interactions with what I have identified here as the malleable, material aspects of the natural world and our understanding of the human *self*. His claim is that the notion of the self is really a composite of several different "selves," including the material self, the social self, the spiritual self, and the pure Ego.[1] The claims that are of most interest here and that are of most importance to the cluster theory of human nature concern what James calls *the material self*. His rationale for the importance of the material self runs something like the following:[2] each person recognizes that his or her physical body occupies a place of special significance in the material world. Whatever the human *self* might eventually be determined to be, there is obviously some sort of intimate involvement with the body to which that self is connected or within which it resides. Thus, each human being *values* and cares about his or her body in a unique way, and indeed, one seems to be more intimately connected to some parts of one's body than to other parts. This recognition of the special place that a person's body occupies in the surrounding physical world provides the initial impetus for understanding how the self is grounded in the material world. James then extends the notion of the *material self* to one's clothes, the members of one's immediate family, one's home, and one's property that is the result of one's wealth and one's labor. For James, the *material self* is thus the result of the interaction of the self with the material world through both the choices that are the result of the exercise of one's "instinctive preferences" and the objects that are the result of ones's investment of time, energy, and physical or mental labor. The loss or destruction of different aspects of one's material self results in a diminution of one's self. While James does not make the explicit distinction between possessions that are acquired and those that are produced by our labor, he does claim that those parts of one's material self that are is "saturated" with one's labor are the most highly valued.

As far as the cluster theory of human nature is concerned, there are several important things to take notice of in James' notion of the *material self*. The most fundamental and important feature of his claim is, at the same time, the most general: to understand who we are and what kind of creatures we are, we human beings must understand something about our relationship to the material world in which we live. Of course, James makes this claim in the context of understanding the notion of the *self*, but it is easy to extrapolate from his observations involving individual selves to the more general notion of human nature. It is hard to imagine, for example, how one might "saturate" one's possessions with one's labor without human intelligence and prehensile hands with opposing thumbs. The politically tainted notion of "labor" must be more fundamentally explained in terms of *species-orientation* and the properties that allow human beings to produce material goods as a result of human *techne*.

In order to capture the contribution of intelligent *techne* to the cluster of properties upon which human nature supervenes, it is necessary and important to distinguish between *the proactive mode of species orientation* and *the reactive mode of species orientation*. The reactive mode of species orientation* has primarily to do with the ways in which the members of a species are acted upon by the *fixed haecceity* of the natural world. Simple hunting and gathering are reactive responses to what is presented by the natural environment. Emphasis upon *the reactive mode of species orientation* encourages attention to theoretical knowledge and does not involve, to any significant extent, the use of intelligent *techne*. For *the reactive mode of species orientation*, it is important for one to *understand* those fixed laws, forces, and patterns of nature in order to act intelligently. By contrast, *the proactive mode of species orientation* has to do with the ways in which members of a species act upon the malleable material aspects of the natural world, i.e., those aspects of the natural world that can be affected by those actions, *given some degree of understanding of the fixed laws, forces, and patterns of the natural world.* Emphasis upon *the proactive mode of species orientation* encourages attention to intelligent *techne.*

While there are obviously some differences between human beings and other animals in terms of the complexity, sophistication, and degree of their respective *reactive modes of the species orientation*, there are, just as obviously, significantly greater differences between human beings and other animals in terms of the complexity, sophistication, and degree of their respective *proactive modes of species orientation.* Other animals acquire or consume different aspects of the material world in ways that are comparable to the ways in human beings acquire and consume. However, no other animal *affects, changes,* or *reconfigures* different aspects of the material world in order to produce "new" objects in any way that is remotely comparable to the ways in which human beings do. Other animals use materials to build beds, nests, burrows, or hives, but no other animal produces a permanent, material culture.

The uniquely human *proactive mode of species orientation* is mainly the product of two factors—human intelligence and prehensile hands with opposing thumbs. Attention will be given to human intelligence in Chapter 8. The focus of attention here is on prehensile hands with opposing thumbs. When one considers all the objects of human material culture produced by intelligent *techne* through the uniquely human *proactive mode of species orientation,* one might easily overemphasize the role of intelligence and overlook the role of prehensile hands with opposing thumbs. However, if one focuses on the fact that the uniquely human *proactive mode of species orientation* is the avenue of the *productive engagement* of human beings with the natural world, it becomes clear that theoretical knowledge or understanding of the natural world is not enough. One must be able to *engage* the natural world physically to affect change in it. This is true of the production of all objects of material culture—from the ancient pyramids to the multifarious aspects of modern, material culture, including such diverse items as paper clips, bobby pins, books, radios, computers, skyscrapers, automobiles, airplanes, rockets, space vehicles, etc. There are also the various products from the fine arts, including the masterpieces of painting, sculpture, music, theater, and architecture. These are all products of intelligent *techne* and represent ways in which human beings have engaged physically with those malleable aspects of the natural world through the *proactive mode of species orientation* in order to affect it and leave their mark upon it.

Human beings are makers, doers, changers. This is the same fundamental quality that explains why primitive peoples drew pictures upon the walls of their caves, or why prisoners in jail write their names on the walls of their cells, or why urban dwellers spray-paint graffiti on sidewalks or in subways, or why lovers carve their initials in trees. And it is the delicacy and precision of the pinching movement made possible by an opposing thumb that can make contact with the finger tips that are responsible for the most instrumentally valuable as well as the most culturally valued objects produced by human *techne*. Indeed, it is exactly this kind of movement that allows for the existence of a written language, discussed in Chapter 9.

The *reactive* and *proactive* modes of species orientation are different ways in which members of a species appropriate what is presented to them by the natural world. In the first case, members of a species merely collect (or otherwise acquire) whatever it is that is provided mainly for the purpose of consumption or other immediate *use*. In the second case, members of a species *use* whatever it is that is provided to produce a new object, the product of *techne*, which is not intended for consumption or other immediate use. There is, to some degree, an aspect of lasting permanence to the products of *techne*. To understand the importance of *techne* to the cluster theory of human nature, it is necessary to understand more thoroughly how the products of *techne* are produced.

Obviously intelligent *techne* must be *intelligent*; so there is no intention here of denying the role of human intelligence in the human *proactive mode of species orientation*; however, intelligent *techne* also is *techne*, i.e., a form of practical knowledge, distinguished from *episteme*, in that it involves the production of some object. *Techne* then is literally a "hands on" form of knowledge, and, as such, requires some attention to the nature of those hands. Human beings without prehensile hands with opposing thumbs, but with human intelligence, would closely resemble brains in a vat. There might be *episteme* in such a situation, but there would not be (nor could there be) very much in the way of *techne*. In Chapter 2, I considered the effect upon human nature of the addition of a third eye to human anatomy; the removal of prehensile hands with opposing thumbs would have an equally serious effect. Arguably, human beings would still be biologically human without prehensile hands with opposing thumbs. In other words, the HAP would still be operative in such a world; however, human nature would be drastically changed.

In other words, the HNAP would not be optimally operative in such a world. Oddly enough then, it is in terms of what might unreflectively seem to be the insignificant anatomical design of the human hand (in the grand scheme of the universe) with its opposing thumb that one can most easily see the HNAP at work. In terms of the biological differences between human beings and other animals, the claim here is that no other anatomical or morphological feature is of any greater importance.

The plasticity of the malleable aspects of the material world varies significantly for different species as the result of several factors as assumed by the notion of *species-orientation*. In the case of human beings, human intelligence and human hands are the two features that are most responsible for the considerably wide range of ways in which human beings, acting in the *proactive mode of species orientation*, are able to affect changes in the natural world. More importantly, *the nature of the changes* affected in the natural world by the production by human beings of various objects of material culture differs from the nature of the changes brought about by species acting in the *reactive mode of species orientation*. Undoubtedly, members of other species of animals are able to affect the world significantly, acting in the *reactive mode of species orientation*. For example, locusts might decimate vast areas of all plant life by consuming it for food, and algae blooms might kill all marine life in vast areas of an ocean by blocking sunlight; however, these effects do not differ from the kind of circumstances that might be produced by natural occurrences. A prairie fire, a flood, a hurricane or an earthquake might just as easily produce similar results. Human beings, acting in the *proactive mode of species orientation* affect the kind of changes in the natural world that are not and cannot be brought about by nature herself. The kind of material objects that are produced by human *techne* are *only* produced by human *techne*.

Furthermore, and perhaps most importantly, the permanent nature of the material objects produced by human *techne* means that these objects can themselves be used to affect further changes in the ways in which human beings act upon and are acted upon by the natural world. The human *species-orientation* sets the natural boundaries of the range of ways in which human interaction with the natural world takes place; however, the material objects produced by human beings, again acting in the *proactive mode of species orientation*, have greatly expanded those natural boundaries. Consider three examples: the production of clothing and footwear and shelters with various means of controlling temperature means that human beings are able to survive and thrive in a considerably wider geographical distribution than any other animal on Earth. Secondly, the production of various vehicles of locomotion means that human beings are able to move about on Earth, above Earth, and beyond Earth to a degree not approximated by any other animal. Thirdly, the invention of instruments that increase the powers and the range of human sense experience (the human *species-sense*), including everything from the most powerful electron microscope to the Hubble Space Telescope, has significantly expanded the range of phenomena with which human beings are able to interact. All of these products are the result of human intelligence and human manual dexterity. There are many other examples.

Human *techne* (literally, the "hands on" practical knowledge of human beings) is thus responsible for producing products that result in a greatly expanded range of ways in which human beings are able to interact with the natural world. Modern man has thus, to a considerable extent, achieved the ambition of Icarus, whatever possible hubris there may be notwithstanding. The unique result of human beings having a wide range of ways of acting through the *proactive mode of species orientation* is thus significantly altered and expanded range of the "natural" ways of acting upon and being acted upon by the natural world determined by the human *species-orientation*. The construction of the aqueducts of ancient Rome, for example, represents a one hundred and eighty degree difference between human beings having to go to where the water is to having the water come to where the human beings are. If one is presented with a river that one wishes to cross on a regular basis and acts through the *reactive mode of species orientation*, one wades or swims across the river. If one acts through the *proactive mode of species-orientation*, one builds a boat or a bridge to cross the river. Whether such changes might be regarded as a good thing or a bad thing, they are a human thing.

This discussion of the importance of the material culture that is produced by human beings acting in the *proactive mode of species orientation* is revealing of an important property that must be included in the cluster of properties upon which human nature supervenes. Several other philosophers and social scientists have emphasized the importance of the fact that human beings are *makers of tools*. Fewer have recognized the importance of the fact that human beings are, for better or worse, simply *makers*. What this discussion of the importance of *techne* and the unique range of activities and the products that are the result of the human *proactive mode of species orientation* reveals is that *Homo sapiens*, *Homo sexus*, and *Homo religiosus* should also be equally recognized as

Homo fabricator, man the maker. As *Homo fabricator*, human beings have more power to influence the permanent nature of the surrounding natural environment than any other creature on Earth. Human beings, through human, intelligent *techne*, have come to the point where we are in the unique position of having the ability to destroy every living thing on Earth and perhaps Earth itself, either slowly through something like global warming or quickly through a nuclear holocaust. On the other hand, human beings, through human, intelligent *techne*, have come to the point where we are in the unique position of having the ability to affect our natural environment to protect the safety and improve the quality of life for other living things on Earth and even the health of Earth itself, which gives a new understanding to what some religious believers call stewardship.

Another important feature about the products of human *techne* is the number of different ways in which human beings *value* those products. Philosophers who have focused their attention upon how human beings value objects have usually been interested in theories of property rights. However, the focus here is not upon the rights of ownership or upon justifying the political protection of private property. Instead, the concern here is simply with the valuing relationship itself and what the importance of that relationship might contribute to understanding human nature. Undoubtedly, human beings value natural kinds, found in nature, including trees, rivers, mountains, plots of land, and precious metals and gems. But the valuing of the products of human *techne* appears to be a characteristic of human beings that gives some thickness to the cluster theory of human nature by distinguishing human beings from other animals—at least by degree.

The examples of the products of human *techne* discussed thus far have all emphasized, or traded upon, the *instrumental value* of such objects. Tools and weapons are examples of objects that are products of human *techne* that are valued instrumentally. Perhaps these were the earliest objects produced by human beings acting in a *proactive mode of species orientation*. The dramatic increase in the sophistication, complexity, and efficiency of the products of *techne* over a relatively short period of time might very well explain what some have called "The Great Leap Forward" during the Pleistocene Period when *Homo erectus* first emerged. Objects with instrumental value—tools and weapons—are the only well-documented examples of items produced by animals other than man acting in the *proactive mode of species orientation*.

For the purpose of identifying the distinctive characteristics of human nature, objects with instrumental value, produced through *techne*, are less interesting since their main purpose is to serve as functional aids to be used to better facilitate acting in the *reactive mode of species orientation*. By using tools and weapons, human beings were and are able to acquire, appropriate, or consume various material aspects of the natural world more effectively, and, to a much more modest degree, some other animals have been known to do the same thing. However, the difference between human beings and other animals is enormous, and the difference lies mainly in the comparative degree to which members of different species act in the *proactive mode of species orientation* versus the *reactive mode of species orientation*. This is why only human beings have produced material culture.

More dramatic differences can be demonstrated between human beings and other animals by considering other kinds of values that human beings attach to the products of *techne*. The main focus here is on different kinds of *attributed* value that human beings place on the products of *techne*. I will postpone consideration of *aesthetic value*, which might be considered an attributed value, until Chapter 9 and will concentrate attention in the rest of this chapter upon what I will call *fetish-value* and *stuff-value*.

Consider first the notion of *fetish-value* since it connects rather directly with the preceding chapter and the notion of *Homo religiosus*. Again, it has been the social scientists—primarily anthropologists and sociologists more so than philosophers—who have been interested in the existence of fetishes in different cultures. However, the peculiar ways in which different peoples have attributed value to fetishes is revealing about human nature. Too use a rather broad definition of "fetish" (one to which some social scientists would want to add some refinement, I am sure), let us say that a fetish is charm, totem, amulet, or other inanimate object to which a person attributes magical or supernatural powers. In what sociologists of religion frequently call "primitive" religions, fetishes are used by magicians, shamans, sorcerers, or witch doctors in various rituals or rites that are intended to influence or control supernatural spirits. Fetishism is closely related to animism, the belief that spirit (or soul) inhabits all forms of matter—humans, other animals, trees, rivers, mountains, etc. While some naturally occurring objects might serve as fetishes, such as stones, blood, or the claws or feathers from animals and birds, the practice most commonly involves the use of objects that are products of some form of *techne*. Fetishism is known to have been practiced in ancient Egypt, and the belief in totems found amongst Native Americans is simply the extension of the belief of the effective range of the magically empowered object from the individual to the clan or tribe.

Some sacred objects are recognized by most modern religions. Questions about the possible exalted status of some material objects and the appropriate veneration of such objects thus still plague modern forms of theism, and the ways in which these questions are answered can serve as a basis for one way of drawing some distinctions between Judaism, Christianity, and Islam. At one end of the spectrum is Roman Catholicism, which recognizes an extensive range of various images, statues, icons, and relics, and at the other end of the spectrum is Islam, which condemns the use of all such objects. The theological differences center around the use of religious icons, relics, and other sacred objects and the sin of idolatry and whether such objects are used in some way to represent God.

Some theologians and sociologists might surely cringe at the broad brush with which I have painted the practice of fetishism and the related use of totems, icons, relics, etc. Undoubtedly, finer distinctions are appropriate and need to be added. However, the importance of this excursion into the sociology of religion is to demonstrate what has been the common human practice, which has occurred often in human history and across different cultures, of attributing to inanimate objects, usually the products of human *techne*, supernatural or magical qualities. Whatever value such objects have is an *attributed value* and constitutes *fetish-value*. Fetishism and the attribution of *fetish-value* is compelling evidence that *Homo sapiens* is also *Homo religiosus* at least partially as the result of being *Homo fabricator*. *Fetish-value* is distinctive in that it is not simply the function of other kinds of value, e.g., intrinsic value or instrumental value. While one might claim that objects of fetishism are instrumentally valuable in that they are thought to have powers to influence either the divine spirits or human events, the objects are also regarded as having exalted status in themselves. Thus, the Ark of the Covenant, for the Jews, was thought to have instrumental value in that it somehow contained the power of God and was thus useful in battle, but it was also thought to be simply a holy thing, in itself, because it contained the tablets upon which, it is believed, Moses deposited the Ten Commandments.

The case was made for considering *Homo sapiens* as *Homo religiosus* in the last chapter. What this examination of *techne* and fetishism reveals is that, in addition to human beings sometimes having what may be regarded as exalted, transcendent experiences accompanied by phenomenological feelings of the sacred or the holy, *material objects* produced by human *techne* are sometimes attributed with the same spiritual or sacred qualities by human beings. Since fetishism requires the production of such material objects by human *techne*, this contribution to the understanding of *Homo religiosus* reveals something of the nature of the causal relations that I have earlier claimed exist amongst the different properties in the cluster of properties upon which human nature supervenes. Just as *Homo sexus* is a function, to some extent, of the biological and anatomical properties of human beings, *Homo religiosus* is a function, to some extent, of *Homo fabricator* and the intelligence and prehensile hands with opposing thumbs necessary to produce the materials objects that result from human *techne*. As indicated earlier, other animals are known to produce some tools and weapons with instrumental value as the result of a primitive form of animal *techne*. In comparison with the tools and weapons produced by human *techne*, e.g., computers and CRUISE missiles, those items produced by other animals are crude, primitive, limited, and unsophisticated. Still, the difference is one of degree, although the difference of degree is one of great magnitude. I know of no evidence from the social sciences that other animals attribute anything resembling *fetish-value* to any objects that are products of animal *techne*.

In addition to *instrumental-value* and *fetish-value*, there are other kinds of value that human beings attach to material objects. Within a particular cultural or economic system, objects are sometimes said to have *monetary-value*, e.g., money or jewelry, a sub-category, perhaps, of *instrumental-value*. Sometimes objects are also regarded as having *intrinsic value* or *aesthetic value*, e.g., the Good, paintings, or sculpture. Some environmental philosophers have argued that some natural objects (such as rivers or forests) have "*natural-value.*" These different kinds of values sometimes overlap and sometimes conflict with each other. I cannot address the relationship of all of these different kinds of value to the cluster theory of human nature here, but I do address the importance of some of these different kinds of value in Chapter 9. The remainder of this chapter is devoted to a consideration of another unique way in which some material objects, nearly always products of human *techne*, are valued by human beings. This way of valuing material objects, which is significantly different from any of the above ways of valuing objects and which has hitherto been neglected by philosophers and social scientists alike, is very revealing to a theory of human nature of the importance of understanding the intricacies of the complicated relationships between human beings and objects in the material world.

The kind of value in question, which is uniquely attributed by human beings to some objects of human *techne*, will be called *stuff-value*. Although this designation might initially disguise the importance of *stuff* for understanding human nature, it is used seriously and advisedly. *Stuff-value* is the result of a relationship between human beings and selective objects produced by human *techne* that is a natural and pre-reflective relationship that produces a unique form of "grounding" of human beings in the natural world. There is a common use of the English word, "stuff," that is usually pejorative and is used to designate an otherwise nondescript collection of relatively worthless physical objects. In this usage, "stuff" is used much like "junk." This use of "stuff" is disarming and misleading. The noun, "stuff," in *stuff-value* is used with a completely different meaning (from the Middle English "stuffe") and conveys a heightened sense of vital importance. According to the *Oxford English Dictionary*, the munitions of an army and the equipment and food necessary for survival, which a soldier took into battle were called "stuffe" as was a person's vital "moveable household property." The use of "stuff" in *stuff-value* is used with this heightened sense of importance. For lack of a more felicitous locution, the phrase "*stuff-value*" is used to capture the elevated sense of perceived vital value that *stuff* holds for a person. A brief examination of the crucial, defining features of *stuff* and *stuff-value* reveals how *stuff-value* is different from the other kinds of value that human beings attach to physical objects and the importance of understanding *stuff-value* to understanding human nature.

An initial feature of *stuff* is one of extreme scarcity, but the scarcity is a self-imposed one. Paradigmatic examples of *stuff-value* involve the attachment that people feel to unique, individual objects, i.e., unique individual objects that are valued in a way such that the value is attributed to that single, specific object, even if other tokens of the same type of object apparently possess very similar or even identical characteristics. *Stuff-value* is usually attached to *this* thing as opposed to *that* thing, even in the cases where *this* and *that* are, for all other purposes indistinguishable, except for being different objects. Compared to *instrumental-value*, for example, if two different hammers are indistinguishable in terms of any of the properties that contribute to their hammering (e.g., size, weight, design, grip, etc.), then there is no instrumental reason to prefer one to the other. However, in the case of *stuff-value*, an object is preferred or valued to another with no relevant, distinguishable differences simply because it is the unique, individual object that it is. Furthermore, in most cases, a person might not be able to identify or specify the *stuff-mak-*

ing quality that a piece of *stuff* possesses that makes it *stuff-valuable*. It might initially seem somewhat unusual, but people frequently apparently value an object as *stuff* without really knowing what makes that object so special. The explanation for this is that *stuff-value* is a Gestalt value—an all or nothing value—that is a function of the total "thisness" or the total individuality of an object. There may be some comparison between the way in which a person attaches to an object of *stuff* and with "love at first sight" where a person loves another person immediately and pre-cognitively. Both require an attribution of value to the object or person in question based upon an immediate, Gestalt experience of the object or person, i.e., the attachment is simply to *that* object or *that* person, *that* one. Examples of *stuff* might include a young child's attachment to a toy or, more famously, a blanket, or a person's attachment to a favorite piece of clothing or a hat. *Stuff* might include other things as a hairpin, a watch, a coffee mug, a book, a pocketknife, a chair or some other piece of furniture, or something else like, in my own case, a high school baseball glove.

Stuff is valued in a manner that is disproportionate to any utilitarian or monetary value that an object might have. *Stuff-value* is an *attributed* value or an *intentional* value because the person develops a special relationship with an object by attributing a special value to that object and elevating that object to the status of *stuff*. An object with *stuff-value* may, of course, have instrumental value or monetary value as well. A single object might be valued in a number of different ways; however, the intentional or attributed value of *stuff* is in addition to and independent of any utilitarian, monetary, or other kind of value that the object might have. A very valuable piece of jewelry might be *stuff* as might a very useful tool, but the value that makes such items *stuff* is independent of whatever other kind of value these items might have.

There is also an obvious comparison to be made between objects that have *stuff-value* and those that have *fetish-value*. Objects with *fetish-value* are attributed with special magical powers that are believed to have the ability of influencing or controlling the spirits or gods. But what sort of power is attributed to an object as the result of that object being assigned *stuff-value*? To answer this question, it is necessary to understand more fully the importance of *stuff* to human nature.

Stuff is particularly fragile and vulnerable to damage, loss, or destruction. The vulnerability of *stuff* is accentuated since the attachment is usually to a unique individual object that cannot be replaced if loss or destroyed. This feature is perhaps most easily illustrated in the case of other living things about which we care. If a pet or a person whom a person loves deeply leaves or dies, seldom can consolation be found in the fact that there are other pets or people around who are very similar. Similarly, by assigning *stuff-value* to objects, human beings commit themselves to an important and intimate relationship of caring about particular aspects of the material world that extends beyond other forms of value that material objects might have. And caring about *stuff* makes one vulnerable in a similarly important and intimate manner. Thus, caring about *stuff* makes a person "vested" in the physical world in much the same way as caring about other people and/or pets does. One becomes especially vulnerable to loss since the loss of *stuff*, like the loss of a loved one or a pet, is a loss that cannot be replaced. Some people have similar attachments to unspoiled rivers or forests or other parts of nature.

An object to which a human being attributes *stuff-value* is usually a one-of-a-kind item (or minimally, an extremely rare item). When a human being is attached to *stuff*, he or she must invest time and energy in caring for it and protecting it. Human beings do care about other kinds of things, of course, but caring about ordinary property seems to be very different. A miser might care for his gold, but if it is lost, it is possible to replace it. Similarly, a carpenter might care about his hammer, but if it is lost, it too might be replaced with one just like it. One might certainly suffer some economic or psychological loss and/or damage if one loses property in some fashion, but the notion that a person can be compensated for the loss of property is a long-lived, tried and true one. In most countries, for example, major social institutions (e.g., insurance companies and tort law) are built upon this notion. The fact that insurance policies and tort law usually explicitly exclude special, "sentimental" or "personal" value indicates that, on some level, the special value of *stuff* is recognized. Having and caring about *stuff* is an important aspect of what it means to be fully human in this world. Having *stuff connects* human beings to the physical world in a unique and intimate manner that is not captured by the possession of property or by the use of tools, weapons, or other implements with instrumental value. By extrapolating from *stuff-value*, one can come to understand more fully how human beings value a specific location, i.e., a "home" or "a place."

Earlier, I suggested that human beings attribute a certain power to *stuff* in a way that is somewhat comparable to the way in which human beings attribute power to fetishes. We are now in a better position to understand exactly what that power is. The *instrumental-value* of tools, weapons, and other objects produced through *techne* is a function of objective and independent factors. A tool or weapon is instrumentally valuable only if it *works*, i.e., only if it functions in such a way to perform whatever purpose for which it was made; however, whether such an object works satisfactorily is determined by the particular form of *haecceity*—the *thisness* or *come-up-againstness*—of the natural world against which, or in the face of which, the object is supposed to work. The natural world thus presents constraints upon how instrumental value of material objects comes about and determines how well such objects work to accomplish their intended purposes. One cannot simply *attribute instrumental-value* to a material object. It either works, or it does not work. Human history is replete with attempts to create material objects with *instrument-value* that have failed. One might argue that much of the "advancement" of human beings has been as the result of figuring out how to produce, through human *techne*, "bigger and better" material objects (e.g., machines) with greater *instrumental-value* to accomplish "bigger and better" tasks in the face of such *haecceity*.

Fetish-value and *stuff-value* are different kinds of value. The *haecceity*—the *thisness* or *come-up-againstness*—of the natural world presents no constraints on *fetish-value* or *stuff-value*. *Fetish-value* is usually the result of a group of human beings—a clan or a tribe—assigning value to an object as the result of certain socially-held beliefs. *Stuff-value* is highly individualistic and is nearly always the result of the imposition of value upon a material object by a single individual by an act of volition. By assigning *stuff-value* to an object, human beings are thus able to autonomously *create* value in the natural world. The result is something such as, "This thing is important and valuable because I say so!" or "I will this thing to be valuable so it is valuable!" Imposing *stuff-value* is raw, unmitigated human volition at work. Creating *stuff-value*, thus anchors an individual in the material world in a unique way that results in a keen sense of belonging and identification with one's surroundings. Some material aspects of the natural world may be alien or even threatening, but not so with objects with *stuff-value*. There are feelings of ergonomic comfort and kinesthetic familiarity that accompany one's associations with *stuff* along with a heightened sense of belonging to or being vested in the material world. With one's *stuff*, one can relax. One is secure. One belongs. One is at one with the physical world. At the other end of the spectrum, is the feeling of alienation from the physical world that is akin to the sensation of tilting back too far in a chair and beginning to fall backwards—a phenomenologically disturbing feeling of being "out of touch," "out of control," or "out of place" in the physical world. *Stuff-value*, after all, is something that the individual has created through an individual act of volition. The *creation* of *stuff-value* is one way of understanding how human beings come to be creatures-in-the-world, i.e., part of human beings being the kind of creatures that we are is to be vested in the natural world in certain ways. *Homo sapiens*, *Homo sexus*, *Homo fabricator*, and *Homo religiosus*, is also, to some extent, *Homo creator*.

The recognition of the importance of *stuff-value* and *Homo creator* adds a new dimension to the notion of *species-orientation*. Through the *proactive mode of species-orientation* human beings appropriate certain malleable aspects of the natural world to create material objects to which value is then attributed by a completely autonomous act of volition. According to top-down, essentialist theories of human nature as Stoicism or Christianity, the attachment to and valuing of material objects are actually contrary to the real, spiritual aspect of human nature. In contrast with those views, the cluster theory of human nature embraces the different ways in which human beings come to be "creatures-in-the-world." Acting in the uniquely human *proactive mode of species orientation*, the production of objects through human *techne*, and the attribution of *stuff-value* (and *fetish-value*) by autonomous acts of volition are all important contributions to the unique pattern of ways in which human beings act upon and are acted upon by the natural world. To a significant extent it is this uniquely human reaction to the *haecceity* of the natural world that makes us the kind of creatures that we are with the kind of nature that we possess. Arguably, the uniquely human *proactive mode of species orientation* is a function of several factors, including a human s*pecies-sense* and a human *species-sensory-integration*, but no factors are more important than human intelligence and prehensile hands with opposing thumbs. Without these two factors, human *techne* would not exist and the human *proactive mode of species orientation* would be drastically different and severely more limited. Human nature, as we know it now and as described by the cluster theory, would also be different. It is easy to imagine a possible world in which the HAP is operative and where creatures that are biologically human exist but with no human *techne*; it is much more difficult to imagine a possible world in which HNAP is operative and where creatures that are biologically human exist but with no human *techne*. The next step is to examine the nature and importance of the *intelligence* that is a part of human *intelligent techne*.

Notes

1. William James, *The Principles of Psychology* (New York: Dover Publications, 1950), Volume I, Chapter X, p. 292. Original copyright, 1890, Henry Holt & Co.
2. *Ibid.*, 292ff.

8

The Human Brain and Human Nature

An astute reader at this point might complain, with some justification, that there has been a large elephant in the room that has not been recognized or commented upon. The elephant in the room of human nature is the human brain. In fact, the brain has recently come to be so significant in terms of understanding human nature that, for many, it now completely dwarfs everything else in the room, i.e., every other factor used to understand or explain human nature. While there is no denying the significance of the contribution of the human brain to the cluster of properties upon which human nature supervenes, as the earlier chapters have shown, it is the combination of a cluster of properties that produces the causal nexus necessary for human nature to exist and not a single factor. Undeniably, in the past few decades, more progress has been made by neuroscientists in understanding the human brain, its functions, and importance than perhaps in any other scientific field related to theories of human nature. One might justifiably say that the last few decades of the twentieth century to the present moment are to neuroscience what the last few decades of the nineteenth century to the present moment are to evolutionary theory.

Neuroscience is a young science, but its revelations to date (as well as its implications for the understanding of human nature) have been truly revolutionary. Still, since, according to the cluster theory, brain morphology and activity, no matter how important, are simply additional properties upon which human nature supervenes, it is necessary to examine and explain how the human brain and its functions are related to the other properties in the cluster discussed thus far in this book. The nature and function of the human brain are causally connected to other properties in the cluster of properties from which human nature emerges, and it is important to sort out and clarify the nature of those causal connections.[1]

It is understandable why some neuroscientists may have made exaggerated claims about the importance of the human brain. It has both a rather odd and, at the same time, an extraordinarily important position and role in the human body. Under normal conditions, unlike the heart or lungs, it does not move. It produces no secretion, unlike the liver or spleen. It provides no structural assistance, unlike bones or muscles. What it does do is function as a powerful dynamo in the body by generating electrical, neuron firings. And, potentially, it does this in the trillions of trillions. With as many as a hundred billion nerve cells in the average human brain and with each of these individual cells having thousands of connections to other nerve cells, there are more potential connections amongst the nerve cells in the human brain, which number in the thousands of trillions, than there are atoms in the universe. Thus, some scientists would say that the human brain is the most complex object known to exist. However, this unique complexity of the brain notwithstanding, while the brain is a significant and unique contributor to the causal nexus created by the combination of properties within the cluster of properties that subvene human nature, it will become clear during the course of this chapter that it is still that complete causal nexus upon which human nature is dependent and not simply any one member of the cluster of properties. It will also become clear that the brain, like the other members of the cluster, is both a contributor to and a product of this causal nexus. Thus, it both shapes and is shaped by those other properties and the causal nexus created by the confluence of those properties.

The first feature of the human brain that must be considered is its size. Comparative morphology indicates that the human brain is not only large, but, when measured as a ratio of average brain size to average body size, the human brain is seven times larger than the brain in any other animal known to exist or to have existed. Such an anomaly in the natural world is, one might say, "mind-boggling" and requires some sort of explanation. Unfortunately, although neuroscientists have made enormous advances in explaining how the brain functions (an issue that will be addressed momentarily), significantly less progress has been made in explaining *how* and *when* and *why* the human brain came to be the size that it is with the design and complexity that it has. While the answers may not be of the nature to satisfy neuroscientists or anthropologists, the cluster theory does provide a framework within which these questions can be answered in a very general fashion.

For present purposes, the main focus is not upon brain size *per se* but upon two directly related consequences of brain size. The first consequence of the unusually large size of the human brain that is particularly significant for the cluster theory is the process of birth and maturation whereby an individual human being comes to possess such a brain. Focusing temporarily just on the size of the human brain, given a naturalistic view to which the cluster theory is committed, some plausible explanation must be given for the benefit of its size since that size comes at some significant evolutionary costs. A larger brain requires a larger skull, and a larger skull means more difficult child birth with greater risk and more potential harm to both baby and mother. A larger brain also must be protected, sustained, and nourished, which means a very heavy demand upon an individual's blood supply and calories. A significant percentage of what one eats goes to feed one's brain. Brains are also very fragile and require a carefully balanced chemical environment within which to operate properly. To maintain this balance the brain produces the *cerebrospinal fluid* to encase the brain and the entire central nervous system. Producing, circulating and maintaining the *cerebrospinal fluid* adds another degree of complexity and vulnerability to the individual human being.

Directly related to the size of the human brain is the fact that it does not develop completely before birth, else the skull would be so large that birth would be impossible without drastic changes in the pelvic structure and the birth canal of women—to say nothing of the major inconvenience and added vulnerability of a significantly extended period of pregnancy. Human babies thus have a slow and prolonged development after birth, much of which is devoted to the development of the brain and the protective skull. New born human infants are underdeveloped physiologically also. They cannot locomote to find food or avoid predators or even cling to their mothers for protection.

The extent to which the underdevelopment of human babies and their corresponding dependency are related to the properties in the cluster of properties upon which human nature supervenes is a topic hotly debated by social scientists. Some comparison with the newborns of other species is informative. The newborn offspring of other species are also sometimes frequently underdeveloped, and nature has evolved various mechanisms for ensuring the protection and nurturing of those offsprings to perpetuate the continuation of the species. Perhaps most illustrative are the circumstances that surround the newborn of the American opossum, a marsupial. When the female opossum gives birth after only thirteen days of gestation, the newborn are *tiny* and significantly underdeveloped, including being completely blind. Several can fit into a teaspoon. The babies immediately crawl into the mother's pouch where each one latches onto a nipple and suckles the mother's milk for a period of up to sixty days without releasing the nipple or venturing from the protection of the pouch. AND, from the standpoint of natural selection, only the thirteen fastest and strongest of the newborn manage to survive, i.e., the ones that are able to secure and defend one of the mother's thirteen nipples. After finally venturing from the mother's pouch, the opossum babies still cling to their mother's back for an additional month or longer while acclimating to the physical world.

Human babies are similarly underdeveloped, dependent, and vulnerable, and nature has not provided a *physiological* adaptation that is, in any way, similar to that of the opossum, for their survival. The argument in the next chapter is that human families and other *cultural* mechanisms provide the means for ensuring the survival of human babies. The present point is that the underdevelopment at birth of what is the unusually large human brain and skull exacts a significantly high cost—both in terms of the cost to an individual's time, energy, and resources and in terms of the social cost to parents, family, and associated relatives. All of these costs include an increased, potential vulnerability to predators both to the individual human infant and to the family, and whereas the development of the newborn opossum consumes a high percentage of the mother's resources, it is only for a total period of approximately three months, and in less than a year, the newborns have reached adulthood and are ready to mate. In contrast, the newborn human infant is dependent for many years, and the final stage of the development of the human brain, which concerns *formal operations*, i.e., abstract reasoning, is now thought by neurophysiologists and developmental psychologists not to be completed until at least age eleven and possibly later. Obviously, a larger brain must have some *significant* benefit to come at such a high cost both to the individual and the species. There may very well also be *benefits* that accrue to the individual and family from prolonged human infancy. These potential benefits are explored in the next chapter.

The second consequence of the unusually large human brain that is of importance to the cluster theory of human nature is the corresponding complexity of the human brain. Although it may not be regarded as "hard" neuroscience, a safe assumption for the purposes here is that increased complexity of brain function is directly proportional to increased brain size. In other words, the greater the number of brain cells in a brain, the greater the number of potential complex functions that brain can perform. Given those hundred billion nerve cells in the average human brain, all of the possible connections amongst those nerve cells, and the trillions of trillions of potential neuron firings of which the brain is capable, the human brain has enormous potential for extraordinarily complex operations. There are at least two disclaimers that must be added to this claim. First of all, one must assume that the brain is functioning normally, and secondly, one must allow for the fact that different brain cells are *specialized* to perform different functions; so the *variety* of different brain cells is also correlated with the overall complexity of brain functions. The first assumption is simply part of a general *ceteris paribus* condition; the second will be addressed later in this chapter.

In the following discussion, as the role of the complexity of the human brain and its operations in the cluster of properties upon which human nature supervenes is explored (along with the resulting causal nexus that arises amongst those properties), it must be remembered that scientists and philosophers disagree about many of the specific claims. In particular, philosophers disagree about what is now called "the hard problem"—the explanation of human consciousness. I do not intend to discuss all of the different theories about the functioning of the human brain or consider the relative advantages and disadvantages of the different explanations of human consciousness. I do intend to develop and defend a theory that is consistent with the cluster theory of human nature. Also, since the subject of this chapter is the *human* brain, I will ignore the claim made earlier that non-human animals may possess human nature to some degree and focus attention mainly on human beings and the contribution made by the *human* brain to the cluster of properties and the causal nexus that exists amongst those properties from which human nature emerges.

One factor about which scientists do agree and about which the scientific data are not vague or indeterminate is the fact that in the natural world greater complexity arises only from lesser complexity. According to top-down views of human nature, the great complexity of the human brain, arguably the greatest complexity in the known natural world, would have been derived from some "higher," other-worldly perfection, i.e., a creator or some other metaphysically distinct source. Such a claim accounts for the complexity of the human brain as deriving from some even greater complexity and thus goes against every other known process in the natural world whereby greater complexity is derived from lesser complexities. On the basis of the best available evidence from the natural and social sciences, the complexity of the human brain is evidence to support the bottom-up, cluster theory of human nature. Any top-down explanation of that complexity amounts to an arbitrary, *deus ex machina* claim. Thus, the complex human brain is best understood as the evolutionary product of a simpler brain, a *protobrain*, that was the product of a ganglia of nerve cells, that was the product of a smaller groups of nerve cells. In this regard the complexity of the human brain is no different than the complexity of the human eye, i.e., each is the product of a very long, slow, and gradual evolutionary process and development from more simple versions.

It is not as though this is an easy, obvious matter to determine. Both Charles Darwin and Alfred Russel Wallace struggled with the question of how something as complex as the human brain could be accounted for on the basis of evolution by natural selection. Wallace abandoned natural selection as a general theory adequate for accounting for the development of the human brain since he regarded the brain as oversized and over-developed, i.e., too complex and too sophisticated, to be accounted for simply in terms of providing whatever abilities might have been necessary for survival. He thought that the "higher level" of human abilities, e.g., language, music, mathematics, and moral and aesthetic sensibilities, were evidence of the intrusion of a "Higher Intelligence," i.e., God, into the natural process of evolution for more "nobler ends" than those that could be accounted for by natural selection. Wallace thus abandoned a bottom-up explanation for the complexity of the human brain in favor of a top-down explanation. At the time, only Darwin stuck with the bottom-up, naturalistic process of natural selection as an explanation for the human brain although, at the time, he could not come up with an adequate explanation for how this occurred.

Working within a bottom-up, naturalistic framework, what does the cluster theory of human nature have to say about the importance of the size and complexity of human brain to human nature? And, given the apparent over-development and complexity of the human brain, is it possible to explain that level of development and complexity as a result of completely natural processes without resorting, as Wallace did, to a *deux ex machina*, top-down principle of some sort that relies upon the introduction of a separate, distinct metaphysical realm? Given that the human brain is not only the largest relative to body size of any brain of any animal known to have existed but also given that complexity of brain functions is directly proportional to brain size (and the number of possible connections amongst brain cells), it follows obviously that the benefit of the larger brain must be found in that increased complexity of brain functions. A consideration of the benefit of brain size thus quickly leads to a consideration of the benefit of those complex brain functions. However, the question immediately arises: Which of the complex brain functions might justify the size of the human brain and its biological costs? The brain must be responsible for some trait that was selected for in the evolutionary process. It is at this point that scientists disagree, and the hard anthropological and neuroscientific data become more vague and opinions become more speculative. While it might seem obvious that creatures with complex brain functions would have some competitive advantage in their dealings with their environments, it is not clear exactly which of those functions might be responsible for that competitive advantage, and it is not obvious, without some explanation, how the advantage, whatever it is, is worth the evolutionary cost.

The most important point to be made initially is that the present interest in the importance of the human brain to the cluster theory of human nature is not confined to the narrow limits of human biology. Both Darwin and Wallace were interested in accounting for the survival and adaptation of *Homo sapiens* as a biological species. So likewise are contemporary biologists. The cluster theory maintains that a distinction must be made between being biologically human and having human nature although, at the same time, the cluster theory maintains that the properties upon which human nature supervenes can be accounted for in term of methodological naturalism. But to which naturally arising properties or traits might the "oversized" human brain be attributed? Some biologists have insisted that the enlargement of the human brain was precipitated by increased sensory input while some anthropologists have attributed that enlargement to the bipedalism of *Homo sapiens*, or the production and use of tools, or to increased social behavior such as the development of language or familial relationships. According to the cluster theory, it is a mistake to try and identify any single ability or trait that accounts for whatever adaptive advantage the human brain might provide for human beings. The correct answer is none of the above and all of the above. It is necessary to consider "the big picture" to understand the role the brain has played both in the survival and adaptive advantage of *Homo sapiens* and in creating the causal nexus amongst the individual properties that allows human nature to emerge.

To understand the development of the human brain and the importance of that development to the cluster theory of human nature, it is important to be reminded of a point made in Chapter 3. Development and evolution of a species are the result of the *interaction* of the members of that species with their environment. The particular natural environment within which and in interaction with which human beings have developed is thus largely responsible not only for the biological features that characterize *Homo sapiens* but also for the properties in the cluster of properties upon which human nature supervenes. This fact holds especially strongly for the development and evolution of the size and complexity of the human brain. To understand the role of the human brain in the emergence of human nature, it is not necessary to introduce any new properties into the cluster of properties upon which human nature supervenes or to wait upon more definite results of neurophysiological research. It is necessary to explain the conditions for the existence of those properties on a "higher" level. While the size and complexity of the human brain (and the number and variety of specialized brain cells) are not *sufficient* to explain the existence of the properties in the cluster of properties and the causal nexus that exists amongst those properties upon which human nature supervenes, they are *necessary* to explain the existence of those properties and that nexus. However, the necessity is a functional necessity and not a biological one.

While the nineteenth-century model of a mechanized human body may be outmoded, it is still useful to think of those trillions and trillions of neuron firings that take place in the brain as the workings of a powerful, energy-generating dynamo that provides the efficacy for the proper functioning of those mechanisms that allow human beings to experience and interact with and our environment—thus allowing human beings to be acted upon by and to act upon that environment. The human brain thus plays a necessary role in consolidating those properties into a *cluster* of inter-related properties, i.e., the human brain is responsible for organizing the individual properties into a related whole by providing the mechanisms that create the *causal nexus* that exists amongst those properties. The human brain thus *unifies* the various properties in the cluster of properties that subvene human nature by providing the mechanisms whereby the *interconnections* amongst those individual properties are established—thereby allowing those interactions amongst the individual properties to produce the causal nexus from which human nature emerges. It is this process that creates the human *species-orientation*.

If the cluster of properties upon which human nature supervenes is analogous to a symphony orchestra, as suggested in Chapter 2, then the function of the human brain may be thought of as comparable to the role of the conductor who *orchestrates* the individual instruments and sections of instruments into something of an organized, united, controlled, regulated, interrelated, smoothly functioning, *synergetic whole*. Just as the multilayered theme of a symphony is produced by the actions of the individual musicians playing significantly different instruments under the direction of the conductor, human nature emerges from the instantiation of the different individual properties under the direction and control of the brain. And just as the conductor ensures that the individual instruments are in tune and each section of instruments is playing the proper notes, at the proper tempo, and at the proper volume, the brain controls the proper functioning of the different behaviors that subvene human nature.

Consider, for example, the role that the human brain plays in human sense experience, human *species-sense*, *species-sensory-integration*, and the resulting *species-orientation*. Specifically, since humans are vision-dominant, consider, for example, the role of the human brain in the case of vision since it is impossible to consider each of the senses in the same detail. Across the animal kingdom, there are many different sensory systems that are photosensitive that result in different organisms being stimulated by light in different ways. These various different photosensitive systems, including the "primitive" systems of flatworms, the compound eyes of insects, and the differing systems of invertebrates and vertebrates, are detailed in most introductory college biology texts. Many animals are *sensitive* to light, but in the case of human beings and other vertebrates, whose eyes famously function like cameras to capture detailed images of the sensory environment, that sensitivity reaches unparalleled heights in the natural world. Vision is an enormously complicated process of interaction between an organism and its environment. In Chapter 3, I have emphasized some of the complexities for which that environment is responsible, and in Chapter 5, I have emphasized the role that sensory experience plays in creating the *species-sense* and resulting *species orientation* of different animals. Each separate sense of each species, which collectively form the *species-sense* for each species, is the result of enormously complicated developmental and anatomical details in the organisms. In humans, the development and role of the various parts of the eye—the cornea, iris, pupil, lens, and retina (with its rods and cones made photosensitive by rhodopsin)—are the subject of much detailed study of human biology.

Less well-known, because until relatively recently less was known about it, is the rather crucial role that the brain plays in human vision.

That role actually begins in the eye itself since, during embryonic development, the highly photosensitive tissue of the human retina is supplied by the brain, which allows the retina actually to begin the neural processing of the visual stimuli before sending them along the optic nerve, through the thalamus, to the visual cortex in the occipital lobe of the brain. The currently often-used comparison of the brain to a computer's central processing unit seems entirely appropriate so far as the brain's role in sense experience is concerned since the brain is far from a passive receptor of the axons arriving from the retina. The information from the two retinas is received by clusters of cells in the occipital cortex—different ones of which are responsible for interpreting different features of the visual field, e.g., color, size, movement, depth, and three-dimensional shape. A properly integrated visual sense experience involving all of these elements requires a properly functioning occipital cortex. The bits of visual information received from the eyes resemble something like a jigsaw puzzle where the pieces have to be assembled by the brain to create a properly integrated, three-dimensional picture of the whole. Color, shape, depth, and movement have to be "bound" together properly to create a proper interpretation of and synthesis of the information received from the two eyes.

Both the neurophysiology of the human brain and its neuro-chemical processes involved in this binding process are much more complicated than anything that can be described here, and it is also this binding function of the brain that is one of the still most mysterious and least understood aspects of the brain. Even minor damage to the occipital cortex, either from disease or injury, can seriously interrupt the process of integration of the axons arriving from the eyes, resulting in the loss of a smooth, "normal," interpretation of one's visual field. As the examples of the anomalies that result from extreme visual agnosia, including prosopagnosia, i.e., face-blindness (discussed in Chapter 5), illustrate, "normal" human vision requires the proper *species-sensory-integration* of one's visual sensory experiences by a properly functioning brain. There are many other anomalies resulting from the breakdown in this process of integration that illustrate this point, including cortical blindness (in which a person "sees" but does not process visual stimuli) and synesthesia (in which stimuli from different senses are mixed, e.g., colors and smells). Of course, *sensory-integration* is not an "all or nothing" process. It can occur to varying degrees across a wide spectrum some range of which is usually characterized as "normal."

What all of this emphasizes is the tremendously important active role of integration that the brain plays in human vision. The same is true, of course, of the remaining four senses. Unlike members of some other species, a human being does not hear, smell, taste, or feel without a properly functioning brain. This is not the place for a detailed biological description of all of the human sensory systems; however, it is the place to make some generalized observations about the importance of those detailed features and the interactive role of the human brain with those systems in producing the human *species-sense, species-sensory-integration,* and the resulting *species-orientation* for human beings. Integration must take place for each of the individual senses as well as the collection of different senses. These are the operations that are crucial for producing many of the properties in the cluster of properties upon which human nature supervenes. For example, consider human hearing. Sound waves traveling through the air arrive at the auditory canal of the ear and are channeled to the tympanic membrane (the eardrum) where they set off a series of vibrations that then travel through the inner ear where the mechanical vibrations are converted by the hair cells of the organ of Corti into electrical impulses that then are then transmitted by the auditory nerve through the thalamus to the auditory cortex of the brain. Again, the brain is not simply a passive receptor of the messages sent through the auditory canal. The brain actually sends messages back to the hair cells on the basilar membrane to help fine tune their sensitivity and to amplify certain sounds. This process allows humans to make very fine distinctions amongst different sounds.

This summarized description of human hearing is very interesting biologically, but what is its importance for the cluster theory of human nature? The point has been made earlier that no single human sense is particularly outstanding in the animal world, and the same is certainly true of human hearing. There are animals with no sense of hearing at all that is comparable to the human sense of hearing, and there are animals whose highly developed sense of hearing, when measured in range or sensitivity, is significantly greater than that of humans.

When the role of the human brain in hearing is considered, however, human hearing begins to take on a more unique nature, and certain aspects of this unique nature are significant contributors to the cluster of properties upon which human nature supervenes. Of primary concern here is not simply the *range* of different sounds that humans are capable of hearing. As noted earlier, the "normal" average human range of approximately 20-20,000 Hz is hardly considered an exceptional one in the animal world. There is the additional obvious feature of human beings having two ears that allow human beings to determine the direction of the source of the sound being heard, but this feature is shared, sometimes to a remarkable degree, by other animals. There is, however, the fact, mentioned earlier, that human beings are able to make very fine distinctions about different aspects of different sounds. Some have claimed that when both subtle changes in the frequency of a human voice (a measurement of the voice's vibrations) and volume are considered, the human ear can detect as many as 400,000 different tones.[2]

Perhaps the most distinctive characteristic of human hearing, this feature is the result of the complexity and plasticity of the human brain, mentioned earlier, which allows different parts of the brain to process different aspects of the sounds and the different patterns of sounds arriving from the ears through the auditory nerve. Illustrative of this specialization and plasticity of the human brain in its processing of sounds is the significantly unique way in which human beings are able to experience music. When the initial stimulus arrives in the auditory cortex, it is divided into tone, rhythm, timbre, melody, and harmony, and different parts of the brain process these different components of the sound. Additionally, the emotional impact of music is processed by the limbic system of the brain. All of which means that human beings are able to experience sophisticated aesthetic reactions to music as well as make subtle distinctions that make oral communication with human language possible as discussed below.

Other animals are able to produce and experience what is appropriately regarded as music. For example, bird songs are commonly distinguished from bird calls, and humpback whales are known to "sing" their whale songs. It is not then that human beings are unique in the animal world in being able to produce and experience music. However, it is the case that the unique anatomical features of human beings as well as the highly complex, specialized, and plastic structure of the human brain allow human beings to both produce and experience music on a level not approximated by any other known living animal. Like the other properties, discussed earlier in this book, which collectively create the causal nexus in the cluster of properties upon which human nature supervenes, human production and experience of music is distinguished from the same abilities in other animals not by a difference of kind but a difference of significant degree of sophistication and complexity that approaches a difference of kind.

A consideration of the relationship between music and mathematics is illustrative of this point. Since Pythagoras, philosophers as well as musicians have been aware of the mathematically structured intervals of the keys, octaves, chords, and scales in music. Whether the metaphysical claims made by Pythagoras about the mathematical structure of the universe and cosmic harmony are correct or not is not at issue here and are still debatable; however, the relationships between mathematics and music are demonstrable and indisputable. While other animals might be taught to paw or peck to count or even add simple numbers, no other animal has a demonstrated mathematical ability that closely resembles the mathematical ability of man. Such a mathematical ability arguably underlies the ability of human beings to produce material culture (discussed in the previous chapter and below), including music. The brain thus provides the "brain power" for the production and experience of music by processing sounds in the auditory cortex, the right and left temporal lobes, and the limbic system and by performing the mathematical operations in the inferior parietal lobe and the intraparietal sulcus.

Even human infants are now known to be able to count and recognize different quantities of objects, and mathematical reasoning obviously has survival value and was selected for at some point in human evolution. The cluster theory of human nature has no difficulty in admitting that other animals may have elementary musical abilities, but nothing that is produced by any other known animal approaches the intricacy of the orchestral scores for symphonies or concerti or the apotheosis of emotion in Bach's *Saint Matthew's Passion* or the grandeur of spirit in the Fourth Movement of Beethoven's *Ninth Symphony*.

The focus in this chapter has been on the role of the brain in the more abstract aspects of music and hearing, but the ability of the brain to control bodily movements, including especially, the precise and delicate movements of the hands with their opposing thumbs, should not be minimized in accounting for the ability of human beings to produce and use musical instruments that, in turn, allows human beings to produce and experience music. This important role of the brain in controlling motor functions is discussed in detail later in this chapter.

The role of the human brain in the production and experience of speech is similar to the one described for music, but, at the same time, it is very different. The concern here is not with linguistic ability or the development of human language as such, although it is admittedly difficult to separate the topics of human speech and human language. A more detailed account of human *language* and human linguistic ability (or what Noam Chomsky called the "language organ") follows in the next chapter. Thus, the focus here is specifically upon the spoken word, *speech*, and the brain's ability to produce and process certain sounds in such a fashion to make human speech and oral communication possible. While human speech does not *constitute* human language or linguistic ability, it is necessary for human language. It is difficult to imagine a species of beings who are otherwise biologically identical to human beings but without the ability to speak or use otherwise use sophisticated oral communication.

The cluster of properties upon which human nature supervenes is not simply a collection of individual, discrete properties like peas in a pod or marbles in a bag. The properties are causally related in such a way to form a causal nexus from which human nature then emerges. Pulling one string thus threatens to unravel the entire fabric, and eliminating one property threatens to destroy the causal nexus. Thus, the fundamental position of human speech in the cluster of properties that subvene the causal nexus upon which human nature supervenes must be examined.

Similarly to what was revealed in the account of music, the human brain is able to both produce and process sounds that constitute human speech as the result of the highly specialized areas of the brain. Speech is produced and controlled by an area at the junction of the frontal and temporal lobes called *Broca's area*. The ability to process, i.e., *understand*, speech is the function of a different, highly specialized part of the brain known as *Wernicke's area* at the junction of the temporal, parietal, and occipital lobes. Because of the lateralization of linguistic ability in human beings, this usually occurs in the left hemisphere for right-handed people, and in the right hemisphere or in both hemispheres for left-handed people.

Since *Broca's area* and *Wernicke's area* are responsible for different aspects of speech, some dysfunction is possible if both areas are not operating properly in a person simultaneously. Damage to *Broca's area*, resulting from disease or injury, can prevent a person's ability to articulate words, while similar damage to *Wernicke's area*, frequently resulting from strokes, can prevent a person from *understanding* language. This illustrates how human speech and human language are integrally related. Human speech consists not simply in issuing certain vocables, but in issuing certain vocables with particular meanings that require *comprehension*. This account of the brain's role in the production and processing of speech is commonly accepted neuroscience.

Of importance for present purposes is the highly specialized roles that these different areas of the brain have in human speech. The roles of the parts of the brain involved in human hearing have already been explained. The human ear (i.e., the human sense of hearing) and the human voice are so closely related and adapted to each other that it is unlikely that one could exist without the other.[3] Along with those areas of the brain involved in hearing, *Broca's area* and *Wernicke's area* of the brain, operating together, are responsible for the uniquely human ability of speech. When compared to other animals, whether this uniqueness is to be accounted for as simply a quantitative difference (i.e., a difference of degree) or a qualitative difference (i.e., a difference of kind) is still hotly debated by linguists and social scientists. For the cluster theory of human nature, the quantitative difference (a difference in degree of complexity) alone is sufficient to explain the uniquely rich, diverse, detailed, abstract, and sophisticated level of communication that is the result of human speech. Whether other animals such as bees, parrots, or chimpanzees are able to communicate by dances, vocables, or grunts or whether they have a "language" is inconsequential to the cluster theory of human nature. While the cluster theory of human nature has no reticence in admitting that other animals have forms of oral communication, no other known form of communication by any other animal approaches the nature of spoken human communication. Some aspects of the diversity, abstraction, detail, and sophistication of human speech are the direct result of those same features in human language; still, the presence of those features in oral communication require the unique anatomical and neurophysiological structures and processes that characterize human speech and hearing. The quantitative difference thus asymptotically approaches a qualitative difference.

The important present consideration is the role the human brain plays in producing and processing what is uniquely human speech (on whatever grounds that uniqueness is explained) and the importance of human speech in the resulting, uniquely human *species-orientation*. However, the impression should not be given that speech is exclusively or even primarily the result of brain activity. The structure of much of human anatomy as well as the respiratory and cardiovascular systems are major contributors to human speech. Contributions by the structures and functions of the diaphragm, lungs, larynx (including vocal cords), jaws, mouth, tongue, and lips must be precisely synchronized before the familiar sounds of a human voice can be produced.

One might say that the human voice, like human nature itself, *emerges* only from a minimal causal nexus, within a limited range, that is the production of a combination of certain anatomical structures and certain properly functioning organs and systems. Consider, for example, the ana-tomical structure of human beings that facilitates breathing, eating, and talking. All mammals except humans have flat tongues with an elevated larynx at the back that allow breathing and eating to occur simultaneously. In contrast, human beings have an arched tongue, and the larynx is located much lower down in the throat. In between is the opening of the vocal tract, an elongated tube that functions like a sounding board for the air that passes through the vocal cords. Through subtle muscle control, the size and shape of the opening can be controlled to produce the richness and variety of different characteristics of human speech from the full, robust notes of an operatic baritone or soprano to the thin, nasal "voice-overs" done for many cartoon characters.

Interestingly, this particular anatomical arrangement in adult humans, so uniquely suited for human speech, is primarily responsible for a higher susceptibility to choking while eating. The location of the larynx in human infants, in contrast, is higher in the throat, connecting directly with the nasal passages, to allow infants to breathe and eat simultaneously. Why would childhood development gradually reposition the larynx lower in the throat thereby creating both the possibility of human speech and, at the same time, a greater risk to the individual's survival? One would think then that human speech must have some significant adaptive value since it comes at the cost of making a person significantly more vulnerable to accidental death.

Of course, the brain's morphology and neurochemical processes responsible for the synergetic relationship between human hearing and human speech do have obvious adaptive value. The richness, complexity, and diversity of human oral communication resulting from both the anatomical features and neurophysiological processes in the brain responsible for human hearing and human speech are unequaled in the animal world. The detail and subtle distinctions possible in human speech allow for a much more useful ability to describe the details of a situation involving the presence and location of a potential prey or predator. The same is true, of course, for the ability to express and understand a greater range of emotions as discussed in the next chapter. Exactly when and how the unique features responsible for human speech evolved from earlier humanoids is still controversial and a matter of some debate amongst social scientists. Some fossil evidence resulting from endocranial casts of skulls suggests that *Broca's area* and *Wernicke's area* of the brain began to develop early in the evolution of *Homo*; however, other evidence concerning the anatomical requirements for an arched tongue and a vocal tract suggests that the development of anything approaching modern human speech was much later. While such matters are of great interest to anthropologists, they are of little concern here.

What this excursion into the brain's role in human sight and hearing reveals is the intricate way in which the brain coordinates, orchestrates, and *integrates* the individual sensory inputs as well as the causal relationships amongst the individual senses. The *species-sense* of human beings thus emerges at a higher level of abstraction and integration than any one of the individual five senses and cannot be accounted for simply in terms of an aggregate of those different senses. The human *species-sense* emerges from the brain's process of *sensory-integration* which, in turn, results from the synergetic interrelationships amongst the different sensory inputs. The *species-sense* is thus an emergent property of members of a species that supervenes upon the sensory causal nexus resulting from the process of *species-sensory-integration* in individual brains. The *species-sense* of human beings is thus unique in the animal world largely because the human brain is unique in the animal world. What this reveals is that at least some of the properties in the cluster of properties upon which the emergent property of human nature supervenes are themselves emergent properties.

Since the *species-orientation* of human beings is partially a function of human *species-sense*, which is turn is partially a function of human *species-sensory-integration*, which finally, is largely a function of the human brain, then the importance of the brain to the properties that produce the causal nexus upon which human nature supervenes is obvious. But that importance is a functional importance. In the natural world in which human beings live and in which we have evolved, it is a biological fact (and hence a contingent fact) that it is the brain that is responsible for *species-sensory-integration*. This reveals that human nature *evolved* and emerged along with the evolution and emergence of the human brain, i.e., the brain of *Homo sapiens*. What does this mean about early humanoids, *Australopithecus*, *Homo habilis*, or *Homo erectus*, members of which lacked the sophisticated brain of *Homo sapiens*? The answer is the same as for human infants, human beings in a permanent vegetative state, as well as those with significant anomalies resulting from disease or injury, such as the case of Laura Bridgman, discussed in Chapter 5. Since human nature is an imperfect, irreducible complexity, it can be possessed in different degrees by different individuals—individuals that are both human and non-human. Early humanoids, *Australopithecus*, *Homo habilis*, or *Homo erectus*, human infants, other animals, and adult *Homo sapiens* that have serious debilitating deficiencies caused by injury or disease that interfere with the integration described above are lacking in human nature to some degree.

What does it require for the property of human nature to be instantiated in an individual and just how much of that property might an individual be lacking and still be said to posses human nature to some degree? The answer to these questions will vary depending upon the exact circumstances and condition of the individual, and definitive answers might not always be forthcoming. Consider again what it means for something to be considered an instantiation of the Fourth Movement of Beethoven's *Ninth Symphony*. When the symphony is performed with a full orchestra and chorus, the answer to this question might be easy. But what if the chorus is missing? Or what if some entire section of instruments in the orchestra is missing? What if someone is simply whistling or humming the theme from the Fourth Movement while walking down the street? Exactly what is it in these cases that one would hear? Or, what if a person hums Tchaikovsky's *1812 Overture* and then at the point where the canons or timpani are supposed to come in, the person just says, "Boom, Boom." What exactly is it that one hears? One might want to say, "I recognize 'that.' 'It' sounds familiar. 'It' sounds like Tchaikovsky's *1812 Overture*." But it is not clear exactly what "it" is. There is obviously a major deficiency. Something is missing. Just how much can be missing from the performance of Tchaikovsky's *1812 Overture* with a full orchestra complete with timpani and cannons and still be that *Overture*? The answer to this question is not so easy. The only answer is that it just all depends upon the judgments made regarding the particular circumstances, and not everyone will agree about such judgments. The same is true when individuals instantiate varying properties in the cluster of properties to different degrees and when the causal nexus (upon which human nature supervenes) that emerges from the instantiation of those properties is seriously compromised. Different individuals possess the property of human nature to varying degrees, and not everyone will agree about the judgments made about which degrees of human nature those different individuals possess.

Most of the examples discussed earlier in this book concern major deficiencies that individuals might have, resulting from disease or injury, in the degrees to which a property is instantiated by those individuals, but the same questions arise about excesses in the instantiation of those properties. Consider the case of Oscar Pistorius, a runner and a double leg-amputee. After being fitted with prosthetics in the shape of long curving blades made of carbon-fiber, Pistorius became known as "the Blade Runner" and was highly competitive, being able often to defeat "normal," highly-competitive runners. However, he was denied permission to participate in the 2008 Olympic Games because officials representing the International Association of Athletics Federation decided that the blades provided him with an unfair advantage over "normal" runners. Ironically, the aspect of Pistorius' *species-orientation* having to do with physical movement of the human body *through* space was skewed on the high end of the scale because he was fitted with "high-tech" prosthetics. In other words, the officials treated his "disability" and his use of the blade prosthetics in the same way in which a person's use of anabolic steroids or other "performance enhancing" drugs would be treated. It is easy to imagine other "performance enhancing" anatomical variations that result in deviations on the excess end of the scale of the "normal" range of human bodily movements, and this is just the beginning. In the future, bioengineering holds the promise of affecting human movements in ways that presently are the subject-matter of science fiction and fantasy. The bottom line is that differing degrees of human nature that individuals possess map onto the differing degrees to which individuals possess differing degrees of human *species-orientation*. Major factors in determining that normal range of human *species-orientation* include the properties resulting from human bodily movements that, in turn, are the result of human anatomy and a properly functioning human brain. More examples of these important bodily movements are discussed later in this chapter.

As recounted earlier, in his *Dialogues Concerning Natural Religion*, while examining what he takes to be the major circumstances that result in pain and suffering in this world, David Hume has Philo complain about the great frugality with which different "powers and faculties" are distributed amongst different animals in the natural world. His point is that animals possess a bare minimum of such powers and faculties necessary for survival and that this creates a situation which results in "misery and ruin" for sentient creatures since there is so little room for error. Philo complains specifically that human beings are the "most disadvantaged in bodily advantages" and that we human beings manage to survive only by our "reason and sagacity." While, on the one hand, this claim correctly recognizes and emphasizes the importance of human reason, on the other hand, it incorrectly ignores and underrepresents the importance of human "bodily advantages" as well as the correlation between human reason and human bodily advantages. The human brain—what has earlier been described as perhaps the most complicated and sophisticated thing that is known to exist in the universe—is of little value and certainly would not have evolved by natural selection unless it accounts for human *movement*. The most obvious immediate examples are the movements that involve the pursuit of prey and the avoidance of predators, but there are many other examples of movements that have significant adaptive value.

Consider those human "bodily advantages" mentioned by Philo. Using the conceptual framework developed in this book for understanding the notion of human nature, human bodily advantages in this context can be taken to include what has been characterized as human *species-orientation*, i.e., the collective range of ways in which human beings are able to act upon and be acted upon by our environment. Some of this range is explained by human *species-sense* and human *species-sensory-integration*, and earlier in this chapter, I have discussed some ways in which a properly functioning human brain is essential to these aspects of *species-orientation*. What has not been discussed to this point is the role that the brain plays with that aspect of *species-orientation* that has to do with bodily movement—the interaction of the human body with its physical environment, i.e, the motor system of the human body.

If Hume intended to include the human motor system in what he calls "bodily advantages," then he has woefully wrong in thinking that human beings are disadvantaged in comparison with other animals regarding "bodily advantages" or that the human motor system is "frugally" constructed. The aspect of human *species-orientation* that is the result of human bodily movement is characterized by an impressive range and variety of different movements. Human beings can crawl, walk, run, and jump, i.e. perform "gross" actions involving moving the entire body *through* space. Human beings can also perform brain surgery, play the piano, use computers, and perform numerous, small muscle, finely-tuned movements. The human brain can direct the body to construct and use delicate medical, musical, and technological instruments and equipment, i.e., perform those "precise" actions that involve manipulating parts of the body *in* space. Undoubtedly, a gazelle may run faster and jump higher than human beings, but a gazelle cannot perform brain surgery. An eagle may fly higher and a dolphin may swim faster than can human beings, but neither of these animals can perform anything like the array of precise movements *in* space that human beings can perform.

Considering the full range and variety of bodily movements of which human beings are capable, human "bodily advantages" are unique in the animal world. Hume's complaint about the apparent disadvantage that human beings experience in this world regarding bodily advantages is explained by the fact that he apparently concentrated upon the gross bodily movements that locomote the human body *through* space. And, in this case, human beings, in something that we might call a "natural state," do not compare well with many other animals. When compared to planarians, slugs, or even ground hogs or mice, the ability of human beings to locomote through space seems to measure up fairly well, but when compared to tigers, horses, or many birds, the locomotion of human beings seems fairly pedestrian. Fish swim. Birds fly. Snakes crawl. Most mammals walk, run, and jump. So, there is a great variety of ways in which different animals move *through* space, and thus, different animals have what might be called their own *species-motor-sense*, i.e., the unique species-specific way in which they "sense" their environments by their movements. What distinguishes human movement and makes it incomparable in the animal world is not simply the ways in which human beings move *through* space but the quality and range of precise manipulations of bodily parts *in* space along with those bodily movements *through* space. Thus, it is the contribution of this combination of the gross and precise bodily movements that creates the uniquely human *species-motor-sense* and partially accounts for the uniqueness of human *species-orientation* and that aspect of *species-orientation* involving "bodily advantages."

Indeed, all of the advantages and the distinctly human products of human *techne* and the *proactive mode of species orientation* discussed in the previous chapter (as well as the cultural products discussed in the next chapter) are the results of the human *species-motor-sense*. Also, as noted earlier, as a result of these significantly more sophisticated and advanced precise manipulations of the body that human beings can perform *in* space, we have managed to alter significantly the range of possible gross movements by which we locomote *through* space. Hume was certainly right that if we imagine a slice in time where a single, individual human being is standing naked and alone in the natural world and then try to evaluate something like that individual's "bodily advantages" compared to those of other known animals in that same slice of time, then that individual human being would appear to be severely disadvantaged. However, the concept of *species-orientation* is a concept that applies to individuals *as members of a species*, and if we imagine that individual with all of what goes into accounting for the evolution of the human *proactive mode of species-orientation* over a significantly period of time, then the apparent disadvantages disappear, and the uniqueness of the uniquely human *species-motor-sense* and the entire *species-orientation* of human beings becomes obvious. Indeed, it is exactly the resulting *proactive mode of species-orientation* that explains the unique position that human beings now occupy in the world compared to every other known animal.

Hume claims that it is human reason alone that sets man apart from the rest of the animal world and provides the slight margin of error that allows human beings to survive. While there is no denying the importance of human reason, this claim ignores some significant human biology.

Human movements—both gross and precise movements—are the result of the synergetic interaction of different features of the human body consisting of the brain, central nervous system, nerves, muscles, tendons, bones, and the sense organs. This collection is what biologists call the human motor system. The current focus of attention is upon the role of the brain and the rest of the central nervous system in the human motor system to explain the uniqueness of human movement and the importance of human *species-motor-sen*se to the cluster theory of human nature. As many school children learn, the central nervous system is composed of the voluntary and involuntary systems. Little will be said here about the involuntary nervous system and only enough detail about the brain and the central nervous system will be said to justify the claim that the range of physical movements of the human body that comprises the human *species-motor-sense* is an important member of the cluster of properties upon which human nature supervenes. This is not an exercise in the philosophy of mind since the position taken here regarding the human brain is a functional one. *Something* has to perform the functions (or something very nearly like the functions) presently performed by the human brain in controlling physical bodily movements. It is a biological and evolutionary fact that those functions are presently performed in human beings by the human brain and only by the human brain. Thus, it is a contingent matter of fact that to the extent that the human *species-motor-sense* is a property in the cluster of properties from which human nature emerges and to the extent that it is a property that exerts a causal influence to produce the causal nexus amongst those properties, then the normal functioning of the human brain is an obvious major contributor to human nature.

Few, if any, of the properties in the cluster of properties that produces the causal nexus upon which human nature supervenes do not depend, at least to some extent, upon a properly functioning brain. Consider, for illustration, some of those properties discussed thus far. Human speech, discussed above, requires a complex set of finely coordinated bodily movements involving the lips, tongue, mouth, jaws, lungs, and diaphragm. Similarly, the production of musical song involves movements. The production of musical instruments as well as the production of music from those instruments results, for the most part, from those precise manipulations of body parts *in* space. All of human *techne*, or, for the sake of argument, *nearly* all of human *techne*, discussed in the previous chapter, is the result of the precise manipulation of parts of the human body *in* space. This is especially and most obviously true of the manipulations of that amazing opposing thumb. Simply having the marvelous, anatomical feature of an opposing thumb is relatively useless unless that opposing thumb can be successfully manipulated in equally marvelous, amazing ways, and it is that manual manipulation for which the brain, the central nervous system, and the rest of the motor system are responsible. Also, frequently overlooked is the importance of a properly functioning brain and motor system in controlling the physical movements necessary for human sexual reproduction and human sexual activity, discussed in Chapter 4. Subtle movements of the human body during sexual intercourse and other intimate sexual activity rival the manipulations of opposing thumbs as distinctive human movements. Both are important aspects of the *species-motor-sense* and the *species-orientation* of human beings.

One last important feature of the human motor system is worth mentioning here. Thus far, the importance of the role of the brain in controlling different bodily movements and creating the human *species-motor-sense* has been emphasized. The importance of these bodily movements to *species-orientation* has, in turn, been noted. However, there is an important aspect of human bodily movements that has not yet been identified, i.e, namely, the learning of complex movements and the *storing* of those learned movements. The storage of complicated *programs* of coordinated bodily movements takes place in the cerebellum (also called "the little brain"), located in the anterior of the hindbrain. It is because of the function of the cerebellum that a person can practice a complicated set of movements over a period of time and store them for quick recall upon demand. It is thus the cerebellum that is responsible for the old adage, "it's just like riding a bicycle," meaning that once one has learned a complicated set of coordinated bodily activities, recall upon demand and performance of that set of activities is easy. Consider the complicated movements of a violinist playing Mendelssohn's *Violin Concerto*, or the movements of a ballerina dancing the final "death scene" of Tchaikovsky's *Swan Lake*, or the movements of a major league pitcher in the game of American baseball winding and throwing a baseball with pinpoint precision. These activities, and many others that are distinctly human in terms of their complexity, would be impossible in they had to be relearned on each occasion of their performance. The storage and coordination of bodily movements by the cerebellum is thus responsible for the distinctive aspect of human *species-orientation* that is the result of human *species-motor-sense*.

Other animals may learn certain movements that can be stored and then repeated upon demand, but no other known animal on Earth has the ability to learn, store, and repeat upon demand physical movements with anything approaching the long, intricate, and complex programs of movements that can be learned, stored, and reproduced by human beings. Finally, it should be noted that bodily movement is inexorably linked to sensory input. An individual's bodily movements must be made on the basis of the nature of that individual's environment and that individual's relationship to that environment. What neurologists call the *association areas* of the brain provide the connection between the areas of the brain that receive the sensory information and the motor cortex that then initiates bodily movements. This integration of different functions of the brain is a further indication of the way in which the complexity of the human brain is responsible for the uniquely human *species-motor-sense* and, in turn, the uniquely human *species-orientation*. I will return to discuss the functions of the association areas of the brain later in this chapter in the treatment of human consciousness.

When Aristotle famously noted that man is a rational animal, he intended this to be an essentialist claim, i.e., he intended rationality to be a qualitatively distinguishing characteristic of human beings. In contrast, the cluster theory takes human rationality (or human intelligence) to be a significant though not an essential property in the cluster of properties upon which human nature supervenes. In further contrast, the cluster theory has no reservations about attributing what is called rationality or intelligence to other animals. To repeat a point made several times throughout this book, the difference between human rationality and that of other animals is one of degree and not kind; however, as also noted earlier, that degree of difference between human beings and other animals is an enormous one. In the particular case of reason, the difference of degree between human rationality and any other known animal is an indispensable desideratum in accounting for the uniqueness of the *proactive mode of species-orientation* of human beings. Human intelligence is spread across a wide spectrum of different forms of reasoning, about which entire books can be and have been written; so, the treatment given here must be admittedly summary and superficial.[4] Even equating rationality with intelligence introduces a degree of ambiguity that would be decried by most specialists. Whatever more subtle distinctions that might be in order notwithstanding, however, it is undeniable that human rationality and/or intelligence depend upon the proper functioning of the human brain.

Amongst the many different aspects of human reason or intelligence, the focus here will be upon only those that contribute to that individual's *species-orientation*. The human *species-orientation* is thus a function of a complex set of causal interrelationships that exist between human beings and our environment, including other human beings. The present focus will be on the role of the human brain in those causal interrelationships between human beings and the environment sans other human beings. The role of the brain in the aspect of human *species-orientation* that involves causal relationships with other human beings is the focus of the next chapter.

The point has been made earlier that the size of the adult human brain and its protective skull necessitate a slow development over several years of childhood. Exactly over how many years this development takes place and in exactly what fashion are still matters of some controversy amongst biologists and psychologists. However, some things seem indisputable. In terms of actual functional ability, a newborn human infant can perform no measurable greater cognitive or reasoning feats than a Golden Retriever puppy, but the human infant does have a human brain. Assuming that an individual's brain functions normally, then gradually and incrementally, the hundred billion or so nerve cells in that individual's brain begin to fire and make some of the possible of trillions upon trillions of possible connections to other nerve cells, and that individual begins to perform some of the complex operations underlying what we call human reason or human intelligence.

Borrowing heavily from the work of the Swiss psychologist Jean Piaget, I will emphasize the operations performed by the brain that are essential for the development of what we call human intelligence and the role that these operations play in producing human *species-orientation* and in turn, human nature. Again, this treatment must be summary in nature. Piaget famously identified different stages though which human cognitive ability develops in childhood, and emphasized that this development takes place in incremental order. Each stage of development provides a significantly and qualitatively richer and more complex understanding of the child's experience of his or her environment. In terms used in this book to explain the cluster theory of human nature, each of Piaget's stages of cognitive development contributes to a more complete and completely human *species-orientation*. The earliest stage Piaget identifies is the *sensorimotor* stage, which occurs from birth until about age two years, during which a child develops a sense of self, i.e., an understanding that one's self is separate from the rest of the world, and a sense of the nature of physical objects, including the concept of object permanence. In the *pre-operational* stage, which occurs from two to seven years of age, children begin to accumulate concepts such as shape, color, and size by means of which they then classify physical objects. The stage of *concrete operations* includes developments that take place between the age of seven and eleven years, and in this stage, children first begin to reason about the properties of objects in the physical world, using the concept of the conservation of property. In this stage children also begin to understand that other people might be the subjects of experiences similar to their own rather simply being the objects of their own experiences. Finally, in the stage of *formal operations*, which occurs beyond the age of eleven, children (or young adults) gain the ability to think abstractly and logically, which enables them to form hypotheses and to reason more hypothetically and generally, e.g., to understand and use general logical laws and the general law of causality.

The cluster theory understands the progression through Piaget's different stages of cognitive and intellectual development (or some such similar development) as an important aspect of the progression towards a full-fledged human nature. The *species-orientation* of newborn human infants is practically non-existent. Some of the development towards full-fledged human nature is the result of physical and biological maturation, and some of it is the result of cognitive and intellectual maturation and the underlying development of the brain.

Philosophers are still divided over whether the concepts and categories necessary for the operations performed in each of Piaget's stages of development are *a priori* or *a posteriori*, and psychologists and biologists still debate and research whether the progression through Piaget's stages is "hardwired" into human biology or whether it is affected by environment and stimulation of the individual child. Another way of posing a similar question is to ask if the development of the human brain allows for a certain level of experience and understanding of and interaction with the world or whether the development of the human brain is the result of such experience and interaction. At the beginning of this chapter, I noted how Alfred Russel Wallace abandoned the general theory of evolution by natural selection when confronted with this issue because he thought that the human brain was too large and complex and its operations too sophisticated to be explained simply in terms of what would be necessary for survival of the species. He thus resorted to a claim of intentional design by a Higher Intelligence, i.e., God, to explain the human brain and human intelligence.

The cluster theory of human nature accounts for the development of the human brain and human reason within a bottom-up, naturalistic framework. Whatever one might think about the rest of the properties in the cluster of properties upon which human nature supervenes, unless human beings are able to understand and interpret our physical environments and are able to interact with and respond to those environments, we cannot survive. Thus, according to the cluster theory of human nature, the human brain and its operations are the result of the interaction of individuals with our environments. There must undoubtedly be some hardwired neural mechanisms in the brain and the central nervous system, but there must also be experiential stimulation of those mechanisms. A perfectly normal human infant that is never stimulated with experience will fail to go through the stages of cognitive and intellectual development successfully, and a child with serious, debilitating maldevelopment of the brain and central nervous system will fail to go successfully through those stages no matter the stimulation. Unfortunately, there are numerous cases of children born with serious, debilitating maldevelopment of the brain and central nervous system; so, the failure of experience to correct those physiological deficiencies is well-documented. The experimental data concerning "normal" children that are not stimulated at all is seriously limited, given the obvious prohibition on controlled experiments with human subjects, but the result of complete isolation and sensory deprivation on very young children is easy to infer from the limited actual cases. The interaction of the normal human brain with its environment is a modern-day interpretation of Kant's dictum that concepts without percepts are empty and percepts without concepts are blind.

If the development of the human brain and human reason and intelligence are the result of the experience of and interaction with the natural world, the question then becomes just what levels of understanding of and interaction with the natural world are necessary to explain the development of the human brain and human reason and, in turn, human survival and flourishing. I will not engage here in speculation about the evolution of neurophysiology except to say that the evolution of the brain and human reason is undeniably the result of a synergetic interaction between organisms and environment.

So far as the cluster theory of human nature is concerned, one of the more important considerations about human reason and intelligence is that it both allows for and promotes the *proactive mode of species orientation*. Given the other limiting characteristics of the human anatomy identified by Hume, the *proactive mode of species orientation* compensates by allowing human beings to act upon and be acted upon by their environments in ways that are not possible given only a *reactive mode of species orientation*. The development of the concepts and the cognitive operations using those concepts in the stages of cognitive development identified by Piaget are essential for the *proactive mode of species orientation*. For example, one cannot build a sophisticated bridge or automobile without dealing with hypothetical and abstract possibilities and adjusting actions to considered hypotheses. And, as indicated earlier, the human *proactive mode of species orientation* actually allows human beings to alter the range of the human *species-orientation*.

The range and the levels of quality and complexity of the *proactive mode of species orientation* are functions of the range and the levels of abstraction and generality of those concepts and operations formed in the formal stage of cognitive development. Those concepts and operations are then obviously adaptive and selected for. Might other animals possess some of those concepts and operations? Undoubtedly, they do. Certainly, other animals exhibit some behavior that appears to involve a *proactive mode of species orientation*, e.g., as noted earlier, some animals build nests or houses or engage in evasive or predatory behavior that appears to be proactive. However, animals in the natural world other than man are generally dominated by a *reactive mode of species orientation*, and those that exhibit proactive behaviors are exceptions to the general rule and do so to a significantly more limited degree than do human beings.

The *proactive mode of species orientation* is not some superfluous luxury for human beings. Upon being birthed or hatched, the young of nearly all species of animals begin their *reactive mode of species orientation*, responding to the particulars of the *come-up-againstness* of the natural world that are then currently manifested in their immediate environments, by avoiding predators or seeking food and shelter. Some adult animals protect and provide for their young for some short periods of time—some of those periods might even extend into months or two or three years. Only human beings have such a prolonged period of development for offspring, and the maturation of the prefrontal lobes of the brain, mainly responsible for rational and cognitive development is one of the slowest processes in that development, extending, according to neruoscientists, into the twenties. Arguably, any species dominated by a *reactive mode of species orientation* would not survive given such a prolonged period of development towards full maturation. Finally, we have arrived at the basis for the designation of human beings as *Homo sapiens*, the wise man, i.e., the development of those concepts and operations, acquired in Piaget's stages of cognitive development, that allow for and promote a uniquely human *proactive mode of species orientation*.

At this point, some readers might be thinking of an objection similar to the one made at the beginning of this chapter. Just as the brain might be thought by some to be the elephant in the room of the cluster theory of human nature, nothing has been said yet in this discussion of the brain about human consciousness. *Consciousness* appears to be the elephant in the room of the brain that has not yet been addressed. Is not consciousness what many philosophers, theologians, and neuroscientists have taken to be the distinctive feature of human nature, and have not entire theories of *mind* been based upon claims about the uniqueness of human consciousness? And do not the operations in Piaget's stages of cognitive development *assume* that the individuals going through those stages are conscious?

Consciousness is the last bastion of top-down theories of human nature. Intuitive self-awareness resulting from introspection is supposedly revealing of a metaphysically distinct soul or mind, the seat of consciousness. Centuries of philosophical debate have brought us no closer to resolving the controversies about such a claim. Given that the cluster theory is committed to a methodological naturalism, the challenge is to provide some account of consciousness without interjecting some *deux ex machina*, metaphysically *ad hoc* feature such as a soul or spirit into the natural world.

It is now commonplace for philosophers and neuroscientists to tackle the problem of explaining consciousness using the distinction, first introduced by David Chalmers, between the easy problem and the hard problem. According to Chalmers, the "easy" problem of consciousness is the one of identifying and explaining the neurochemical processes in the brain that are functionally correlated with what are regarded as conscious experiences. The "hard" problem is the one of explaining why these neurochemical processes in the brain produce or are accompanied by a *subjective feeling*. To illustrate the difference between the easy and hard problems and to drive home the difficulty of the hard problem, Chalmers introduces the hypothetical notion of *zombies* that behave in exactly all the ways that human beings behave but who have no conscious experience. Presumably, the possibility of zombies means that what are typically regarded as conscious experiences are superfluous so far as human survival is concerned and then would not have been selected for.

What is the position of the cluster theory of human nature regarding the easy and hard problems of consciousness? The first observation is that what Chalmers calls the easy problem is not all that easy. Perhaps part of the issue here is that it is a philosopher who is characterizing what is primarily a problem of neuroscience as "easy," and arguably, as some of the above discussion reveals, neuroscientists have made some progress towards resolving the easy problem though that progress is the result of years of painstaking research. More and more data are now available correlating what are reported as conscious experiences with different neurochemical processes in the brain, and the effects of injury, disease, surgery, electrical stimulation, and drugs on those processes are becoming increasingly well-known. But what of the "hard" problem? How and why do these processes produce subjective feelings rather than simply producing or allowing whatever behavior is correlated with them?

I approach the hard problem of consciousness with a high degree of trepidation since this problem has, to date, stumped the most highly-regarded figures in the philosophy of mind and neuroscience. In fact, there is not even a consensus of agreement that the hard problem is really a legitimate problem, or, if it is a legitimate problem, what form a legitimate solution might take. Some prominent figures such as Daniel Dennett have denied that consciousness even exits while others, such as Thomas Huxley, have regarded it as nothing short of miraculous, comparing it to the genie that appears from Aladdin's magic lamp. Exactly what conscious experience amounts to has also been understood differently by different authorities. Some have taken it to mainly consist in self-awareness, "privileged" first-person access to "private" information about the self, or qualitatively subjective experiences (*qualia*), or some combination of all three kinds of experience. This dispute will not be resolved here, but hopefully, the cluster theory can provide some small insight into both the nature of and the importance of conscious experience.

Within the cluster theory of human nature, one way of approaching the hard problem of consciousness is by focusing on the difference between the *reactive mode of species-orientation* and the *proactive mode of species-orientation*. I have argued that human beings are dominated by a *proactive mode of species-orientation* whereas other animals are generally dominated by a *reactive mode of species-orientation*. How does this difference in the two modes of *species-orientation* come about, and how have human beings evolved to the point where the *proactive* mode is the dominant mode of *species-orientation*? And what does this distinction and the dominance of the *proactive* mode have to do with human consciousness? Consider again Piaget's *sensorimotor* stage, the first stage of cognitive development that occurs between birth and age two. In this stage, amongst other changes, human infants acquire the distinctions between self and non-self and the concept of object permanence. Without these concepts in place, there would not be and could not be any conceptual difference for an infant between the pain produced by touching the ubiquitous hot stove and having an itch or some gastronomical pain. A young infant's *species-orientation* is completely in the *reactive mode*, which is one of several important factors that severely limits the infant's degree of human nature. The same is true for those in a permanent vegetative state. Injury, disease, drugs, and alcohol can be responsible for an individual's loss of the conceptual distinction between self and non-self and thereby losing (or severely restricting) the ability to behave in a *proactive mode of species-orientation*. Even trances induced by hypnosis or meditation can have the same result, and neuroscientists can now identify and measure the parts of the brain that are affected.

Presumably, even though the pain from touching the hot stove and from indigestion might both be experienced subjectively, there is a significant difference between the two. The main difference is that the pain from touching the hot stove results directly from an individual's interaction with his or her environment, i.e, from the specifics of the *come-up-againstness* of the individual's immediate surrounding environment. Lacking the recognition of this fact, an individual can never develop a *proactive mode of species orientation*, and given the admitted limitations of other human "assets" in dealing with a dangerous, threatening, and sometimes hostile environment, without the distinction between experiences that are caused by one's environment and ones that are "internal," the species could not survive. The recognition of this distinction requires an individual, or an individual's brain, to monitor, analyze, and evaluate his or her experiences. In other words, there must be meta-level experiences that take as their objects other experiences, or, if one prefers, there must be brain processes that are "about" other brain processes. It may well be that it is on this meta-level of experience, experience about experience, that human consciousness first emerges. This might explain what some neuroscientists mean when they claim that consciousness is an emergent property, i.e., that it is a complex property whose unique nature emerges at a certain level and is not possessed by or explained by its component properties at a "lower" level.

The sense of *proprioception* (sometimes called "the sixth sense") is the sense that a human being has of the location of the appendages of one's body in surrounding space. Proprioception also contributes to one's sense of balance and the location of one's physical body in space. It is the sense of proprioception that allows a person to touch his or her nose in the dark, to scratch an itch without looking at the bodily location, or to sit down in a chair without holding on or looking at it first. Proprioception thus provides certain perspectival information—a physical "point of view" in respect to the location and position of one's body vis-à-vis space and the objects in the external, physical world. The sense of proprioception thus locates and orients one's body and one's bodily movements in and to one's surrounding environment.

What does this discussion of proprioception have to do with consciousness? The suggestion here is that human consciousness is a form of *mental proprioception*, i.e., the monitoring, anaylzing, comparison, and evaluation of experiences provides *perspectival* information (or establishes a *perspectival* view) about those experiences that has the consequence of locating those experiences in time and space and orientating them to each other in time and space. Consciousness is thus an experience *locator*, an experience *orientator*, i.e., consciousness locates and orientates experiences to other experiences and time and space. It is thus a "second order," meta-experience and emergent property that emerges from a causal nexus that is established amongst experiences through the processes of locating and orienting experiences to other experiences. When a person has an experience, one must learn to recognize the source of the experience and what sort of information is being provided in the experience and to make some judgment about the experience. The perspectival view of consciousness provides a person with the meta-level recognition that this experience is *mine*, and this information is about *this* or *that*. It also allows a person to engage in directed experiments to test the meta-level conclusions about the experience and the information provided in the experience by moving certain body parts or engaging in certain behavior, i.e., by *acting* on the meta-level judgment, to determine what happens.

It is thus the emergence of this perspectival view that gives rise to the sense of self-awareness, privileged access to information about experience, and the subjective "feeling" that accompanies experience. Comparing *pain, here, now* and *touch, stove, there* gives rise to an understanding of the experience of pain caused by touching a hot stove and the orientation of one's body to one's physical environment, a perspectival view whereby that orientation is established. "I, me, mine," is *here*, and the hot stove is *there*. The same is true of the establishment of a temporal perspective and the orientation of one's experiences in time, e.g., the pain is *now* and touching the hot stove was *then*. Consciousness thus emerges not just from the bundling of experiences together into a collection but from the processes of monitoring, analyzing, and comparing experiences. Like the cluster theory's understanding of human nature, consciousness arises from a causal nexus amongst experiences, and it is the perspectival nature of this causal nexus that explains the subjective feelings of self-awareness and privileged access. Human consciousness is an emergent property similar to the property of being flammable in the natural world. Before scientists understood the explanatory principles of combustion, they posited the existence of phlogistine in things that burn in similar fashion to the way in which a spirit or soul is now posited by some to explain human consciousness. But scientists now understand that no special, "hidden" substance is required to be present in an object or a bit of material in order for that object or bit of material to burn. Similarly, the perspectival view of consciousness, developed here, shows how it is possible to explain consciousness without appeal to some metaphysically distinct entity such as a soul or spirit that is introduced into the natural world on an *ad hoc* basis.

Most top-down theorists, because of theological considerations, reserve consciousness for human beings, but a consequence of this *perspectival view* of consciousness resulting from the *proprioception* of experience is that different individuals possess different degrees of consciousness, and "different individuals" is intended to include individuals of the same species and of different species. Obviously, different animals have perspectival views of some degree. They are able to orientate themselves and their experiences to their environments and to each other. Through a comparable sense of *proprioception*, they are able to orientate their bodies in space, and through a comparable sense of *proprioception* of experiences they are able to monitor and compare their experiences to each other to avoid predators, to seek food, or to find their way back to their nest or lair. The cluster theory has no qualms about attributing some degree of consciousness to other animals. Arguably, many animals have a much more highly developed perspectival view of their places in their environments resulting from the *mental proprioception* of their experiences than do human infants. The cluster theory of human nature is thus on the opposite end of the spectrum from Descartes in attributing sentient experiences to other animals.

The difference between human consciousness and the consciousness in other animals is thus explained in terms of the degree of the complexity of that perspectival view that is established and the extent, complexity, and degree of abstraction that is the result of the sense of *proprioception* amongst experiences. The causal nexus that is established amongst human experiences from which human nature emerges is, on the basis of the best available evidence from neuroscience and the social sciences, significantly different from any found elsewhere in the animal kingdom. Human beings are simply "aware" of a significantly greater range of ways in which they and their experiences are situated in their environments, i.e, they have a greatly expanded perspectival view of the universe, and the expanded view is expanded in terms of complexity and, in particular, abstraction. The uniquely human perspectival view of the universe in which the sense of *mental proprioception* amongst experiences of an individual and between those experiences and that individual's environment functions to orientate those experiences in space and time is a major component of the uniquely human *species-orientation*.

The complexity of human consciousness is a direct function of the complexity of the human brain (discussed at the beginning of this chapter)—in particular, the complexity of the thalamus, thought by some neuroscientists to be the seat of consciousness since it functions something like a "Grand Central Station" distributing incoming stimuli to other parts of the brain. The ubiquitous example of the subjective feeling of pain, although critically important, is a crude and elementary conscious experience shared by many animals and human infants. Simple sentience, by itself, e.g., the experience of qualia, is likewise a crude and elementary form of consciousness—what one might call *consciousness simplicter*. After all, of what *use* is the experience of pain to a newborn infant? The infant can do nothing to alter its state. It can only *react*. Similarly, the simple recognition of oneself in a mirror (in what scientists call "the mirror test") is a poor test for self-awareness. Chimpanzees, dolphins, elephants, and parrots have "passed" the mirror test, but whatever self-awareness this is evidence of is crude and simple.

The more sophisticated aspect of human consciousness involves the difference in the degree and range of complexity of the persepctival view that results from the *mental proprioception* of experiences—what some neuroscientists call *extended consciousness*. Other animals and human infants undoubtedly feel pain, but they do not understand nerves, the brain, or the central nervous system. They do not understand what causes pain, how it is caused, or the use of anesthesia. The recognition of oneself in a mirror does nothing in itself to explain *species-orientation*. The differences in the complexity, range, and degree of abstraction of consciousness between human consciousness and the consciousness in other animals results in the same differences in terms of what can be understood and explained ostensibly, and this complexity is a function of *extended consciousness*, i.e., the ability to monitor, analyze, compare, relate, order, and evaluate a large number of different kinds of experiences. Other animals may ostend (i.e., subjectively identify and sense one's relation to) *this* food, *this* pain, *this* nest, *this* predator, and perhaps, even *this* forest, *this* migration route, or *this* moon (shiny light). However, there is no evidence that other animals (or human infants or humans in a permanent vegetative state, for that matter) can ostend (be conscious of) anything related to the complexities and principles of agriculture, medicine, architecture, geography, or astronomy. If there is no *proprioception* amongst human experiences, then there is no human speech, no music, no reason, no intention, and no *proactive species-orientation*.

Other animals may be conscious of *this* mate or *this* offspring, or even *this* "family," or *this* colony. However, again, there is no evidence that other animals are conscious of anything related to the complexities and principles of societies, culture, genetics, or heredity. The uniquely human understanding of personal and social relationships and human culture are direct functions of the complexity of human consciousness, which is a direct function of the complexity of the human brain. The *mental proprioception* and the perspectival view of the world that is human consciousness includes, most importantly according to some, the set of ways in which human beings act upon and are acted upon by other human beings. Thus, discussion of the importance of human society and culture to the cluster theory of human nature is the subject of the next chapter of this book.

Notes

1. The following treatment of the human brain and neuroscience is informed by and gleaned from several important sources, including the following: *Life: The Science*

of Biology, Fifth Edition, William Purves, Gordon H. Orians, H. Craig Heller, and David Sadava (Sunderland: MA, 1998), especially Chapter 30; *What Is Special about the Human Brain?* R. E. Passingham (Oxford: Oxford University Press, 2008); *Conversations on Consciousness: What the Best Minds Think about the Brain, Free Will, and What It Means to be Human*, edited by Susan Blackmore (Oxford: Oxford University Press, 2006); *The Evolving Brain: The Known and Unknown*, R. Grant Steen (Amherst, NY: Prometheus Books, 2007); *The Blank Slate: The Modern Denial of Human Nature*, Steven Pinker (London: Penquin Books, 2002).

2. Peter B. Denes and Elliot N. Pinson, *The Speech Chain* (Gordonsville, VA: W. H. Freeman, 1993).
3. Alfred A. Tomatis, *The Conscious Ear* (New York: Station Hill Press, 1991).
4. See Ian Glynn, *An Anatomy of Thought* (Oxford: Oxford University Press, 1999) and Steven Pinker, *How the Mind Works* (New York: W. W. Norton & Company, 1997).

9

Human Society, Human Culture,
and Human Nature

The *species-orientation* for members of a particular species covers the range of ways in which the members of that species are able to act upon and be acted upon by their environment. The point has been made earlier that the range of ways in which those actions take place should be understood to include the ways in which members of a particular species are able to act upon and be acted upon by other members of their own species. In fact, members of different species in the animal world seemed to be "hard-wired" to recognize their own kind—which means, that members of different species engage in a unique range of behavior towards their own kind.

In terms of the conceptual distinctions that have been introduced in this book in an attempt to elucidate the cluster theory of human nature, one would say that there is a unique and distinct sub-range of ways of each *species-orientation* that appears to be reserved by nature for acting upon and being acted upon by members of the same species. The *haecceity* of the external world (i.e., the *come-up-againstness* of the natural world) that provides the resistance that allows human beings to become agents by acting to bring about intentions comes in many forms. Many of those different ways—some of which are fixed and some of which are malleable—in which the *haecceity* of the natural world is presented to human beings has been treated in detail earlier. Amongst the varied ways in which human beings must learn to adjust our actions to the *come-up-againstness* of the natural world, are the ways that are the result of relating to—acting upon and being acted upon by—members of our own species. This sub-set of actions that is a part of the human *species-orientation* is so important for understanding the cluster theory of human nature that it will be designated as the human *species-haecceity*, i.e, the specific *thisness* or *resistance* that is presented to human beings by other human beings. The concept of *species-haecceity* significantly broadens Jean-Paul Sartre's notion of *the Other*, discussed in Chapter 6. In addition to the importance of interaction with the significant, intimate, other person there is the wide range of interactions with *the Others*, i.e., the other living things like *me*. It is the unique range of the *species-orientation* of human beings, which consists in the unique set of ways in which human beings, i.e., *the Others*, are able to act upon and be acted upon *only by* other human beings, that is captured by the notion of *species-haecceity*.

Emphasizing the *resistance* presented by *species-haecceity* is not intended to mean, of course, that *species-haecceity* is especially dangerous or poses some sort of threat to the development of human nature. On the contrary, like other aspects of the *haecceity*, the *come-up-againstness*, presented to human beings by the natural world, *species-haecceity* may sometimes be dangerous and threatening, at other times benign, and at other times, helpful, complimentary, or nurturing. Also, like other aspects of *haecceity*, *species-haecceity* is simply a part of the natural world presented to human beings that we must somehow accommodate and to which we must adjust. Just as the biological traits of human beings were selected for, as discussed in Chapter 4, as the result of the interaction of human beings with the environment of evolutionary adaptation (EEA), the properties in the cluster of properties upon which human nature supervenes came about only as a result of human beings acting upon and being acted upon by our environment. What attention to *species-haecceity* emphasizes is the rather crucial position in that environment that other human beings occupy.

Species-haecceity is simply one of many ways—but an extremely important way, to be sure—in which the natural world says to human beings, "Here. Now deal with this!" And the unique ways in which human beings "deal with" other human beings result in important contributions to the cluster of properties that creates the causal nexus upon which human nature supervenes. To complete the examination of those properties upon which human nature supervenes, it is thus necessary to examine those properties and the causal relationships amongst those properties that are generated by the ways in which human beings act upon and are acted upon by other human beings. The general results of such interactions are what social scientists and philosophers call "human society" and "human culture."

There is one further introductory comment that is worthy of mention at this point, although it will not be pursued at any great length here. This examination will hopefully shed new light on the nature/nurture debate. Biologists and social scientists often make a sharp distinction between the biological and cultural contributions to human nature and then argue the relative importance of each. Human society and human culture are obviously usually counted on the culture side of such an equation. The cluster theory of human nature recognizes the contributions of both the biological and cultural aspects of human nature to the different ways in which human beings are able to act upon and be acted upon by our environment. The main difference between the two simply being the different parts of that environment that acts upon or is acted upon by the individuals or the different ways in which those actions take place. The cluster theory of human nature thus considers the biological and cultural influences upon human nature simply to occupy different positions on the same continuum and not to be qualitatively different from one another. However, the cluster theory does recognize that on the continuum of the different ways in which the *haecceity* of the natural world is presented to human beings, the *come-up-againstness* for which other human beings are responsible does occupy a privileged position. For the most part, human beings experience and act upon other human beings using the same *species-sense* and *proactive mode of species-orientation* with which the rest of the environment is experienced and acted upon. However, there are some unique and discrete aspects of the human *species-sense* and the human *proactive mode of species-orientation* that are reserved for *species-haecceity*, i.e., there are unique ways in which human beings act upon and are acted upon only by other human beings. Some of these ways involve the sexual behavior, human sexuality, and sexual reproduction discussed in Chapter 4. The additional aspects of *species-haecceity* discussed here involve the ways in which an individual acts upon or is acted upon *by groups* of other human beings or the ways in which groups of human beings act upon and are acted upon by other such groups, i.e., the aspect of *species-haecceity* that are *social* instead of personal.

Perhaps the most important of the unique ways in which human beings act upon and are acted upon by other human beings is the use of human language. The roles of the brain and the anatomical features that make human speech possible have already been discussed in detail in the preceding chapter; therefore, the focus here is upon the social aspects of human language.[1] Perhaps the most significant initial point to be made is that human language is, by its nature, a social phenomenon, and a crucial aspect of the social nature of language is the fundamental role of the recognition of *species-haecceity* by human beings. Biologists and social scientists alike have realized for some time that members of different species recognize members of their own species and begin relating to them in unique ways early in infancy. Like many other animals, we humans recognize our own kind, i.e., we develop a *species-identity*. Human infants do this to an amazing degree and at very early ages—concentrating on adult faces, mimicking movements, and imitating sounds. Perhaps it is the extreme dependency of human infants necessitated by their inability to locomote to find food or avoid predators that brings about the early social interactions between human infants and adults. In this regard, the role of the large and complex human brain and its stages of development cannot be minimized. Whatever the complete and final explanation might be, the social interaction of human beings is far more complex and results in a much earlier and more sophisticated degree of learning than that of any other known animal.

The impact of social interaction on learning is nowhere more important and apparent than in the learning of language. Perhaps human beings do have what Noam Chomsky called a "language instinct," i.e., an innate, "hard-wired" linguistic ability. Or, alternatively, it is as if human beings come with a default software program, what Chomsky called a "Universal Grammar" that allows people to decode natural languages, encode them into a single, underlying grammatical structure, and to *generate* completely novel sentences from new combinations and arrangements of words. While there is enormous controversy surrounding Chomsky's theory about language, the weight of the evidence from the social sciences now supports his claim of an innate, language instinct, but this is not the place to recount the evidence or to engage in the controversies. For the purposes of understanding the importance of language to the cluster theory of human nature, it is enough to point out that even if human beings do have an innate, hard-wired language instinct, this does not mean that human nature or any property in the cluster of properties upon which human nature supervenes is the result of a top-down process. On the contrary, granting the existence of an innate language instinct does not explain the existence of human language. Social scientists have proven that, like many other morphologically structured and neurochemically explained abilities possessed by human beings, the ability to speak and understand human language requires the proper experiences—the proper stimulations—at the proper times–during the proper stages of cognitive development. Unfortunately, several examples of children who were socially isolated for prolonged periods of time have demonstrated that—language instinct or not—without the proper social stimulation, children never develop the ability to speak and understand human language.

Emphasizing the fundamental social aspect of language is the point of Wittgenstein's initially enigmatic comment about a lion speaking, discussed in Chapter 2. Suppose that one were to encounter a lion in the jungle that offered a greeting, in common English, "Top of the morning to you, madam." Could a normal human adult ever come to the point where she would attribute the unaided locution to the lion and "understand" it? Why does such a suggestion seem so conceptually odd and even impossible? Wittgenstein's answer to these questions would be that it is impossible to bridge the conceptual gap between what one takes to be the conditions for the meaningful uses of human language—including, perhaps most importantly, the intentions and other "states of mind" attributed to human speakers—and lions. Including lions in the class of creatures capable of using human language meaningfully would violate human *species-identity*. Human language is not some isolated phenomenon that can exist independently of a context. As indicated earlier, the meaningful use of language is, in Wittgenstein's term, part of a *form of life*. In terms that have been used to explain the cluster theory of human nature, human language is integrally embedded in the *species-haecceity* that human beings present to other human beings, which, in turn, is integral to developing a *species-identity*, which, in turn, is embedded in human *species-orientation*. In other words, recognizing the range of ways of being able to act upon and be acted upon by other human beings, i.e., recognizing human *species-haecceity*, leads to a *species-identity*, which is an essential aspect of human *species-orientation*. Acting upon and being acted upon by other human beings using human language is an essential aspect of that *species-haecceity* and is thus a major contributor to the development of an individual's *species-identity* and *species-orientation*.

There is still much speculation and disagreement amongst biologists, social scientists, linguists, and philosophers about when, where, and how human language developed. Those disputes will not be engaged here. There is also disagreement about whether human language is qualitatively unique since other animals have and use languages. That dispute will also not be engaged here. Whether it is qualitatively distinct or not, human language provides human beings with the ability to describe, understand, and communicate information about a much greater range of data about our environments—from subatomic particles to distant galaxies in the far reaches of the universe—than is possible by any other known creature. Human language is also largely responsible for human beings being able to engage in a *proactive mode of species-orientation* to alter and expand the human *species-orientation* with the result that human beings have a much greater range of *species-orientation* than any other animal. But these more obvious consequences of the use of human language are not the primary focus of the present discussion.

For the present purpose, the important aspect of human language to emphasize here is the way in which its development and uses were and still are essentially social. *Species-haecceity* is presented to human beings in various ways, but no way is more central or important than through the use of human language. In other words, if it is true that we human beings recognize our own kind, then the use of language is one of the most important ways, if not the single most important way, in which we are able to do that. This is because the use of human language is so essentially embedded in human *species-haecceity*. This integral relationship between language and human *species-haecceity* explains why some philosophers have insisted that human infants develop a "philosophy of mind" at very early ages which they use to attribute mental states–intentions, emotions, etc.–to other people. Consider the well-known and widely-spread use of what some social scientists call "Motherese," the soft, soothing, sing-song, nearly-hypnotic tone of voice that mothers use to talk to their infants. What explains the effect of "Motherese" on infants? There is perhaps the simple physical effect of a pleasant sound. Maybe Motherese soothes the fussy infant in much the same way that music soothes the savage beast. But what happens when the infant comes to attribute the source of the pleasant sound to its source and associate it with the different circumstances in which it occurs? The soothing sounds do not come from the chair or table or from the dog or the cat. They come only from that other creature that is a lot like *me*—but much bigger. At some point the child comes to develop a theory of mind according to which those sounds originate only from another individual who thinks, feels, and understands in roughly the same ways in which other human beings do and never from a lion. Developing a theory of mind thus is a fundamental step in developing a *species-identity*. Admittedly though, both cybernetics and possible encounters with extra-terrestrial beings may well challenge this view in the future; so the present privileged place that human language holds in human *species-haecceity* is a contingent one.

With a theory of mind in hand (or in mind, so to speak), the human infant begins developing a more robust understanding of human *species-haecceity* along with a more robust human nature, i.e., the properties in the cluster of properties that produce the causal nexus upon which human nature supervenes begin to accumulate. Exactly what it is that provides the final, magical catalyst that then produces that causal nexus may never be determined. It is simply the synergetic interaction amongst some minimal number of properties. However, it is difficult to imagine this occurring without a sense of *species-identity* and some understanding and appreciation of human *species-haecceity*, and it is difficult to imagine such an identity occurring and such understanding and appreciation occurring without the accompanying understanding and appreciation of human language and a theory of mind.

Consider again, for example, David Chalmers' suggestion of the existence of zombies, mentioned in the previous chapter, to illustrate the "hard problem" of consciousness. *Zombies*, according to Chalmers' suggestion, are automata who are functionally identical to human beings but with no subjective, sentient experiences. The original point of Chalmers suggestion was to focus on the questions of if or how and why the neurochemical processes in the brain that produce sentient experiences are accompanied by conscious experiences at all. What additional work does consciousness do? But consider now this different aspect of Chalmers' suggestion: What would it be like for a person really to believe that all other human beings are really *zombies*? This might be called the epistemological version of the *zombie* hypothesis. Is such a belief possible? In some ways, this is not such a fanciful supposition. Descartes, on the basis of his top-down view that an immortal soul was responsible for sentient experiences in human beings, believed that animals are automata, i.e., animal *zombies*, programmed to behave functionally as if they were sentient creatures and "programmed" to emit screams or moans in circumstances in which human beings might emit screams of pain or moans of pleasure.

It is difficult to imagine Descartes having a full-blown, robust human nature if he really believed and acted on such a view of animals; however, *a fortiori*, it appears that a human being would be severely deficient in the human nature department if he or she held and acted upon such a view that regarded other human beings as *zombies*. Something extremely important and very fundamental to the ways in which such a person would act upon and be acted upon by the *haecceity* presented by his or her environment (particularly the *species-haecceity* part of that environment) would be distorted. The theory of mind that a person develops that results in a *species-identity* and helps to explain *species-haecceity*, i.e., the uniquely human *thisness* or the uniquely human *come-up-againstness* presented by other human beings, is a vital ingredient in producing the causal nexus amongst the properties in the cluster of properties upon which human nature supervenes. Creatures that are functionally equivalent but with no conscious experiences just would not presently do the job of allowing a person to develop a *species-identity* or explain the subtle nuances of *species-haecceity*. Furthermore, the use and understanding of human language is perhaps the single most important aspect of that human *species-haecceity* that is responsible for a person developing a theory of mind and attributing conscious states to other human beings.

Understanding the importance of the use and understanding of human language and the accompanying development of a theory of mind to human *species-identity* helps to explain the significant differences between the cases of Laura Bridgman and Helen Keller. The case of Laura Bridgman was discussed at length in Chapter 5, and with the necessary additional conceptual framework now in place, it is possible to draw a sharp contrast between her case and that of Helen Keller. Born in Alabama in 1880, Helen Keller was, like Laura Bridgman, a normal child until the age of nineteen months when she was apparently stricken also by scarlet fever (although some accounts say that Keller's maladies existed from birth). The disease left her both blind and deaf. Keller's progressive parents contacted the Perkins Institute for the Blind in Boston on the basis of the report given by Charles Dickens in his *American Notes* of the treatment and education of Bridgman by Dr. Samuel Gridley Howe at the institute. Keller's famed teacher, Anne Sullivan, was trained at the institute in the same methods that had been used by Howe in his treatment of Bridgman. Sullivan taught Keller in the privacy of the family home in Alabama and did not have to cope with the puritanical theology that surrounded Howe's treatment of Bridgman in Boston. There is no evidence that anyone associated with Keller regarded her deaf-blindness as the corruption of some metaphysically distinct soul that was the result of divine punishment, the result of God's wrath, or possession by evil demons. She exhibited extreme behavioral problems, and although she had learned a few ad hoc signals for communicating with other human beings, she suffered from severe limitations in her *species-orientation,* including obvious severe limitations in her *species-identity.* Her family tried to train her to behave acceptably in much the same way that one might attempt to train a pet to behave acceptably. The success of Sullivan's instruction of Keller was famously immortalized in *The Miracle Worker.*

According to Sullivan's account, Keller's breakthrough came when Sullivan made the motions in the mechanical language for water as she ran water over Keller's hand. Suddenly, she "got it!" The *word* symbolized the *thing*—the cool, wet stuff touching her hand. Keller's progress in learning human language progressed at an accelerated rate after this initial conceptual breakthrough. She learned to read Braille—and in several different languages. Sullivan taught her to speak using the Tadoma method in a manner that allowed her to communicated orally. Eventually, Keller attended and graduated from Radcliffe College. She traveled widely. Lectured to large audiences. Wrote books. Became a suffragette and an activist for the disabled. Developed and maintained close friendships with Sullivan and others. In other words, Keller acquired a rather robust human nature.

Although already biologically human, Keller became more fully human by developing her human nature, and she did this by developing a more robust human *species-orientation* (by approximating the unique range of ways in which human beings act upon and are acted upon by the environment), including a more robust *species-identity* (by coming to understand more fully and identify more closely with her fellow human beings). The development of her *species-identity* came about by the persistent presence of the uniquely *human haecceity* presented to her initially in the person of Anne Sullivan and then by her family and companions. The most salient and effective form of interacting with that *human haecceity* and the resulting cause of her "breakthrough" was through the use of human language.

Although still severely limited in her *species-sense,* Keller compensated for her seriously compromised *species-sense* by developing the other properties in the cluster of properties upon which human nature supervenes. Exactly how and why Keller was successful in doing this while Bridgman was not can probably never be completely determined. Whatever subtle differences and nuances there might have been in their respective brain morphologies or the neurochemical processes taking place in their brains, or whatever subtle differences there might have been in the teaching techniques, or other environmental influences have never been determined (and now, in all probability, never will be determined). The end result is that Keller, even with the severe limitations to her *species-sense*, managed to develop a *species-identity* and a *species-orientation* within the general range or normalcy while Bridgman did not. This does not mean, of course, that one must write books or travel widely to develop a *species-identity* or a human *species-orientation*. It does mean that one must develop a minimum of understanding of and identification with one's own kind (a *species-identity)*, which includes attributing sentient experiences to other human beings using a theory of mind, and the most overwhelmingly convincing evidence for doing this is by participating in the meaningful use of language with others.

When a child goes through the process of developing a *species-identity* and a theory of mind by which to attribute sentient states of mind to others, he or she frequently makes mistakes by attributing similar sentient states of mind—motives, feelings, moods, to pets or even inanimate objects. Eventually, a normal child comes to distinguish other human beings from other things in the universe and develops a *species-identity*. The development of a *species-identity* is the first step in developing a sense of *social proprioception*, i.e., the sense of how one stands in relationship to other human beings. Just as the sense of *proprioception* indicates the orientation of one's body and limbs in the physical world and just as consciousness (*mental proprioception*) indicates the orientation of one's experiences to one another in space and time, *social proprioception* is the perception of oneself vis-à-vis others like oneself. *Species-identity* and the sense of *social proprioception* are also the beginnings of what the American pragmatists William James and George Herbert Mead called "the social self," i.e., that part of one's self-identity that is determined by one's personal, social, and political relationships. Biologists regularly use the notion of *social proprioception* when describing the features of different species on non-human animals. For example, the notion of "alpha male" to describe the relationship of an individual to siblings or other members of a group is one such characterization.

Consider once more (and for the last time) Wittgenstein's comment about our inability to understand a lion if it were to speak. Using and understanding a human language is part of a *form of life* that includes, to use the conceptual framework developed in this book, a *species-orientation*, including a *species-identity*, that is developed in reaction to the *haecceity* presented by the natural world, including especially the *species-haecceity* presented by other human beings. Helen Keller acquired such a form of life, and Laura Bridgman did not. Evidently, Laura Bridgman's relationship to other human beings represented a conceptual conundrum that could not be resolved. She thus apparently never fully developed an understanding of *species-haecceity* or a *species-identity*. The same, unfortunately, is true of those children that are the victims of extreme isolation for long periods in early childhood with similar consequences for their *species-sense*, their sense of *social proprioception*, their *species-orientation*, their *species-identity*, and finally, their *human nature*. The comparative adaptive advantages of a normally developed child with a "normal" human *species-sense*, a "normal" *species-identity*, a "normal" sense of *social proprioception*, a "normal" *species-orientation*, and a "normal" human nature certainly implies that human language offers significant adaptive advantages and was selected for by natural selection.

Whenever, wherever, and however human language developed and on whatever grounds it is explained today by social scientists and linguists, the important point for the cluster theory of human nature is that, on a very fundamental level, the development of a *species-identity* in human beings is directly correlated with the development of human language. All of this is a social process and does not happen in isolation from others. Also, as I have argued, another fundamental aspect of developing a *species-identity* and a sense of *social proprioception* is the development of a theory of mind according to which young children attribute to other people sentient experiences to account for, amongst other things, the *meaningful* uses of human language and their communication with others using language.

A significant aspect of one's sense of *social proprioception*, i.e., the sense of the unique range of reciprocal interactions that are possible with fellow human beings, is the development of a theory of mind, according to which one attributes similar mental states as one has oneself to others. This means the recognition of intentions and motives in oneself and the attribution of intentions and motives to others, and such recognition and attribution are the beginnings of the recognition and the attribution of *emotions*. It is a short, easy step from the attribution to others of the understanding a word or gesture or having a motive for a word or gesture to the attribution to others of such emotions as fear or love. And the attribution of emotions to other human beings is as much a part of a theory of mind as is the attribution of intentions, motives, or understanding.

Unlike the meanings that lie behind language and gestures, the *expressions* of emotions are taken by many, including famously, Charles Darwin, as "natural" and, in some cases at least, universal amongst different human cultures. In *The Expression of the Emotions in Man and Other Animals*, published in 1872, just one year after *The Descent of Man*, Darwin meticulously gathered and documented data concerning the different facial expressions, changes in volume, pitch, and tone of voice, body posture, etc., associated with the expression of different emotions. He also did very similar research on the different behaviors taken to be the expression of emotions by domesticated animals. Darwin had no reticence about attributing emotions to animals. Certain behaviors of a dog, cat, or other domesticated animals are as easily understood as the expression of emotions, e.g., fear, as can the behavior of a person. While there is still some controversy amongst social scientists about whether the particular forms of expression of emotions are universal or not, it is clear that enough of the behavior expressing emotions that is presented to an individual human being by other human beings is "natural" enough that it represents a significant aspect of the *species-haecceity* and the *come-up-againstness* presented by the natural world.

In particular, being presented with the expression of emotions by other human beings as part of the *species-haecceity* with which an individual is faced, presents a unique opportunity (and perhaps necessity) for an equally unique range of behavior in the *proactive mode of species-orientation*. I have argued earlier that human beings are characterized by a unique range of experience and behavior that constitutes the human *proactive mode of species-orientation*. What is now obvious is that a significant portion of that range of behavior that constitutes the human *proactive mode of species-orientation* is devoted to acting upon and being acted upon by other human beings. Furthermore, a significant portion of that range of behavior that is devoted to acting upon and being acted upon by other human beings results from the expression of emotions and the perception of the expression of emotions. It is the beginning of what some call "the social brain." There will be no effort here to provide a complete theory of human emotions; however, by focusing on some particular emotions and some particular aspects of how those emotions are expressed or recognized, it is possible to provide some insight into how human emotions factor into the cluster theory of human nature.

Like much of the other uniquely human properties in the cluster of properties upon which human nature supervenes, the human brain is especially adapted for the expression of emotions and the recognition of the expression of emotions. It is easy to understand how such an ability was selected for by natural selection since the recognition of such expressions identifies another individual as friend or foe—as ally or enemy. The accurate attribution of emotions to others is an important aspect of the theory of mind. The ability to recognize at least some expressions of emotions seems to be *hard-wired* into the human psyche. Such attributions of emotion are features of the human *proactive mode of species-orientation* as responses to the very specific ways in which *species-haecceity* is presented by other human beings. While it may be not be a very attractive prospect for a proponent of some top-down theories of human nature (where human emotions are regarded as the result of some metaphysically distinct spiritual quality), neuroscientists now believe that the limbic system, lying deep within the brain at the juncture of its two hemispheres, is the part of the brain that is mainly responsible for human emotions. Similar structures are thought to be present in all mammals. The human limbic system is composed of the hippocampus, the amygdyla, and the hypothalamus with each part responsible for a particular aspect of recognizing and expressing emotions. For example, fear that is the result of a sudden, surprising, threat is produced by the amygdala, which then stimulates the hypothalamus that, in turn, stimulates such physiological reactions as a rise in heart rate and breathing. Both the recognition of the threat and the immediate bodily expressions of fear are the results of neurochemical processes in the brain and central nervous system. A malfunctioning amygdala, resulting from disease or injury, leads to regressive, infantile, anti-social behavior, subdued, "flat," emotions, and the inability to recognize the expression of hostility from other human beings or animals. It is this same limbic system that allows for the kind of "supernatural experiences" discussed in Chapter 6 that are characterized by a sense of heightened and elevated emotional feelings. The experiences that some described as "transcendent"—aesthetic experiences, experiences of the sacred or the holy, experiences of horror or terror, and experience of extreme personal intimacy—are all functions of the limbic system in the human brain.

None but the most devout closet Cartesians would probably have difficulty in attributing such an emotion as fear to other animals. It is non-threatening to attribute such feelings as surprise or fear to animals. For example, it is common to attribute such emotions to dogs that exhibit the familiar expressions in domesticated dogs, as Darwin noted in *The Expression of the Emotions in Man and Other Animals*,[2] such as trembling muscles, raising of hair, tucking of the tail between the hind legs, and flattened ears. However, things become a bit more controversial when it comes to other emotions such as love. It should be noted though that all mammals have very similar general brain morphologies—although with some admittedly significant differences is size and shape—as well as very similar neurochemical processes in those brains. In contrast with those theories of human nature that attribute the "higher" emotions to some other-worldly, spiritual source, the cluster theory of human nature has no difficulty in anchoring the "higher" emotions such as love, empathy, joy, and devotion, in human biology and the neurochemical processes of the human brain. Thus, the cluster theory has no difficulty in attributing those "higher" emotions to some other animals as well given the similarities that exist between the brain morphologies and neurochemical processes between human and non-human animals.

Scientists are in near universal agreement that human beings, like other animals, have a strong drive to reproduce. Whether it is "the selfish gene" that accounts for this drive or some more general and vague principle of biology, it is clear that the human species (and consequently human nature) would not survive without widespread procreation amongst members of the species. Biological clocks tick, people mate, and babies are born. However, more than simple mating and sexual reproduction are necessary for the perpetuation of the species. Given the long period of infant development after birth and the extreme helplessness and vulnerability of human infants, some social arrangements are necessary for their safety, health, and normal development.

While there may theoretically be many different kinds of social arrangements to provide for the protection and care of human infants, the most common kind of arrangement involves some sort of pair-bonding between the two parents with some sort of extended familial connections with whatever siblings of the child there may be and whatever relatives of the parents there may be. And while there my be some degree of flexibility in terms of what particular personal and social arrangements are deemed most suitable for the care and protection of children, the view that human sociology is infinitely malleable and completely culturally determined has been undermined by the evidence from the research in neuroscience that shows that a great deal of those personal and social relationships are "hard-wired" into the human brain. Contra the view of the "blank slate" nature of human beings, the cluster theory embraces the view that some of the most fundamental and important properties in the cluster of properties upon which human nature supervenes are the functions of innate, biological features and processes (and, in this case, neurochemical processes in the brain). Nurture is thus thoroughly informed by nature.

This discussion, of course, centers around the primary sociological group called "the family." But what provides the bond between the parents and the family ties that unite certain groups of people? The most common answer from most social scientists is *emotional* connections. Very little in the way of emotion is required for the simple act of mating to produce children. Impregnation can occur easily, even in an act of violence, with no emotional connection between the two parties (expect perhaps passion, lust, anger, or even rage). Lust and love excite completely different areas of the brain. As described in some detail in Chapter 4, human sexuality is far more sophisticated, luxurious, and intimate than what is required for simple, lustful procreation. Reciprocal emotions such as love and feelings of attachment are usually involved between the parents and between the parents and child when human procreation is a matter of reflective choice. This is all a good thing for human infants since pair-bonding resulting from mutual love and commitment provides the stability and social environment necessary for the kind of healthful and normal child development described in the preceding chapter. While most social scientists are reluctant to say that any aspect of human psychology or any form of human relationships is universal, some recognition of human romantic love has been documented in nearly all human cultures, and, contrary to much public opinion, permanent pair-bonding amongst non-human animals that contributes in any significant way to the raising of offspring, although it does occasionally occur, is quite uncommon. Something is obviously unique about human romantic love and the complicated social arrangements that are the result of that emotion.

Arguably, whatever it is that is that mysterious, unique quality about human romantic love, it has been the subject of more poetry, novels, essays, and, more recently, scientific research than perhaps any other topic. What explains such an interest in the emotion of romantic love? It is something of an unromantic understanding of romantic love that the fixation on romantic love might well be the result of its extremely fundamental biological basis and its important evolutionary function. Part of the recent scientific research focusing on brain chemistry on the part of neuroscientists has produced considerable evidence that the human emotion of love (in this case, what is called "romantic" love) is the result of the brain's production of different chemicals in certain concentrations, especially dopamine, serotonin, and norepinephrine.[3] Romantic love is often associated with behavior that closely resembles addiction—extreme fixation on the object of one's affection, often resulting in emotional exhilaration, anxiety, and loss of sleep and appetite. Interestingly, these chemicals are also associated with such behavior.

Furthermore, brain scans have indicated that the areas of the brain most exercised by strong emotions of romantic love are the caudate nucleus, a part of what is considered to be one of the earliest developing parts of the brain called "the reptilian brain," and the ventral tegmental area (VTA). These areas of the brain are important "reward areas" of the brain, responsible for a person's recognition of a reward and the development of preferences for certain rewards over others. They are responsible for motivation towards achieving rewards and the feelings of satisfaction upon that achievement. The elevated levels of dopamine and norepinephrine are responsible for the single-mindedness and stick-to-itiveness that are often necessary for obtaining rewards. Individuals who are "love sick" are often driven to desperate measures that are not always beneficial to the individual, but which, evidently, serve the species well. Although it is not a very romantic picture, much of the same brain chemistry appears to be involved in a person's addiction to drugs or compulsive pursuit of fame and fortune as is involved in the pursuit of one's romantic love interest. That same chemistry may well explain why failed romantic love often ends in violence and tragedy.

Cybernetics and cloning may well threaten this view of the role of romantic love in the future. Given the evolutionary history of human beings, the brain has evolved to the point where it functions to produce and recognize the production of human emotions. Might those emotions be produced artificially by yet to be invented means? Perhaps. The impact on human nature will depend upon how drastic the changes are. Some people already are treated with drugs that alter or control the chemical processes in the brain to regulate psychological moods and emotions within what is considered to be a "normal" range. It is known that different drugs or different concentrations of drugs can produce extremes of moods and emotions that seriously alter or destroy a person's *species-orientation* and often have tragic consequences. This illustrates that it is possible to destroy human nature with drugs that have disastrously damaging effects on the brain. In such cases, the remark is often made that the person is just no longer normal or is not really "human." Using the cluster theory of human nature, this description is understood to mean that the individual's *social proprioception* has been seriously damaged and altered beyond the range or normalcy and that the individual no longer possesses human nature or possess it only to a very minimal degree. It is easy to imagine that the current, normal human *species-identity* (and the naturally occurring *species-haecceity*) could be "stretched" in the future as the result of drugs or cybernetics.

Of course, none of this means that an individual must experience romantic love to have human nature. While the focus here has been on romantic love, it is just one of a full range of human emotions, and it seems reasonable to say that any individual who feels *none* of those emotions or an extremely limited number of those emotions throughout an entire lifetime is missing an important property in the cluster of properties upon which human nature supervenes. Would completely missing all human emotions be enough to collapse the causal nexus that is generated amongst those properties? What would one say if a person never felt any anger, fear, love, or any other human emotion? The answer to this question must come on an individual case basis. In the once-popular television series *Star Trek*, Mr. Spock, the Vulcan, feels no emotions. In terms of the property of human reason emphasized both in Chapter 3 and Chapter 8, Mr. Spock apparently was able to act upon and be acted upon by his environment in many of the same ways as did the human characters in the show—except with a much higher ability and to a greater degree of sophistication. However, amongst the most obvious differences between Spock and human beings was the fact that he was completely devoid of feeling emotions. This illustrates the fact that human nature is not the result of any one property or any small, definitive set of properties in the cluster of properties that subvenes human nature. Spock may have possessed several of those properties—perhaps even a majority of them. However, if he felt no emotions at all, his *species-identity* would have been so different from the *species-identity* of human beings that one most likely would say that he was missing a significant degree of human nature. As described in the shows, Spock lacks a human *species-identity* and is seriously lacking in a human *social proprioception*. It is common to make the same sort of judgment about psychopathic killers who murder other human beings in particularly gruesome ways while having no emotional responses at all.

If human beings are, in some sense, "hard-wired" to express and recognize the expression of emotions, what does this mean for the cluster theory of human nature? The answer to this question is to be found in the inextricable relationship between the expression and recognition of the expression of emotions and the moral nature of human beings and the social and political arrangements that human beings have devised on the basis of that moral nature. Darwin famously claimed that human beings are the only moral animal. What is the basis for such a claim and what is the evolutionary basis for man's moral nature? And if the cluster theory is grounded in empirical scientific theories of the natural and social sciences, how can the development of man's moral nature be accounted for in light of what appears to be the brutal, amoral mechanism of natural selection? At least part of the answer to these questions is to be found in considering the role that sexual selection, which Darwin considered to be a separate evolutionary mechanism from natural selection, has played in the evolution of human beings.

Earlier, I have emphasized the immaturity, helplessness, and vulnerability of newly-born human infants and the very slow process of development that eventually results in independence and self-sufficiency. For the human species to survive, obviously some sort of arrangement is necessary to provide for the care and protection of human infants and young children. One does not have to go so far as to accept Richard Dawkins' notion of "the Selfish Gene" to realize that adult human beings have some significant investment in our offspring and attribute some significant value in their safety, survival, and flourishing. This notion of parental investment in offspring, arguably first introduced by Robert Trivers, has now become the operable paradigm for social scientists and the theoretical analysis of Darwin's notion of sexual selection and the resulting personal, familial, and social relationships.[4] There is much of interest in the notions of sexual selection and parental investment, but the main emphasis here is upon how these aspects of the biological nature of human beings contribute to the eventual development of the moral and social nature of human beings and the role these properties play in the cluster theory.

The commonly accepted view of human sexual selection amongst social scientists of an evolutionary bent is that women have a significantly greater parental investment than do men. This disparity can be accounted for on several grounds, including the relative scarcity of female eggs compared to male sperm, the frequency with which women can reproduce compared to men, and the increased inconvenience and possible danger resulting from pregnancy and birth. Again, the commonly accepted view is that this difference in female and male parental investment has contributed to women being more choosy than men about their sexual partners and making those choices on different grounds. Generally, on strictly evolutionary grounds, men are primarily interested in maximizing the production of offspring and therefore desire sex with as many productive women as possible while women are primarily interested in security and protection during possible pregnancy and childbirth. Of course, much of this characterization is still controversial and the subject of a great deal of research in the social and natural sciences, and there is no effort here to develop a comprehensive theory—based on Darwinian evolution or otherwise—of how moral theory developed based upon these claims. It is possible, however, to make some somewhat tentative suggestions that are open to review and revision on the basis of future research in the social sciences and theories developed by moral philosophers. It is not vital to the cluster theory of human nature that human morality be based upon natural selection; it is important to recognize the existence of human morality and to provide some plausible explanation of how moral judgments, beliefs, and codes factor into the cluster of properties upon which human nature supervenes without assuming a special moral sense that is based upon a non-natural metaphysics.

Whatever controversy and disagreements there may be notwithstanding, it stands to reason that because of the degree and character of their biological and personal investment, women are likely to attribute significant value to their babies. Generally, people care about that in which they have invested a great deal. Thus, in what is an admittedly fast and loose connection, a mother's significant investment in her offspring generally promotes valuing that promotes caring that promotes affection and promotes loving that promotes certain moral values.

The parental investment and the connection between parental investment and sexual selection in men is perhaps not so obviously or so easily drawn. If men are interested primarily in maximizing their offspring, this cannot mean simply impregnating as many women as possible. This might be the case with species that produce hundreds or thousands of offspring that are then cast to the winds (or tides) for survival; however, if newborn human infants are cast to the winds (or tides), none survive. So, to insure the survival of their offspring, men must have some interest and investment in more than simply the impregnation of females. They must have some investment in ensuring the survival, safety, and maturation of their offspring. It is this investment that most plausibly accounts for the parental investment of men in their children on evolutionary grounds. Again, fathers care about that in which they are invested, and caring about their offspring promotes caring about those who protect those offspring and promote their welfare; so some valuing of mothers by fathers is the result. These biological and evolutionary interests are obviously open to various interpretations; however, this sense of investment at least provides a plausible explanation for the beginnings of such human social arrangements as the family with the accompanying and underlying emotions that are attached to those arrangements—feelings of attachment, commitment, romantic love, jealousy, parental love, and empathy. Where such emotions and social attachments occur, morality is sure to follow.

It is not necessary for the cluster theory of human nature to provide a naturalistic account of the origin of human emotions and social structures. That is a job for the social scientists and perhaps the neuroscientists. I have claimed in Chapter 4 that human sexuality is overly designed for mere reproduction. The peculiarities of human sexuality promote personal intimacy quite independently of the "natural" consequence of pregnancy, reproduction, and preservation of the species. The fundamental point for the cluster theory of human nature is that coming to recognize the range of unique connections to other human beings, i.e., developing a *social proprioception*, is the basis for human emotions and human morals. This comes about by being presented with and reciprocally presenting a uniquely human *species haecceity*. The unique set of ways in which human beings act upon and are acted upon by other human beings includes the use of human language, the expression of and the recognition of the expression of emotions, entering into certain social arrangements, and the recognition that some actions are beneficial to other human beings while other actions are harmful to them.

The recognition of the distinction between actions that are beneficial to others and those that are harmful would seem to be a rather primitive and fundamental stage in the development of human moral psychology. While "human moral psychology" may seem redundant to some, I wish to leave open the possibility that other animals also have a moral psychology and experience, to some degree or other, moral sentiments. However, this is not a claim that I will defend at any length here. The crucial step, which has occupied psychologists and moral philosophers for centuries, is how what may be described as the cognitive and detached recognition of the distinction between beneficial and harmful acts comes to be accompanied by feelings of positive inclination or judgments of approval and feelings of aversion or judgments of disapproval respectively. Several prominent moral philosophers as well as Darwin bridged this step by attributing a "moral sense" to human beings. Hence the origin of the designation of human beings as "the moral animal." Darwin's view was that the moral sense of human beings arose from human sexual and parental instincts—a view that is fundamental to the position developed by the cluster theory of human nature.

Biologists tend to emphasize the importance of sexual reproduction, i.e., *meiotic* reproduction, for the rich diversity of traits that exist in a species resulting from a mixing of genes from the two parents compared to the uniformity that results from asexual reproduction. However, from the standpoint of a theory of human nature, it is equally important to emphasize that human sexual reproduction (and the sexual selection that accompanies sexual reproduction) necessitates a connection of one human being to another. Indeed, it obviously necessitates a *physical* connection of one to another. In addition to the physical connection, however, there are the connections involved as a part of sexual selection having to do with courtship, pair-bonding, and parental investment. Even without the considerations having to do with reproduction, the psychological connections resulting from the personal intimacy can be understood as providing the biological basis for romantic love. As discussed in Chapter 4, the peculiarities of human sexuality seem to encourage such emotional and psychological connections. Such relationships can easily be taken to be the origin of Sartre's notion of *the Other*, discussed in Chapter 6, as well as the notion of *the Others*, discussed above, i.e., those like oneself with whom one has collaborative and corporative interests and arrangements. While there may be significant cultural variation in the nature of those social arrangements and the related moral feelings or judgments, the social nature of human beings appears to be natural. And given the importance of that social interaction to the normal development of human infants and young children, it is hard to imagine that any individual could develop a full, robust human nature in the complete absence of such interactions. Thus, the development of a *social proprioception*, at least to some minimal degree, is a vitally important property in the cluster of properties that produces the causal nexus upon which human nature supervenes.

To return to the thought experiments of the early chapters of this book, imagine a human infant Robinson Crusoe, Jr., stranded by whatever means on a deserted island. Again, by whatever means (except with no Friday or any contact with any other human being whatsoever), imagine that the infant survives to adulthood. Although biologically human, it is difficult to imagine that such an individual would have the minimum of predicates to generate the causal nexus upon which human nature supervenes. Even adult human beings that exist in complete isolation from other human beings (such as prisoners in long-term solitary confinement) are bound to lose some degree or other of their human nature. Whether such a person can ever fully regain his or her human nature will depend upon the particulars of the individual situation and is a matter for social scientists to investigate.

The same point suggests that the last human being left alive, if he or she lives long enough, is sure to lose most of his or her human nature, and, in this case, barring some miraculous intervention, such an individual will never regain his or her human nature before death. This illustrates the fundamental point that a significant number of the properties and the resulting causal nexus amongst those properties that produce human nature are the result of an organism's *social proprioception*, the subrange of an organism's *species-orientation* that is species-specific. A vital aspect of the *species-orientation* of human beings is the human *species-identity* that is generated only by the *species-haecceity* presented by other human beings. A fundamental claim of the cluster theory of human nature is that human nature emerges from a range of ways in which human beings act upon and are acted upon by our environment. A consequence of this view is that a dramatic change in that environment would naturally eventually result in a dramatic change in human nature, and a dramatic enough change would result in a significant enough deterioration of the causal nexus that exists amongst the properties upon which human nature supervenes that a complete loss of human nature might result. What the foregoing discussion indicates is that the complete absence of other human beings in one's environment and the complete loss of *species-haecceity* and the resulting loss of *species-identity* and *social proprioception* would represent just such a dramatic change.

I will not engage here in an investigation of how the primary and fundamental social connections of human beings, e.g., the family, develop into more complex social and political ones. I will leave such matters to the sociologists and the political anthropologists. There is obviously considerable conventional and cultural variation in those complex social and political arrangements that human beings have devised. The specificities of those arrangements are not important here. What is important is that human biology—and particularly human sexuality—push man towards engaging in collaborative and cooperative social arrangements and endeavors with other human beings.[5] Living with and interacting with other human beings and engaging in projects in concert with other human beings, e.g., developing a sense of *us*, is thus an important property in the cluster of properties upon which human nature supervenes. While an individual might maintain the fragile integrity of the causal nexus that is created amongst those properties while living in complete isolation from other human beings for some period of time, the chances are that after a significantly prolonged period of such isolation, the causal nexus would break down. This is evidence of the importance of *social proprioception* for a robust and healthy human nature.

In the remainder of this chapter, I will address the importance of *human culture* to the cluster theory of human nature—a final development of the discussion of human *techne* in Chapter 7. The emphasis there was on *material* culture and the productions of the practical—physical or mechanical—endeavors of human beings acting in the *proactive mode of species-orientation*. The emphasis here will be upon what might described as the more intellectual endeavors that produce human culture. While artists, musicians, authors, other creative artists and aestheticians continue to debate the difference between "the arts" and technology, i.e., between what I call here the more "intellectual" endeavors and what I discussed in Chapter 7 as human *techne,* that debate and those arguments will not be enjoined here. Drawing the difference between art and *techne* explicitly in theoretical terms is not an important issue for the cluster theory of human nature. Explaining how each kind of endeavor contributes to the cluster of properties that subvene the causal nexus upon which human nature supervenes is the main concern at the moment.

The point has been made that the products of human *techne* far exceed the products of any other species in the degree of their scope and complexity and that human *techne* is result of a significant difference between human beings and any other species known to exist on Earth. This difference is accounted for in terms of the degree to which members of different species interact with their environment on the basis of a *proactive mode of species-orientation*. The same claim is perhaps more obviously true of the products of human intellectual endeavor—the human *arts*.

Some have made the claim that human beings are distinguished from other animals by our creative abilities, our aesthetic sense, and our phenomenological experience of beauty. John Dewey is one such philosopher. As explained earlier, Dewey maintained that aesthetic experiences are the "highest" form of human experience since they stir into action deep resonances of the primitive dispositions of human beings. Aesthetic experiences are transcendent for Dewey in that they introduce meanings and values that transcend ordinary sense experience. Such experiences have "depth," and are what some people call "spiritual" or even "religious" experiences. The focus here goes beyond simply the notion of aesthetic experience, however, to whatever "primitive disposition" there may be in human beings to produce the objects of such experiences or in promoting the having of such experiences.

It is commonly agreed that the earliest examples of hominid art to have been discovered by archeologists are the paintings found in different caves in France. Chauvet Cave has paintings that are claimed to be over 30,000 years old while the more famous, extravagant, and detailed paintings in Lascaux, France, are said to be over 15,000 years old. While archeologists emphasize the importance of the paintings as evidence for the communal and cooperative arrangements in which the early hominids who produced these paintings lived, the emphasis here is on their aesthetic qualities. This is not meant to deemphasize the importance of the social element of art. In fact, quite to the contrary, this entire chapter is devoted to the social and cultural aspects of human nature, and whatever aesthetic sensibilities human beings have are an aspect of a *social proprioception*. There is a *range* of human art that is distinctively human, and art, in its most general form, is both a result of and a contributor to a human *species identity*. There is abundant anthropological evidence of social and cooperative behavior amongst early homimids, and while there is justifiable concern amongst anthropologists and sociologists in pinpointing the earliest period and location of such behavior, that is not the concern here. The fundamental questions for the cluster theory about such early examples of art (including cave paintings, pottery, etc.) concern the aesthetic sensibilities of human beings, the creative artistic qualities in man, the relationships amongst human beings, and the development of human nature.

These early Lascaux paintings of animals—bulls, horses, and deer— are informative and illustrative about a certain aspect of human nature in that they seem to go far beyond whatever might be deemed to be any practicable, functional purposes involved in the hunting of the animals. Some of these paintings are simply magnificent, and the scale is staggering with some measuring several feet in length. Some of the animals depicted are realistic characterizations of actually existing animals (and hence, targets of the hunt) while others seem to be clearly imaginary ones. These paintings are not "battle plans" for the hunt or simple, stick diagrams for purposes of the instruction of neophyte hunters. They are much too elaborate and were much too labor-intensive to have been produced simply for such practical purposes. The paintings are best taken as tokens of adoration, as expressions of the human creative spirit, or as possible empirical evidence of some human aesthetic sense. The same points can be made about other elaborate "artifacts" of early man from locations in Spain, Germany, Russia, and Turkey, amongst other places.

Again, all of this is not to deny that other animals perhaps "sense" beauty or have something of an aesthetic sense. Visual displays during mating, the "songs" of birds, and the decoration of the bowers of

Australian bower birds, amongst other examples of animal behavior, strongly suggest that other animals produce and value aesthetic experiences. However, it is obvious and inarguable that no other animal has produced objects or aesthetic experience that come close to rivaling those produced by human beings in terms of scale, sophistication, complexity, and permanence. News accounts have reported how a Vietnamese potbellied pig (named Smithfield), when supplied with the proper supplies, has managed to create "paintings" by using its body (mainly its drooping belly) to rub paint on a canvas. Some may wish to call such a process "art." For the cluster theory of human nature, whether such a process or product qualifies as art in some abstract, theoretical sense does not matter. Even if other animals engage in creative artistic processes and even if the products of those processes are regarded as art, nothing produced by any other species of animal on Earth even remotely approximates the products of human artistic creative endeavors. Consider, for comparison, the Mona Lisa, the ceiling of the Sistine Chapel, Starry Night, David, Venus de Milo, the Parthenon, Beethoven's *Ninth Symphony*, Mozart's *Fortieth Symphony*, or even various examples of what is considered "pop" culture.

As these examples illustrate, aesthetic sensibilities in members of different species of animals and the products of those sensibilities and abilities are species-specific. In other words, there is a range of such sensibilities and products of those sensibilities that is distinctively human. Bower birds decorate their long, tunnel-shaped bowers for other bower birds, and human beings produce their paintings, sculptures, symphonies, and novels for other human beings. To produce and appreciate such aesthetic works is a part of the human *social proprioception*, i.e., a distinctive aspect of the ways in which human beings are able to relate to other human beings.

This aesthetic component to the human *social proprioception* is a result of intellectual, emotional, and/or spiritual proactive responses to conditions and circumstances in one's environment, i.e, a distinctive version of the *proactive mode of species orientation*. In the *proactive mode of species orientation*, members of a species engage in proactive behavior to a set of circumstances by acting upon materials or resources to rearrange or reconfigure those materials in a novel way to address the *haecceity* that is present in those circumstances rather than simply *reacting* it. As I have argued in Chapter 7, this is the same kind of behavior that underlies human *techne*. While both are forms of the uniquely human *proactive mode of species orientation*, the significant difference between human *techne* and human art is that the practical application of the respective behavior for addressing the *haecceity* present in the circumstances is readily apparent in the case of human *techne* while, in the case of human art, the behavior is not practical *per se* but is fundamentally an expression of a more abstract, intellectual, emotional, or spiritual (and thus, less practical) reaction. The blurry line between art and crafts represents the grey area of this distinction.

The enormous differences in scale, scope, sophistication, and complexity between the products of human artistic endeavors and those of other animals are instructive of at least two important, salient, and distinctive features of human art and human aesthetic sensibilities for the cluster theory. These two features give clues as to how human art and aesthetic sensibilities might be seen as part of the human *proactive mode of species orientation* and a human *social proprioception*. First, such artistic endeavors across such a wide spectrum—visual art, sculpture, music, literature, and, more recently photography and film and other "new" art forms—have required and continue to require enormous expenditures of time and energy. Such endeavors make heavy demands on both the individual level and the level of the human species. The "practical" aspects of crafts or human *techne* may be regarded as making significant contributions to the preservation of the species, but if there is some practical feature of the arts that might hold adaptive value, it is not readily apparent. However, it is equally obvious that such endeavors and the products of such endeavors must hold great value to human beings to justify the investment of time and energy they require.

Aestheticians have struggled with these issues for centuries (at least since the time of Plato), and the cluster theory of human nature has no unique theory to offer regarding the adaptive value of human art or human aesthetic sensibilities. However, the enormous investment of time and energy in such endeavors is clear evidence of the significant value of those endeavors and, in the absence of any evidence of immediate practical value, the value must derive from the human psyche and human emotions, i.e., from the limbic system. In addition to physical actions, human art is produced by a significant investment of emotional energy, and the products that result from that investment of emotional energy also engage human emotions. Given what has been said earlier in this chapter about the unique range and depth of human emotions and the natural *expressions* of those emotions, one clue about the proactive value of art is to be found in the ways in which it might benefit human beings in addressing the *haecceity*, the *come-up-againstness*, of the human condition. In other words, the human *proactive mode of species orientation* includes emotional reactions to the *haecceity* in addition to mere physical actions. Whatever the synergetic interaction may be between the two has been and continues to be the subject of much research in psychology. Those emotional responses, however, represent something of a universal component to being human, i.e., they are a component of the "natural" range of ways in which human beings are related to other human beings.

Secondly, the enormous investment of emotional energy in the production of art and the emotional responses evoked by the various products of artistic achievements, i.e., the human aesthetic sensibility, are evidence of the great breadth and depth of the range of the human *proactive mode of species orientation*. Just as the examples of "supernatural" experiences (discussed in Chapter 6) are evidence of the heightened nature of some human experiences, so human *techne* and human aesthetic sensibility are evidence of the uniquely human range of ways that human beings are able to act upon and be acted upon by their environments in the *proactive mode of species orientation*.

Consider, for example, the *come-up-againstness* often present in the human *species haecceity* of being presented with another human being that one loves. How is one to deal with such a highly emotionally charged situation of "resistence" from one's environment? The answer is that there is not a single answer to this question nor are there definitive right or wrong answers. Perhaps the only answer is that it just all depends, i.e., it depends a great deal upon the specifics of the individuals involved and the specifics of the situation; however, it is distinctively human to associate the products of human aesthetic sensibilities, e.g., paintings, poems, novels, music, into whatever specific behavior that is the result to such situations in a *proactive mode of species orientation*. The difficulties and ambiguities of such emotionally-charged aspects of *species haecceity* probably account for why such a topic has been so ubiquitous for poets, novelists, and other artists. The same sort of account can be proffered for death—perhaps the most threatening and certainly the most unavoidable form of *haecceity* presented to human beings by the natural world. Elaborate pyramids and mausoleums and, more commonly, death liturgies, poems, requiems, religious masses, and other rituals are aesthetic products that have resulted form human attempts to respond to the *haecceity* of death through an emotional or a more abstract, spiritual aspect of a distinctively human *proactive mode of species orientation*.

Whatever aesthetic sensibilities human beings might have and whatever the range of the products of aesthetic endeavors might be, they are functions, to a significant extent, of a uniquely human *species-orientation* resulting from a uniquely human *species-sense* and the unique set of phenomenological experiences (especially emotional experiences) that are produced through this *species-sense*. The production of, the appreciation of, and the emotional and/or spiritual or religious attachments to such endeavors or products is an important aspect of human *social proprioception*. These aesthetic endeavors and the products thereof have thus given rise to *Homo artifex*.

That same human sense of *social proprioception* is responsible for the political relationships and organizations that have been produced by human beings through a *proactive mode of species orientation*. It is such a sense developed to a certain level of abstraction that has made man a social and political animal. As Aristotle noted, "Man is by nature a political animal," a sentiment echoed by Cicero who said, "*inter homines esse*," i.e., human beings are meant to "live in society." The treatment here of man as a political animal, the ultimate stage of the human sense of *social proprioception*, is brief and summary in nature. Attention is focused here only on demonstrating how the abstract social and political relationships amongst human beings factor into the cluster of properties upon which human nature supervenes.

Other animals are well-known to live in groups of varying sizes and degrees of organization, but no other animal has exhibited the degree of abstraction and sophistication in various social and political organizations as have human beings. The complexity, sophistication, and degree of abstraction of those social and political organizations are the ultimate consequences of human *social proprioception* and the human "social brain." The "social brain" begins with the development of a "theory of mind" and attributing mental states to other human beings. It then leads to the ability to express and recognize the expression of emotions in others of one's own kind, which then leads to the attributing of value to significant others. The culmination of this process is the organization of various social and political structures to protect and nurture those other human beings to which one attributes value, e.g., mates, offspring, and extended kin. The final result is the production of complex social and political arrangements.

Top-down theories of human nature tend to explain the sophisticated political lives of human beings on metaphysical grounds. The democracy of ancient Athens was to have been a gift from Athena, and Augustine claimed that the City of Man is derived from and depends upon The City of God. Such explanations that rely upon a supernatural metaphysics are not available to the cluster theory of human nature, which is committed to methodological naturalism. The cluster theory explains the social and political aspects of human nature in completely natural terms. The beginning of that explanation lies in human biology and neurophysiology. The physiological and morphological bases for the sophisticated social brain that exists in human beings are found in the amygdala, the cingulate gyrus, and the orbitofrontal cortex of the brain. Neurochemical processes in these areas of the brain account for the following human behavior: the ability to express and recognize the expression of human emotions within some range that is considered normal, the ability to engage in appropriate social interaction with other human beings, and the ability to monitor and control social behavior by considering its effects on others. Whether all social and political behavior is completely biologically determined or not, it is obvious that such behavior is at least largely a function of human brains and would be impossible without the proper morphological and neurochemical underpinning. This is another indication of the interplay between nature and nurture and how nurture (in this case, the provisions provided by complex social and political arrangements) is grounded in nature.

The usual explanation on biological terms for the complex human social and political organizations begins with the interest in protecting and nurturing one's offspring (whether this interest is explained on the level of individual organisms or individual genes). In order to achieve this goal in a social setting where an individual is unavoidably faced with the *species haecceity* presented by other human beings in a group, one cannot act completely selfishly or simply to promote one's own self-interest or the exclusive interest of one's genetic offspring. *Enlightened* self-interest requires that to promote one's own interests one must cooperate with others, which means that, on occasions, an individual must sacrifice one's own immediate and short-term interests for the welfare of others in order to preserve (and hopefully promote) one's long-term interests. Developing such a state of political equilibrium may well explain the beginnings of altruism and the kind of reciprocal consideration necessary for political affiliations.

Exactly how such a state of political reflective equilibrium comes about is still a controversial issue and a matter of some considerable debate. Human beings may indeed be social creatures, and complex political organizations and interactions may require a properly functioning orbitofrontal cortex, as does all social behavior. However, beyond that, the basis to explain exactly how and why human beings came to enter into political arrangements, construct such things as governments, and engage in reciprocal behavior towards others is still a matter of considerable philosophical disagreement.

Given the commitment of the cluster theory of human nature to a naturalistic methodology, the most plausible explanation for human political behavior may lie along the lines suggested by Robert Wright.[6] Wright borrows from the results of a computer competition designed by Robert Axelrod to explain how one might gain some theoretical purchase on the process of explaining the origin of reciprocal altruism. Taking the prisoner's dilemma as a point of departure, Axelrod asked game theorists to design computer programs to represent the various different possible ways in which human beings might decide whether to cooperate with other human beings.[7] In other words, these were programs designed to explain the different possibilities for successful cooperative social interaction or reciprocal behavior amongst human beings. After a prolonged competition, the winning program, called TIT-FOR-TAT and designed by Anatol Rapoport, was declared. TIT-FOR-TAT is a very simple program that requires that one be nice to others initially and thereafter requires that one treat others as one has been treated. If A is benevolent to B, then B is benevolent to A, and if A is malicious to B, then B is malicious to A. When generalized, this simple program proffers the beginnings, at least, to a solution to Thomas Hobbes' "war of all against all" by providing what evolutionary biologists call an *evolutionarily stable strategy* for explaining the origins of reciprocal altruism and, in turn, political affiliation amongst human beings. TIT-FOR-TAT would promote and protect cooperative well-being and benevolent behavior amongst the participants while, at the same time, discouraging and threatening the selfish and malicious behavior of others. It promotes self-interested cooperation while punishing cheating. Presumably, in the long run, the good would thrive and the bad would not survive. The reciprocal altruism found in TIT-FOR-TAT is not the result of applying some abstract or theoretical concept of altruism. If there is such a concept, it is the *result* of the behavior and not the cause of it. As Wright points out, such emotions as gratitude and obligation, anger and disapproval, and forgiveness are all tied to the different actions required by TIT-FOR-TAT.

The selection of reciprocal altruism through some such mechanism as TIT-FOR-TAT provides at least a plausible evolutionary explanation for *Homo civilis* or *Homo politicus*, i.e., political man. Such selection, involving reciprocal altruism amongst non-kin, might well have emerged from such a simple set of interactions as described by TIT-FOR-TAT and preserved in individual genes. There is little doubt that *Homo civilis* or *Homo politicus* represents the most advanced, complex, and abstract manifestations of *species haecceity* and *social proprioception* and the corresponding social properties in the cluster of properties upon which human nature supervenes. The cluster theory thus provides at least a partial explanation for Aristotle's claim that man is a political animal.

Notes

1. In addition to those references mentioned in Chapter 8 (fn1), the following sources have informed the present treatment of the role of the brain in human language and social relationships in this chapter: *The Language Instinct: How the Mind Creates Language*, Steven Pinker (NY: W. Morrow and Co., 1994) and *The Neuroscience of Human Relationships*, Louis J. Cozolino (NY: Norton, 2006).
2. Charles Darwin, *The Expression of the Emotions in Man and Other Animals*, Third Edition (Oxford: Oxford University Press, 1872), pp. 122-23.
3. See Helen Fisher, *Why We Love: The Nature and Chemistry of Romantic Love* (New York, NY: Henry Holt and Company, 2004), Chapter 3.
4. Robert Trivers, "Parental Investment and Sexual Selection," in *Sexual Selection and the Descent of Man*, edited by Bernard Campbell (Chicago, IL: Aldine de Gruyer, 1972).
5. This is not to deny the importance of other cooperative endeavors such as hunting. It is also not to deny the possible influence of other evolutionary forces such as kin selection.
6. Robert Wright, *The Moral Animal: Evolutionary Psychology and Everyday Life* (New York: Pantheon Books, 1994), pp. 196ff.
7. In fact, the competition was amongst the computer programs themselves, but the programs modeled human behavior.

10

Conclusion

Since ancient times, philosophers have perhaps speculated about human nature more than, or certainly as much as, any other single topic. A key aspect of the explanation for this philosophical attention is perhaps the uniquely human urge to classify and organize the objects of one's experience—the urge to characterize and then distinguish objects from one another in an organized manner that then allows those objects to be compared with one another and placed in conceptual "pigeon-holes" to facilitate understanding. This is perhaps especially true of classifying man and understanding man's unique place in the natural world. To a significant degree, the same process characterizes scientific inquiry. For example, the earliest and perhaps still the most fundamental stage of biology is classification. In the history of intellectual thought, the attempts to explain and classify human nature are spread across a broad spectrum. For the most part, what are characterized here as *philosophical* attempts (or *theological* attempts) are at one end of this spectrum and scientific ones from the natural sciences are at the other. The crucial difference to be noted between the philosophical and scientific approaches is that, as indicated, philosophers have generally *speculated* about what it means to be human while scientists have tried to construct a scientific explanation of what it means to be human.

The uniqueness of human beings has, for the most part, been taken as a given. Even a casual observation of human beings and our place in the natural world leaves the very strong impression that there is something unique about the human species and that we human beings are significantly alike one another even given the many equally obvious differences that exist amongst us. Some thinkers, identified in Chapter 1 as *anti-essentialists*, have denied that there is such a thing as human nature and have claimed that whatever there is that is considered as such is really socially and culturally *constructed*. Even amongst those scholars—philosophers, theologians, scientists—who have defended human nature, the basis (or bases) upon which to explain the uniqueness of human beings has been a matter of continual debate and disagreement. For various reasons, elaborated upon throughout this book, both earlier philosophical and scientific approaches to the study of human nature have proven to be inadequate. Speculative, philosophical, and theological attempts to characterize human nature have too frequently relied upon the introduction of metaphysical distinctions, or quasi-metaphysical distinctions, that do not meet the ontological "sniff-test" of modern science, i.e., such theories have tended to introduce and thus multiply ontological entities beyond the natural world.

There is also an ontological spectrum along which such extra-natural or supernatural have been distributed. For example, what are characterized in Chapter 1 as "top-down" theories of human nature have sometimes claimed that the uniqueness of human beings is the result of the possession of a spiritual, immortal soul introduced into the natural world from some metaphysically-distinct realm. Another equally speculative claim, based upon a similarly ontologically generous basis, is that human beings are unique in the natural world because we are "made in the image of God." Top-down theories of humans also tend to be *essentialist* theories, attempting to account for human nature in terms of a single essential characteristic or a set of defining characteristics. Such theories also tend to be "thick" theories, attempting to identify a qualitative difference between human beings (usually a difference accounted for in metaphysical terms) and other living creatures in the natural world.

The cluster theory, developed in this book, is committed to a naturalistic methodology and thus rejects the metaphysical, essentialist, and "thick" claims of top-down theories of human nature. The cluster theory is *non-essentialist* and is to be distinguished from the denial of the existence of human nature by the *anti-essentialists*. Thus, the view of human nature based upon Christian theology is rejected as well as the Platonic view along with the Aristotelian view based upon the uniquely human *telos* of *eudaimonia* since such views are not compatible with methodological naturalism. Such attempts to explain human nature wind up basing the elusive notion of human nature with significantly more elusive metaphysical notions, including teleological notions. Such ontological misdirections have normally been the result of misguided commitments to essentialism. Attempts to identify the elusive single essential characteristic in terms of which the uniqueness of human beings is explained have led to supernatural, metaphysical realms and beings.

Since the cluster theory is methodologically committed to a naturalistic ontology, it may then seem that the cluster theory of human nature is nothing but a scientific theory; but this is not the case. In many ways, the cluster theory finds straightforward scientific attempts to explain human nature as inadequate as it does top-down theories, even though scientific theories tend to be descriptive, bottom-up, "thin" theories. This is especially true of biological attempts to explain human nature. *Human nature* cannot be explained simply in terms of classical biology or even evolutionary biology. Even though the cluster theory embraces both, it maintains that there is a conceptual divide between understanding what it means for human beings to be *biologically* human and for human beings to *be human*, i.e., to have human nature. The best that biology can do is to explain what it mean for the biological species, *Homo sapiens*, to exist and to have evolved into existence, but there is much more to be said about why the members of the biological species, *Homo sapiens*, have (and how we came to have) the unique *nature* that we do.

While it may offend the delicate sensibilities of some people, the distinction that the cluster theory defends between being biologically human and having human nature means that not all individuals that are biologically human have human nature. For example, newborn human infants and individuals in a permanent, vegetative state have little or no human nature. Since the cluster theory of human nature maintains that human nature can be instantiated in different individuals to varying degrees and in some individuals who are biologically human to no degree or to practically no degree, there is no conceptual difficulty in admitting on the one hand that an individual is *human*, i.e., *biologically human* but has no *human nature*. If fact, this distinction is a major asset of the cluster theory since it accounts for various conceptual distinctions revealed in the kinds of things that people regularly say and intuitions that they have. Parents, for example, routinely say such things as "Little Johnny (or little Susie) is becoming more and more human every day." And people regularly characterize the vile, contemptible, abominable acts of psychopathic villains as "inhuman" or "inhumane" even though the individuals committing such acts are clearly biologically human. Biology and the other natural sciences alone cannot explain human nature (or a great deal of other human phenomena, for that matter), which explains the development of the social sciences. While the cluster theory borrows heavily from the social sciences to explain human nature, it does so from biology as well. Whatever the actual effects of nurturing are upon human nature, that nurturing and those effects are heavily conditioned by and is a function of the underlying biology.

The point has been made repeatedly throughout this book, however, that the connections between the properties that create the cluster of properties upon which human nature supervenes according to the cluster theory is a contingent one. In fact, a major advantage to the cluster theory is that it allows for human nature to be instantiated to varying degrees in individuals that are not biologically human. While this claim may initially seem to be counterintuitive, a moment's reflection confirms its accuracy. Remember that the cluster theory takes as its point of departure in its understanding of human nature, Plato's claim expressed in the foreword of this book:

> Ought we not to consider first whether that which we wish to learn and to teach is a simple or multiform thing, and if it is simple, then to inquire what power it has of acting or being acted upon in relation to other things, and if multiform, then to number the forms, and see first in the case of one of them, and in the case of all of them, what is the power of acting or being acted upon which makes all of them to be what they are?
>
> —(Plato, *Phaedrus*, 270d)

Applying Plato's insight to the concept of human nature has revealed that to understand human nature, we must understand the place of those individuals said to possess human nature in our environments and understand the range of interactions between those individuals and our environments. This fundamental commitment led to the recognition of the importance of the particular characteristics of the natural world in which human nature has developed, i.e., what some evolutionary biologists have called "the environment of evolutionary adaptation" (EEA). More conclusions will be drawn about the importance of the EEA momentarily. Following Plato's lead also led to the development of the notions of a *species-sense* and a *species-orientation*, which are used by the cluster theory to explain how individuals with human nature are able to act upon and be acted upon by our environments within a unique range. With the notion of *species-orientation* and the recognition of its importance in place, it is easy to understand how some non-human animals may possess human nature to a greater degree than some individuals who are biologically human. For example, some people frequently attribute human-like qualities to their pets, and this process is more than a thoughtless form of anthropomorphism. Again, some delicate sensibilities and political correctness notwithstanding, there is little doubt that the collective ways in which some non-human animals act upon and are acted upon by their environments, i.e., their *species-orientation* is more "human like" than the severely diminished or undeveloped human *species-orientation* of some individuals who are biologically human.

A major advantage of the cluster theory of human nature thus is that it captures and explains many common expressions in ordinary language and many distinctions embedded in common sense. Since the cluster theory is a descriptive, *thin* theory of human nature, it divorces the notion of human nature from the trailing, heavily anthropocentric influences of ancient (and now outmoded) philosophical and theological claims that tie human nature to some metaphysical distinction between human and non-human animals. The commitment to methodological naturalism means that whatever differences there may be between the ways in which human nature is instantiated in individuals who are biologically human and other individuals need not appeal to anything metaphysical in nature but can be accounted for on the basis of a naturalistic ontology and differences of degree. This places the cluster theory squarely in mid-stream so far as the social sciences are concerned and gives it a significant methodological advantage over overly-ontologically generous, top-down theories of human nature.

Considering the impact of the variations in the *species-sense* and *species-orientation* in individuals who are biologically human caused by disease, injury, and/or developmental abnormalities and considering the similarities and differences between such individuals and non-human animals provides some additional conceptual purchase on the notion of human nature. Thus, the abnormalities in the "normal" human *species-sense* (considered in Chapter 5), such as various forms of agnosia, including prosopagnosia, resulting from a breakdown in *species-sense-integration*, are illustrative of how human *species-orientation* (and thus human nature) is a function of sensing and interacting with one's environment within a certain range. Perhaps, more effectively, simply considering the modalities of various changes that might conceivably, or, in some cases, might realistically occur over time provides a more general approach to understanding the parameters of human nature. In this regard, it should be clear that not all intuitions will agree, but even if there is not complete agreement, considering the possibilities at least clearly focuses attention on the points of dispute and further distinguishes having human nature from being biologically human.

Consider, for example, the "Twin Earth" thought experiment first suggested by Hilary Putnam.[1] In this thought experiment, Putnam proposed that we imagine a twin of Earth that is exactly like this actual Earth except it contains no water. Twin Earth does contain a substance that has all of the physical properties that water has on Earth, but instead of being chemically composed of H2O, it is composed of chemicals XYZ—the exact nature of which is unimportant. We are to further assume that the thought-experiment occurs some time ago before it became known that water is H2O. The following question is then asked: If a human on Earth and that human's twin on Twin Earth each use the term "water," do they mean the same thing? Putnam uses his thought experiment of Twin Earth to illustrate what has become known in the philosophy of language as "semantic externalism," i.e., the position that maintains that meanings of terms are not intentional concepts "inside a person's head."

With only some slight modifications and remembering that yesterday's science fiction is today's scientific fact, Putnam's thought experiment involving Twin Earth provides a promising avenue for understanding some important consequences of the cluster theory of human nature. Also, Putnam's suggestion of the thought experiment of Twin Earth is along the same lines as considering the possibility of a third human eye (Chapter 2), Wittgenstein's point about the possibility of a speaking lion (Chapter 2) and Hume's speculation about the possible ways in which human nature might have been tweaked (Chapter 5). All of these different scenarios involve thinking counterfactually about the ways in which human nature might be different and how human nature is conceptually distinct from being biologically human. However, the Twin Earth suggestion is far more subtle in that, if we replace "water" in Putnam's thought experiment with the phrase "human being" then it becomes especially illustrative of the uniqueness of the cluster theory of human nature. If we adapt the Twin Earth thought experiment to apply to the use of the phrase "human being" instead of the word "water," then we are to imagine twin human beings using the expression "human being" to apply to individuals (twin humans) that are functionally equivalent to human beings on Earth but which are composed differently "chemically." Twin humans on Twin Earth use the expression "human being" in exactly the same ways in which human beings on Earth do (with presumably the same disagreements that exist on Earth).

What might it then mean in the case of human nature to imagine twin human beings that are functionally identical to human beings but are constituted differently in some way that is comparable to water's being XYZ instead of H2O? Well, there are two possibilities to consider—a naturalistic one and a supernatural one. Consider the supernatural possibility first, i.e., an example of some version of a top-down theory of human nature that claims that human beings are the result of the possession of an immortal soul or on the basis of some other metaphysically distinct element. Then what might the differences be between the meaning and application of the phrase "human nature" to twin human beings on Twin Earth if they are understood, for the sake of argument, as *not* possessing that metaphysically-distinct element, e.g., an immortal soul, etc., that characterizes human beings on Earth? Remembering that twin human beings on Twin Earth and human beings on Earth are functionally identical, the answer seems clearly to be none. Meaningful uses of the phrase "human nature" on Twin Earth would have the same meaning and refer to the same cluster of properties as do such uses on Earth, whatever disputes there may be about semantic externalism and the meaning of "human being" notwithstanding. Maintaining that human nature would be different because twin humans do not have souls would be defending a distinction without a difference.

Consider then the possible naturalistic explanation of the possible ways in which twin human beings and human beings might differ. What might this mean? Remembering again that twin humans and humans are functionally identical, on naturalistic grounds twin humans and humans might differ in terms of genetics or DNA. On Earth, human DNA is distinctively and uniquely *human*; so, on Twin Earth, twin humans might be thought of as having distinctively and uniquely *twin human* DNA, which is different from *human* DNA. If so, what difference might this mean in the ways in which we would understand the meanings of the different uses of the phrase "human nature" on Earth and Twin Earth? The answer again clearly seems to be none since human beings on Earth and twin human beings on Twin Earth are functionally equivalent.

What this little thought experiment confirms is the way in which an individual's having human nature is different from water being water and from a human being being a human being. Human nature is a property that emerges at a "higher level," supervening upon the existence of other things and properties. Human nature on Earth is comparable to *buoyancy* on Earth and Twin Earth, and the meaning of "buoyancy" would be the same on Earth and Twin Earth since water and twin water are functionally identical. Likewise, human nature would be the same on Earth and Twin Earth since human beings and twin human beings are functionally identical.

As argued in Chapter 2, buoyancy is not a property of discrete, individual objects, i.e., it is not a single-place property, but it is a multi-value property that is a function of the causal relationships between objects, liquids, and various natural features of the environment, i.e., what are collectively called in Chapter 3 the *fixed haecceity* of the natural world, e.g., gravity. Objects float because the force of the weight of the object exerted by gravity is canceled by the pressure that the liquid exerts on the objects. Since the thought experiment imagines Twin Earth to be exactly like Earth except in the single respect in which human beings are different in some undetectable, "hidden" property (e.g., genetics or DNA), the *fixed haecceity* of Twin Earth will be identical to the *fixed haecceity* of Earth. Without prolonging the argument unnecessarily, it is clear that if Twin Earth is exactly like Earth except in the one respect mentioned, then human *species-sense,* human *species-sense-integration*, and human *species-orientation* will be identical to their counter parts on Twin Earth. This means that Twin *Homo sapiens* will also be Twin *Homo sexus* (Chapter 4) and Twin *Homo religiosus* (Chapter 6) and Twin *Homo fabricator* (Chapter 7) and Twin *Homo artifex* (Chapter 9) and Twin *Homo civilis* or *Homo politicus* (Chapter 9) in ways that are identical to those demonstrated by the cluster theory to characterize *Homo sapiens* on Earth. In other words, there would be no difference between Twin human nature on Twin Earth and human nature on Earth because human nature *floats* upon the underlying properties produced by the causal relationships between individuals and the environment.

But what about the existence of human nature in other worlds and other environments that may not be as friendly as that found on Twin Earth, i.e., environments that are significantly different from the natural environment found on Earth? The recognition of the importance of the environment of evolutionary adaptation (EEA) for the selection of certain traits that have been preserved over time is explicit in evolutionary biology. This means that—without something bordering on a miraculous coincidence or a series of major mutations—the biological species *Homo sapiens* could only have evolved in a natural world that might have deviated from the actual world only within a very narrow window. This means that it is important to recognize an evolutionary version of the Anthropic Principle (AP), which circumscribes the narrow range of circumstances within which the biological species, *Homo sapiens*, evolved, i.e., a Human Anthropic Principle (HAP). However, since the cluster theory separates human nature from being biologically human, while the HAP may explain the evolution and emergence of *Homo sapiens*, it does not explain the evolution or emergence of human nature. The set of whatever conditions responsible for allowing the emergence of human nature is not a discrete subset of those conditions in HAP (although there may be some significant overlap of those two sets of conditions); thus, as argued in Chapter 3, it is necessary to also recognize a distinct Human Nature Anthropic Principle (HNAP), which delimits those conditions under which human nature was able to evolve and emerge.

Recognition of the importance the role of EEA and the differences between the resulting HAP and the HNAP has some potential significance for gaining some conceptual purchase on some puzzling questions prompted by possible events and developments facing human beings in the foreseeable future—events and developments that are likely to have important consequences for our understanding of human nature. The cluster theory provides a framework which offers some significant advantages for dealing with such thorny issues, which can only be hinted at here. First, consider the potentially cataclysmic climate changes that are predicted by many scientists to occur on Earth over the next few millennia as the result of global warming. The exact nature of such changes is still debatable as is the probability or timing of such changes; however, even with such debates notwithstanding, it is unreasonably sanguine to expect the Earth's climate and the HNAP to remain relatively unchanged over a prolonged period of time. A strike by a large meteorite could cause similar changes as could a nuclear war. Even if human beings manage to survive such cataclysmic climate changes—perhaps by becoming subterranean—it is clear that human nature would change. If human beings became subterranean creatures, for example, the human *species-sense* would obviously change over time and then so would the human *species-orientation*. The brain would obviously begin to process the sensory information differently. Vision might disappear altogether, depending upon what sort of artificial lighting might be available, and if vision goes, so probably would bipedalism. It is very doubtful that human nature, as it has been described in this book could survive with human beings living underground. Predicably, too many of the properties and the causal connections amongst those properties that produce the causal nexus upon which human nature supervenes would be lost.

Other kinds of changes brought about by different events would similarly threaten human nature. A pandemic that results in a large number of human deaths and requires quarantine involving severe, prolonged isolation of large numbers of people could easily undermine human *species-haecceity*, alter human *species-identity*, and ultimately destroy human *social proprioception* necessary for the existence of social and political institutions. Whatever the nature might be of surviving human beings, the chances are that it would be significantly different from the kind of human nature captured by the cluster theory in this book.

A different kind of change that is facing human beings in the more immediate future involves space travel. Human beings are already spending extended periods of time in space, and unmanned space vehicles have already left our solar system. Extremely extended periods of time in space for human beings—extraterrestrial living—poses many of the same issues for human nature as does subterranean living. It is not possible to address these issues in any detail here, but much will depend upon how successful space scientists are in providing an artificial environment that captures the crucial features of our natural environment on Earth that preserves the human *species-sense* and the human *species-orientation* (and the other properties discussed in this book). The causal nexus upon which human nature depends might then be preserved as well. At some point attention will have to be given to such concerns. If human advances continue so far as space travel is concerned at the staggering pace established over the past hundred years (a result of the human *proactive mode of species-orientation*), then, in the next hundred years, large numbers of human beings may well be living in space for long periods of time. Also, given that astrophysicists have now discovered hundreds of extrasolar planets and dozens of "Super-Earths" (extrasolar planets that are dense, like Earth) and talk regularly of "habitable zones" outside our own solar system, it is becoming more and more reasonable to believe that there are places in the universe other than Earth that might sustain life—even possibly human-like life.

What *kind* of creatures might human beings become if we lived for prolonged periods, e.g., millennia, in space? What kind of nature might we then have? Would it be the same kind of human nature described in this book captured by the cluster theory? And, what *kind* of creatures might we encounter in the different "habitable zones" scattered across the universe? And, what kind of nature might such creatures have? And, how might encounters with and interactions with other forms of extraterrestrial life affect our own nature? The answers to these questions must await a careful, detailed examination of the specific circumstances of the different possible scenarios, but the cluster theory provides a framework within which such inquiries might take place in the future.

All of these different possible eventualities pose puzzling questions about what kind of creatures we human beings might become given significant enough changes in the environment in which we find ourselves and significant enough differences in the ways in which we are acted upon and are able to act upon that environment. Whatever kind of creatures we might become will be a function of the patterns of those interactions. Whatever answers might eventually be forthcoming to the questions about what *kind* of creatures human beings might become in the future (the kind of human nature we might have) will come from extrapolations from the *kind* of creatures we are now. The cluster theory, developed in this book, provides the most complete understanding of that presently existing human nature to date.

Since I have used various metaphors throughout this book to explain the cluster theory and how human nature supervenes upon the causal nexus created by the relationship amongst a cluster of properties, it is appropriate to finish the book with one last metaphor. Consider *flight*, i.e., the ability to fly. What explains the ability of a non-human animal or an inanimate object to pass through space *in the air*? Flight is instantiated in different ways in different individuals in this natural world. Birds obviously fly. But kites and balloons do as well. What of *winged* flight? Gliders and airplanes fly. Airplanes have some mode of power resulting in *powered* flight while gliders do not. Rockets and missiles are said to fly. So does the space shuttle. What is importantly illustrative about flight is that these different instantiations of flight are the result of different complex sets of properties—some of the natural environment and some of the individual object—that causally interact in such a manner that flight occurs. Thus, gravity, the nature of the atmosphere, and speed as well as the shape of wings or the power produced, in different instances, causally contribute to the production of flight. Flight is a complex matter. There is, after all, the science of aeronautics.

The result of the causal nexus created by a successful combination of such properties is that a bird, a balloon, an airplane, or the space shuttle is able to rise above the ground and move through space. Flight is not a single-placed property of an individual but a multi-placed property resulting from a complex set of properties—some of which pertain to the individual, some of which pertain to the individual's environment, and some of which pertain to the relationship between the two. Thus it is with human nature. When a critical mass of the underlying properties are in place (those discussed throughout this book), the causal interactions amongst those properties create a causal nexus that then produces and supports human nature. As we have seen, some of those properties pertain to the individuals, some pertain to the environments of those individuals, and some pertain to the relationships between those individuals and their environments. Human nature then emerges and ascends from the properties occurring in the natural world. Its emergence has been explained as a result of the causal nexus produced by a cluster of properties in the natural world, but human nature itself is instantiated at a "higher" level of complexity than those naturally occurring properties. Human nature thus *ascends* from the natural world, and the *ascent* of human nature is the *ascent* of man.

Note

1.   Hilary Putnam, "Meaning and Reference," *Journal of Philosophy*, 70, 1973, 699-711.

Selected Bibliography

Barrow, John D. and Tipler, Frank J., *The Anthropic Principle and the Cosmo-logical Argument* (Oxford: Oxford University Press, 1986).

Berry, Christopher J., *Human Nature* (Atlantic Highlands, NJ: Humanities Press International, 1986).

Brown, Donald, *Human Universals* (New York, NY: McGraw-Hill, 1991).

Buber, Martin, *I and Thou* (New York, NY: Touchstone, 1970).

Buller, David J., *Adapting Minds: Evolutionary Psychology and The Persistent Quest for Human Nature* (Cambridge, MA: MIT Press, 2005).

Campbell, Bernard, ed., *Sexual Selection and the Descent of Man*, (Chicago, IL: Aldine de Gruyer, 1972).

Chomsky, Noam & Michel Foucault, *The Chomsky-Foucault Debate: On Human Nature* (New York, NY: New Press, 2006).

Cozolino, Louis, J., *The Neuroscience of Human Relationships*, (New York, NY: Norton, 2006).

Csikszentmihalyi, Mihaly, *Flow: The Psychology of Optimal Experience*, (New York, NY: Harper & Row, 1990).

Darwin, Charles, *On the Origin of Species by Means of Natural Selection* (Garden City, NY: Doubleday & Company, Inc., 1859).

_____, *The Descent of Man, and Selection in Relation to Sex* with an introduction by John Bonner and Robert M. May (Princeton, NJ: Princeton University Press, 1981).

_____, *The Expression of the Emotions in Man and Other Animals*, Third Edition (Oxford: Oxford University Press, 1872).

Dawkins, Richard, *The Selfish Gene* (Oxford: Oxford University Press, 1976).

Denes, Peter B. and Pinson, Elliot N., *The Speech Chain* (Gordonsville, VA: W. H. Freeman, 1993).

Dennett, Daniel C., *Darwin's Dangerous Idea: Evolution and the Meanings of Life* (New York, NY: Simon & Schuster, 1995).

_____, *Consciousness Explained* (Boston, MA: Little, Brown, 1991).

Dewey, John, *Art as Experience* (New York, NY: Perigee Books, 1934).

_____, *Experience and Nature* (New York, NY: Dover Publications, 1958).

Diamond, Jared, *The Third Chimpanzee: The Evolution and Future of the Human Animal* (New York, NY: Harper Collins Publishers, 1992).

Dugatkin, Lee Alan, *The Altruism Equation: Seven Scientists Search for the Origin of Goodness* (Princeton, NJ: Princeton University Press, 2006).

Farb, Peter, *Human Kind* (Boston, MA: Houghton Mifflin Company, 1978).

Feinberg, Todd, *Altered Egos: How the Brain Creates the Self* (Oxford: Oxford University Press, 2001).

Fisher, Helen, *Why We Love: The Nature and Chemistry of Romantic Love* (New York, NY: Henry Holt and Company, 2004).

Freeberg, Ernest, *The Education of Laura Bridgman: The First Deaf and Blind Person to Learn Language* (Cambridge, MA: Cambridge University Press, 2001).

Fukuyama, Francis "Transhumanism," *Foreign Policy*, 144, Sept.-Oct., 2004.

Glynn, Ian, *An Anatomy of Thought: The Origin and Machinery of the Mind* (Oxford: Oxford University Press, 1999).

Hamer, Dean, *The God Gene* (New York, NY: Doubleday, 2004).

Harris, James F., *Analytic Philosophy of Religion* (Dordrecht, The Netherlands: Kluwer Academic Publishers, 2002).

Herrigel, Eugene, *Zen in the Art of Archery*, translated by R. F. C. Hall (New York, NY: Vintage Books, 1953).

Huron, David Brian, *Sweet Anticipation: Music and the Psychology of Expectation* (Cambridge, MA: MIT Press, 2006).

Kainz, Howard P., *The Philosophy of Human Nature* (Chicago, IL: Open Court Publishing Co., 2008).

Karpf, Anne, *The Human Voice: How This Extraordinary Instrument Reveals Essential Clues about Who We Are* (New York, NY: Bloomsbury Publishing, 2006).

Kinget, G. Marian, *On Being Human: A Systematic View* (New York, NY: Harcourt, Brace, Jovanovich, 1975).

Langford, Peter, *Modern Philosophies of Human Nature: Their Emergence from Christian Thought* (Dordrecht, The Netherlands: Kluwer Academic Publishers, 1986).

Levitin, Daniel J., *This Is Your Brain on Music: The Science of a Human Obsession* (New York, NY: Dutton, 2006).

Loptson, Peter, *Theories of Human Nature* (Peterborough, Ontario: Broadview Press, 2001).

_____, *Readings on Human Nature* (Peterborough, Ontario: Broadview Press, 1998).

Marks, Jonathan, *What It Means to Be 98% Chimpanzee: Apes, People, and Their Genes* (Berkeley, CA: University of California Press, 2002).

Morris, Desmond, *The Naked Ape* (New York, NY: McGraw-Hill Book Company, 1967).

Nott, Kathleen, *Philosophy and Human Nature* (London: Hodder and Stoughton, 1970).

Otto, Rudolf, *The Idea of the Holy* (Oxford: Oxford University Press, 1923).

Pagels, Elaine, *Adam, Eve, and the Serpent* (New York, NY: Vintage Books, 1988).

Passingham, R. E., *What Is Special about the Human Brain?* (Oxford: Oxford University Press, 2008).

Pinker, Steven, *The Blank Slate: The Modern Denial of Human Nature* (London: Penquin Books, 2002).

_____, *The Language Instinct: How the Mind Creates Language* (New York, NY: W. Morrow and Co., 1994).

_____, *How the Mind Works* (New York, NY: W. W. Norton & Company, 1997).

Pojman, Louis P., *Who Are We?* (Oxford, Oxford University Press, 2005).

Purves, William, *et. al.*, *Life: The Science of Biology*, Fifth Edition, (Sunderland, MA: W. H. Freeman, 1998).

Richards, Janet Radcliffe, *Human Nature after Darwin: A Philosophical Introduction* (London: Routledge, 2000).

Rouner, Leroy S., editor, *Is There a Human Nature?* (Notre Dame, IL: University of Notre Dame Press, 1997).

Sacks, Oliver, *The Man Who Mistook His Wife for a Hat and Other Clinical Tales* (New York, NY: Touchstone, 1970).

Sarles, Harvey B., *Language and Human Nature* (Minneapolis, MN: University of Minnesota Press, 1985).

Steen, R. Grant, *The Evolving Brain: The Known and Unknown*, (Amherst, NY: Prometheus Books, 2007).

Stevenson, Leslie, *The Study of Human Nature*, 2nd ed. (Oxford: Oxford University Press, 1999).

Stevenson, Leslie and Haberman, David, *Ten Theories of Human Nature*, 4th ed. (Oxford: Oxford University Press, 2004).

Tomatis, Alfred A., *The Conscious Ear* (New York, NY: Station Hill Press, 1991).

Wilson, Edmund O., *On Human Nature* (Cambridge, MA: Harvard University Press, 2004).

Wittgenstein, Ludwig, *On Certainty* (New York, NY: Harper Torchbooks, 1969).

Wright, Robert, *The Moral Animal: Evolutionary Psychology and Everyday Life* (New York, NY: Pantheon Books, 1994).

Index